The KINGFISH and the Constitution

Recent Titles in
Contributions in Political Science

Securing the Covenant: United States Israel–Relations After the Cold War
Bernard Reich

Why the Cold War Ended: A Range of Interpretations
Ralph Summy and Michael E. Salla, editors

Presidential Leadership and Civil Rights Policy
James W. Riddlesperger, Jr., and Donald W. Jackson, editors

The Eagle and the Peacock: U.S. Foreign Policy Toward India Since Independence
M. Srinivas Chary

Japan's Role in the Post–Cold War World
Richard D. Leitch, Jr., Akira Kato, and Martin E. Weinstein

Botswana's Search for Autonomy in Southern Africa
Richard Dale

Contested Terrain: Power, Politics, and Participation in Suburbia
Marc L. Silver and Martin Melkonian, editors

After Authoritarianism: Democracy or Disorder?
Daniel N. Nelson, editor

Ethics and Statecraft: The Moral Dimension of International Affairs
Cathal J. Nolan, editor

Social Security Programs: A Cross-Cultural Comparative Perspective
John Dixon and Robert P. Scheurell, editors

International Organizations and Environmental Policy
Robert V. Bartlett, Priya A. Kurian, and Madhu Malik

Cautious Revolution: The European Union Arrives, Second Edition
Clifford Hackett

The KINGFISH and the Constitution

Huey Long, the First Amendment, and the Emergence of Modern Press Freedom in America

Richard C. Cortner

Contributions in Political Science, Number 365

GREENWOOD PRESS
Westport, Connecticut • London

Library of Congress Cataloging-in-Publication Data

Cortner, Richard C.
The Kingfish and the Constitution : Huey Long, the First Amendment, and the emergence of modern press freedom in America / Richard C. Cortner.
p. cm.—(Contributions in political science, ISSN 0147–1066 ; no. 365)
Includes bibliographical references (p.) and index.
ISBN 0–313–29842–4 (alk. paper)
1. Long, Huey Pierce, 1893–1935. 2. Freedom of the press—United States—History—20th century. 3. United States—Constitution—Amendments—1st. 4. Press law—Louisiana—History—20th century. 5. Louisiana—Politics and government—1865–1950. I. Title. II. Series
E748.L86C67 1996
323.44′5′0976309043—dc20 95–31340

British Library Cataloguing in Publication Data is available.

Library of Congress Catalog Card Number: 95–31340
ISBN: 0–313–29842–4
ISSN: 0147–1066

First published in 1996

Greenwood Press, 88 Post Road West, Westport, CT 06881
An imprint of Greenwood Publishing Group, Inc.

Printed in the United States of America

The paper used in this book complies with the Permanent Paper Standard issued by the National Information Standards Organization (Z39.48–1984).

10 9 8 7 6 5 4 3 2 1

Copyright Acknowledgments

The author and publisher gratefully acknowledge permission to use selected excerpts from the *New Orleans Times-Picayune* and the *Baton Rouge Morning Times-Advocate*.

Every reasonable effort has been made to trace owners of copyright materials in this book, but in some instances this has proven impossible. The author and publisher will be glad to receive information leading to more complete acknowledgments in subsequent printings of the book and in the meantime extend their apologies for any omissions.

For Leo

I must believe that Willie Stark was a great man. What happened to his greatness is not the question. Perhaps he spilled it on the ground the way you spill a liquid when the bottle breaks. Perhaps he piled up his greatness and burnt it in one great blaze in the dark like a bonfire and then there wasn't anything but dark and the embers winking. Perhaps he could not tell his greatness from ungreatness and so mixed them together that what was adulterated was lost.

—Jack Burden in *All the King's Men*

A free press stands as one of the great interpreters between the government and the people. To allow it to be fettered is to fetter ourselves.

—Justice George Sutherland in *Grosjean* v. *American Press Co.*, 1936

Contents

Preface

♦ Huey Pierce "Kingfish" Long was killed some two months before I was born, and consequently I had no opportunity to form any impressions of the man during his lifetime. As a youth growing up in southern and south central Oklahoma during the 1930s and 1940s, however, I remember adults who held Huey Long in high esteem as a rare politician who had sponsored programs that helped the common people. As I became a professional political scientist, I, of course, became more acquainted with the career of Huey Long as governor of Louisiana and later its U.S. Senator, but even then I had no detailed knowledge of his political career. I regarded him as a somewhat clownish political figure whose principal value to me was as a source of humorous anecdotes that were useful in lightening up my lectures in political science classes. My impression of Huey Long was probably one shared by large numbers of others who possessed only a vague knowledge of his political career and regarded him as a comic and rather colorful figure from our political past.

Franklin D. Roosevelt, who had received crucial support from Long in securing the Democratic nomination for the presidency in 1932, had a much different and more definite opinion of Huey Long. After receiving a telephone call from Long at his Hyde Park home following his nomination for the presidency, Roosevelt commented to his guests, "It has its funny side but actually Huey is one of the two most dangerous men in the United States today. We shall have to do something about him." An adviser later asked Roosevelt who was the other most dangerous man in the country, and Roosevelt replied, "Douglas MacArthur."[1]

In undertaking the research for this book, I was for the first time required to examine Huey Long's life and career in some detail, and, consequently, to form my own more definite opinion of him as an American politician. The reader should be aware, since it may well color what follows, that I have come to fully share Franklin Roosevelt's assessment of Huey Long. Although he doubtless possessed an intelligence of a high order, Huey Long totally lacked the core values—what political scientists sometimes call respect for "the rules of the game"—that politicians must possess if any nation is to successfully maintain a democratic republic. Those values include a recognition of the sanctity of the democratic process and a respect for the fundamental principles that are essential to the preservation of this process in any society, and an awareness that any public policy or practice that subverts the democratic process, or breaches the principles upon which it rests, are illegitimate and out of bounds.

For Huey Long, however, nothing was out of bounds if it was perceived by him as necessary to increase his political power or to advance his political ambitions. The democratic process and the fundamental constitutional principles essential to that process were treated by him as any other obstacle or opponent, to be destroyed if possible or brushed aside if not.

The Kingfish's assault on the freedom of the press in 1934, which is the subject of this book, is a case in point. When it became apparent in 1934 that he faced the implacable and virtually unanimous opposition of the urban daily press of Louisiana, Huey Long struck back with a tax on newspaper advertising. If the newspaper advertising tax had been sustained in the courts, and had he lived, there is little doubt that the Kingfish would have increased the tax to the point that the state's daily press would either have been constrained to drop its opposition to him and his programs or have faced bankruptcy. The press, as perceived by Long, was just another source of opposition to be destroyed or neutralized if possible, without his acknowledgment or recognition that a free press is an essential element in the preservation of a democratic society. That Huey Long totally lacked any appreciation of this fact was further demonstrated by his subsequent ruthless censorship of the student newspaper at Louisiana State University, which had sought to publish what was a relatively mild criticism of his antics.

The focus of this book is the relationship between Huey Long and the press, from his successful race for governor of Louisiana in 1928 until his death in 1935, and the crisis for the constitutional protection of freedom of the press that ultimately occurred in Louisiana. While Long enjoyed significant support from Louisiana's urban daily press during his campaign for governor in 1928, any support he had received from them quickly evaporated, and by 1934 the Kingfish faced vehement and virtually unanimous opposition from the daily press. Long struck back by imposing a tax on newspaper advertising in papers that printed at least 20,000 copies per week—a tax that fell only on his critics in the daily press—as an obvious attempt to develop a weapon with which he could bludgeon his press critics into silence.

The daily press of Louisiana, however, closed ranks behind a constitutional challenge of the state's newspaper advertising tax in the federal courts. Fortunately for the press, in 1931 the U.S. Supreme Court had held in *Near* v. *Minnesota* that freedom of the press, which had been protected from abridgment by the federal government since the adoption of the Bill of Rights, was also protected from invasion by the states under the Due Process Clause of the Fourteenth Amendment.[2] Although the *Near* case meant that the Louisiana newspapers could attack the advertising tax in the federal courts under the federal Constitution, the press still faced considerable obstacles to successfully persuading the courts to invalidate the tax as an abridgment of freedom of the press.

The most formidable obstacle to a successful constitutional challenge on free-press grounds was the rather narrow, traditional interpretation of the scope of constitutional protection afforded the press by the courts. In construing the scope of freedom of the press, the courts had traditionally held that the primary purpose of the First Amendment was to prohibit governmentally imposed prior restraints on the press; that is, restrictions that required prior government approval of what was to be published before publication occurred. This had been the scope of protection for freedom of the press under the English common law at the time of the adoption of the First Amendment, and the U.S. courts traditionally ruled that the First Amendment was intended to codify the common law meaning.

The Louisiana newspaper advertising tax, however, was not a prior restraint as defined by the common law. Hence, the Louisiana newspapers and their counsel faced the formidable task of persuading the federal courts, and ultimately the U.S. Supreme Court, to expand the scope of constitutional protection of freedom of the press beyond its traditional meaning. This they ultimately accomplished when the Court's decision in *Grosjean* v. *American Press Company* invalidated the Louisiana newspaper advertising tax in 1936. The Supreme Court unanimously rejected the concept that the First Amendment was limited to prohibiting only prior restraints of the press, and thus took a major step in laying the basis for the modern interpretation of the constitutional protection of freedom of the press in the United States.[3]

What follows, therefore, is an analysis of the evolving relationship between the Louisiana press and one of the most colorful, and in my view, dangerous, politicians the United States has produced—a relationship that culminated in a major constitutional battle over freedom of the press in modern America. The ultimate victory of the press over Huey Long's attempt to impose censorship by taxation was not only a significant contemporary event but it also forms an important chapter in the constitutional development of the United States.

With great appreciation, I would like to acknowledge the many sources who provided assistance in my research for this book. I extend my thanks to the staffs of the University of Arizona Library, the Library of Congress, the Seeley Mudd Library at Princeton University, the Southwest Regional Records Center of the National Archives, Ft. Worth, Texas, and the Hill Memorial Library at Louisiana State University at Baton Rouge. I am equally grateful to the many Louisiana law firms that searched their files for records on the *Grosjean* case and especially to Ms. Gwen Horner from the Lafayette, Louisiana, law firm of Davidson, Meaux, McElligot & Swift, for giving me access to a crucial memorandum on the strategy of newspaper counsel in the *Grosjean* case. My manuscript was reviewed by persons associated with newspapers and law firms in Louisiana, and I am indebted to them for their comments, although their assistance must be acknowledged anonymously at their request. I also extend my appreciation to Deborah Griffis of the Department of Political Science, University of Arizona, for her valuable assistance. And finally, I thank my old friend, Leo Sonderegger, who meticulously reviewed the manuscript and subjected it to the critical eye of a veteran newspaperman and editor. Leo represents all that journalists should aspire to be, and it is to him that this book is gratefully dedicated. As always, I am alone responsible for any errors of commission or omission that may appear in the pages that follow.

NOTES

1. Arthur M. Schlesinger, Jr., *The Age of Roosevelt: The Crisis of the Old Order, 1919–1933* (New York: Houghton Mifflin, 1957), pp. 417–18.
2. *Near* v. *Minnesota*, 283 U.S. 697 (1931).
3. *Grosjean* v. *American Press Co.*, 297 U.S. 233 (1936).

Chapter 1

Introduction: Huey Long, the Press, and the First Amendment in 1930

> Louisiana is confronted today by a situation which, we believe, has no counterpart in American history for impudent disregard for constitutional . . . [protection] of the press or even common decency in political affairs affecting business.
>
> —*Editor & Publisher,* June 21, 1930

> [W]hen men have realized that time has upset many fighting faiths, they may come to believe even more than they believe the very foundations of their own conduct that the ultimate good desired is better reached by free trade in ideas,—that the best test of truth is the power of the thought to get itself accepted in the competition of the market; and that truth is the only ground upon which their wishes safely can be carried out.
>
> —Justice Oliver Wendell Holmes, Jr., dissenting in *Abrams* v. *United States,* November 10, 1919

♦ In June 1930, there were introduced in the Louisiana legislature what the American Newspaper Publishers' Association denounced as "the boldest and most flagrant measures ever aimed at the freedom of American newspapers." Louisiana in 1930 was the realm of Huey P. "Kingfish" Long, who headed one of the most powerful political machines ever to dominate the politics of an American state. The legislative measures so vehemently denounced by the publishers' association were an indication that the relations between the Louisiana press and Huey Long and his organization, relations that had been strained at best since the Kingfish's election as governor in 1928, had increased in hostility to the verge of open warfare that would ultimately create a crisis for freedom of the press in Louisiana.[1]

The first measure introduced in the legislature at the behest of Governor Long would have imposed a 15 percent tax on the gross revenues received by Louisiana newspapers from sales of advertising. The second measure, denounced by publishers as "an opinion-smothering gag law" and a "padlock law," would have allowed the suppression by court-issued injunction of any newspaper or publication that was "obscene, lewd or lascivious" or that was "malicious, scandalous or defamatory." The bill authorized local Louisiana district attorneys to bring suits for injunctions in the state courts against such publications if petitioned to do so by any reputable citizen, or if the district attorneys failed to act, the injunction proceedings could be initiated by the state attorney general. If both the district attorneys and the attorney general failed to act, the bill authorized private citizens to initiate injunctive proceedings themselves.[2]

If the tax on the gross receipts derived from the sale of advertising by newspapers were sustained by the courts, Huey Long and the Louisiana legislature would possess a powerful weapon by which they could bludgeon the newspapers of the state into hewing to the political line that Long and the legislature desired. If the tax were upheld, it could be increased until the newspapers either complied and followed the correct political line or were driven into bankruptcy. The injunction-gag law proposal could also be used for the same purpose. Any newspaper found to be publishing malicious, scandalous, or defamatory material could be permanently enjoined from publication under the terms of the gag law measure, even if future issues of the paper might not have included the kind of material prohibited by the proposed law. The political purposes to which such a measure could be used against an opposition press were thus also obvious.

Arthur G. Newmyer, the general manager of one of the leading daily newspapers of New Orleans, the *Item*, dispatched letters to leading publishers throughout the country, alerting them to the gravity of the threat to press freedom posed by the Louisiana measures. Newmyer especially denounced the proposed advertising tax as a threat to the economic survival of the state's newspapers. "A reading of this [tax] bill," he said, "I think, will convince every newspaper man, who has an elementary conception of the dignity and independence of our profession, and the importance of the preservation of the liberty of the press, that the measure is most vicious."[3]

The result of Newmyer's warning was a "barrage of editorial opposition" to the Long-backed bills by newspapers throughout the country. The Association of National Advertisers warned Governor Long on June 17 that sales of advertising by newspapers was vital to the continuation of low-cost, widespread circulation of newspapers, while *Editor & Pub-*

lisher, the voice of the American Newspaper Publishers' Association, declared that "Louisiana is confronted today by a situation which, we believe, has no counterpart in American history for impudent disregard for constitutional . . . [protection] of the press or even common decency in political affairs affecting business." The proposed legislation in Louisiana, *Editor & Publisher* continued, was "Gov. Huey P. Long's plug-ugly answer to newspapers that have conscientiously criticized his administration" and was "a politician's low revenge against his critics." "No incident in modern times, in our opinion," it declared, "better illustrates the indispensable value of a free and independent press. We congratulate the people of Louisiana on possessing newspapers of sufficient independent character to stand for public right no matter how greatly this policy may imperil their own business futures."[4]

Joining in the outcry against the proposed legislation in Louisiana, the *New York Evening Post* denounced the bills as "an open attempt to penalize men whom . . . [Governor Long] has been unable to intimidate or coerce," which should be "resisted by every American worthy of the name," while the *New York Herald Tribune* urged that the "force of public opinion, state and national, should be brought to bear upon the legislators before whom this precious piece of political vindictiveness is pending. Its passage would be a menace to a free press and a disgrace to the State of Louisiana." Organized by Charles Manship, publisher of the *Baton Rouge State-Times* and *Morning Advocate*, forty-six newspaper men met in Baton Rouge, the state capital, to develop a strategy to fight the bills in the legislature. The conclusion of the meeting was that these measures, plainly done out of "spite" against the press, would be defeated if they were brought to a vote. "Governor Long has brought chaos into affairs of state," Manship's *Morning Advocate* said the following day. "He has brought turmoil and bitter strife to Louisiana." Noting that Long was always surrounded by armed bodyguards, the *Advocate* predicted that "he is not going to bully and blackmail the independent members of the . . . [legislature], not even with the threat of [an] armed guard."[5]

Questioned regarding the reasons the threatened assault on the press had occurred in Louisiana, Marshall Ballard, editor of the *New Orleans Item*, attributed the move against the press by Long forces to the newspapers' opposition to a $68 million bond measure, sponsored by Governor Long, for building bridges and paving highways in the state. To defuse their opposition, the governor had invited the New Orleans newspapers to propose appropriate safeguards to prevent the money raised by the bond issue from serving as a slush fund for the Long organization, and the papers had proposed appropriate measures that Long had initially accepted but subsequently repudiated. "Since his repudiation of his agreements he has been denouncing and berating the newspapers in general as reprobates and liars," Ballard said. "No legislation for such discriminatory newspaper taxation and press-gaggery ever was undertaken before in Louisiana."[6]

Colonel Robert Ewing, publisher of the *New Orleans States* and the *Shreveport Times*, agreed with Ballard that press opposition to the bridge and highway bond issue was partially the reason for Long's attack on the press. Over the opposition of the press, Long "insists on a political highway commission controlled by himself and with freedom to spend money as he wills," according to Ewing. In addition to the bond issue as a source of conflict between the governor and the press, Ewing pointed out that Long had attempted to force the New Orleans Democratic organization, the "Old Regulars," to support the bond measure by cutting off the city's credit and denying it the power to collect taxes. The newspapers had supported the city against the governor in that situation, Ewing noted, so "the governor has had two spite bills introduced. . . . He has a following in the legislature, many members of which he put on the state payroll until the [state] supreme court unanimously decided against his right to do so. Some of them will vote any way he dictates, but he cannot control all his men, and I feel confident in saying that both [antipress] bills will be beaten."[7]

Colonel Ewing's analysis of the prospects for the Long antipress bills in the legislature proved to be correct, since the ways and means committee of the house of representatives unanimously reported the advertising tax bill unfavorably on June 26, despite its sponsor's attempt to salvage the measure by lowering the tax rate from 15 to 5 percent. The newspaper injunction-gag bill was also subsequently allowed to die a quiet death in the judiciary committee of the Louisiana senate.[8]

As these events transpired, James M. Thomson, publisher of the *New Orleans Item*, expressed the gratitude of the Louisiana newspapers to the national press and pointed out that the "Louisiana newspapers and advertising interests are under the deepest obligation to the newspapers and advertising interests of the United States because of their immediate and splendid reaction to Governor Long's newspaper spite bills." It was difficult, Thomson said, to determine what objectives Long had sought through the antipress measures, but the governor probably had two objectives in mind. "Primarily, he would have been glad to pass them if they could have been passed," he continued. "Secondly, the introduction of bills of this kind is calculated to frighten some people because of the direct threat to their own business, and to divert attention from the main issue which with us and most of the newspapers of the state has been opposition to putting more funds in the hands of Governor Long." The overwhelming majority of both the Louisiana and national press had united in opposition to Long's attack, Thomson noted, and the result of the brief conflict might well be to the advantage of newspapers everywhere. "I think what he has attempted to do to the press of Louisiana will be additionally valuable," he concluded, "as it will cause newspaper workers and men who really love and respect the ethical and professional side of their business everywhere to be more actively and effectively on guard to protect the freedom of the American press."[9]

Thomson was correct in his assessment of Long's motive in initiating the antipress attack in 1930, at least with regard to believing that the attack had been intended as a threat to the state's press and a warning to cease its unremitting opposition to him and his policies. When that warning was not heeded, Long would renew his attack on the press in 1934, an attack that would precipitate one of the most important episodes affecting the emergence of the modern protection of freedom of the press in America in the 1930s.

When Huey Long initially attacked the Louisiana press in 1930, the status of freedom of the press under the federal Constitution was largely undeveloped. The First Amendment to the Constitution, of course, provided that Congress "shall make no law . . . abridging the freedom of speech, or of the press." It had been added to the Constitution in 1791 as a part of the Bill of Rights, but prior to World War I the First Amendment remained largely uninterpreted by the U.S. Supreme Court. At the time he introduced the proposals that would become the Bill of Rights in the first Congress in 1789, James Madison had included a proposed constitutional amendment that would have also protected the right to trial by jury and the right of religious freedom, as well as the freedom of the press, from abridgment by the governments of the states. Despite his belief that this proposed amendment was "of equal, if not greater importance" than his other proposals to add a Bill of Rights to the Constitution, the Senate failed to adopt Madison's proposed amendment to restrict the powers of the states over basic rights, including freedom of the press.[10]

The understanding of those who participated in the proposal and ratification of the Bill of Rights was consequently that the Bill of Rights constituted restrictions upon the powers of the federal government alone and did not restrict the powers of the states. This understanding was given authoritative status as constitutional doctrine when Chief Justice John Marshall, speaking for a unanimous Supreme Court in 1833, held that none of the basic rights contained in the Bill of Rights applied as restrictions on state and local governments, but rather were applicable to the national government alone. The Bill of Rights contained "no expression indicating an intention to apply them to the State governments," Marshall said. "This court cannot so apply them."[11]

Despite the vehemence of the denunciations of Huey Long's tax and gag law proposals of 1930 as violations of freedom of the press, at that time there was in fact no federal constitutional guarantee of freedom of the press applicable to restrictions upon that freedom by the states. If those measures had been enacted into law and a federal constitutional challenge of them had been brought in the courts, the result would have been the dismissal of the suits, since there was no valid basis in federal constitutional law for their maintenance in the courts.

In addition to the restriction of the First Amendment's applicability to actions of the national government alone, with the attendant severe restriction on the opportunities the Supreme Court had for its interpretation, on those few occasions on which the Court had interpreted the meaning of freedom of the press and its twin right, freedom of speech, it adopted a narrow view of the scope of the freedom. Generally speaking, the Court adopted the view that the First Amendment's guarantee of freedom of expression only prohibited prior restraints of expression by the government. That is, the Court held, only if the government attempted to require its prior approval of the content of expression before it occurred would a violation of the First Amendment be triggered. But after expression occurred, the government was free under the First Amendment to punish abuses of freedom of expression, since such punishments were not governmental censorship of the content of expression prior to its occurrence.

This distinction between previous restraints of expression, which were constitutionally prohibited, and its subsequent punishment, which was not prohibited, formed the basis of one of the most important debates regarding freedom of expression in America prior to the twentieth century. That debate had been occasioned when the Federalists, who controlled the national government during the formative years of the Republic following the ratification of the Constitution, enacted in 1798 the Sedition Act, which criminally punished as seditious libel criticism of the national government and its officials. The Sedition Act was a transparent attempt by the Federalists to suppress criticism of the national administration under President John Adams by the Jeffersonians, led by Thomas Jefferson. The premise of the Sedition Act, Jeffersonian leader Albert Gallatin declared on the floor of the House of Representatives, assumed that those who criticized the incumbent administration or its policies were enemies of the Constitution and ought to be punished. The act, he declared, was plainly intended to suppress criticism of the Federalists and to "perpetuate their authority and preserve their present places."[12]

When the Sedition Act was denounced by the Jeffersonians as a blatant violation of the free-press and free-speech guarantees of the First

Amendment, the Federalists answered that the First Amendment only protected freedom of expression to the extent recognized under the common law in England. They pointed out that Sir William Blackstone, in his *Commentaries on the Laws of England,* had correctly summarized the scope accorded freedom of expression under English law. "The *liberty of the press* is indeed essential to the nature of a free state," Blackstone said, "but this consists in laying no *previous* restraints upon publications, and not in freedom from censure for criminal matter when published. Every freeman has an undoubted right to lay what sentiments he pleases before the public: to forbid this would destroy the freedom of the press: but if he publishes what is improper, mischievous or illegal, he must take the consequences of his own temerity."[13]

Since the Sedition Act did not seek to require government approval before expression occurred, thus imposing a prior restraint, the Federalists argued, but rather imposed punishment for seditious libels of the government after they had been published, the act conformed to the free-expression guarantees of the First Amendment. The Jeffersonians answered that the First Amendment had not been intended merely to codify the English law governing freedom of expression, but rather to afford a much broader freedom for Americans. The First Amendment, James Madison contended, was intended to protect the "right of freely examining public characters and measures, and of free communication among the people thereon, which has ever been justly deemed the only effectual guardian of every other right." If this were so, then the First Amendment not only prohibited previous restraints of expression, as the Federalists argued, but most subsequent punishments of expression as well.[14]

No Supreme Court test of the validity of the Sedition Act of 1798 occurred, since the act expired in 1801, but every lower federal court before which the Sedition Act prosecutions were brought upheld the constitutionality of the act. On those lower federal courts also sat three of the justices of the Supreme Court. Upon his assumption of the presidency in 1801, Thomas Jefferson pardoned all of those convicted under the Sedition Act, and years later Congress voted to refund the fines of at least two of those convicted under the act. While the Jeffersonians had lost the initial battle over the validity of the Sedition Act, in response to the defense of the act by the Federalists they had formulated a broad concept of freedom of expression that was available for consideration, and perhaps adoption, by the people and most especially the courts in generations to come.

One of the most important events of the nineteenth century having the potential for constitutionally enlarging the applicability of freedom of expression was the adoption of the Fourteenth Amendment to the

Constitution in 1868, in the wake of the Civil War. Unlike the Bill of Rights, the Fourteenth Amendment was plainly intended as a limitation of the powers of the states, and included in its provisions was the Due Process Clause, which prohibited the states from depriving any person of life, liberty, or property without due process of law. Soon after its ratification, litigants began to assert in the courts that the "liberty" or the "due process of law" protected from deprivation by the states under the Fourteenth Amendment included rights protected in the Bill of Rights. In addressing such arguments, the Supreme Court initially rejected them out of hand and adopted reasoning that would have precluded any ruling that the Due Process Clause of the Fourteenth Amendment guaranteed any of the rights in the Bill of Rights as restrictions on the states. In 1897, however, the Court ruled that the Due Process Clause did require the states to provide just compensation for private property taken for public use, a right also included in the Fifth Amendment of the Bill of Rights. By the turn of the century, consequently, it appeared to be an open question whether the Due Process Clause of the Fourteenth Amendment might be held in the future to apply additional rights in the Bill of Rights as restrictions on the powers of the states.[15]

In the early years of the new century, however, the Supreme Court continued to reject arguments that the Fourteenth Amendment applied rights like those in the Bill of Rights to the states, and on the few occasions in which the Court addressed freedom of expression issues, it adopted a narrow, restrictive approach. In *Patterson* v. *Colorado*, decided in 1907, the Court upheld a decision of the Colorado Supreme Court convicting Patterson, a newspaper publisher, of contempt of court for publishing articles and a cartoon critical of the Colorado court's decision regarding an election dispute. Writing for the U.S. Supreme Court, Justice Oliver Wendell Holmes, Jr., sidestepped an argument that the Due Process Clause of the Fourteenth Amendment made the First Amendment right of freedom of the press applicable to the states. "We leave undecided," Holmes said, "the question whether there is to be found in the 14th Amendment a prohibition similar to that in the 1st." But even if the Court assumed that the freedoms of the press and speech were protected by the Fourteenth Amendment, Holmes continued, "the main purpose of such constitutional provisions is 'to prevent all such *previous restraints* upon publications as had been practised by other governments,' and they do not prevent the subsequent punishment of such as may be deemed contrary to the public welfare." Since Patterson had been convicted and fined for contempt of court, he had been subjected not to a previous restraint of his right to publish what he wished, but to subsequent punishment for publishing material that would "tend to obstruct the administration of justice," Holmes concluded, and his conviction should therefore be affirmed.[16]

The Supreme Court's decision in the *Patterson* case revealed that the scope of freedom of expression was still regarded, at least by the Court, as essentially the same as that advanced by the Federalists in their defense of the Sedition Act in the 1790s. Constitutional guarantees of freedom of expression were still limited to prohibiting governmentally imposed prior restraints of expression. The opinion of the Court by Justice Holmes also embraced another restrictive doctrine with regard to expression, the "bad tendency" concept. Subsequent punishments could be imposed, Holmes had held, upon those whose expression either was "deemed contrary to the public welfare" or might "tend to obstruct the administration of justice." Under such a test, expression that might at some future, indefinite, remote time have the tendency to produce undesirable, antisocial, or illegal effects or prove harmful to the public welfare could thus be subject to subsequent punishments because it was beyond the legitimate scope of constitutional guarantees of free expression.

One year following the decision in the *Patterson* case, the Supreme Court decided another case that had a profound effect upon the applicability of the guarantee of freedom of the press and, indeed, on guarantees of civil liberties generally. In 1908, the Court decided *Twining* v. *New Jersey* and again rejected a claim that a right in the Bill of Rights, this time the Self-Incrimination Clause of the Fifth Amendment, applied to the states via the Fourteenth Amendment. But in its discussion of the meaning of the Due Process Clause of the Fourteenth Amendment, the Court conceded that the Due Process Clause guaranteed against deprivation by the states of every fundamental principle of "liberty and justice which inheres in the very idea of free government and is the inalienable right of a citizen of such a government." So interpreted, the Court said, the Due Process Clause might guarantee against the states rights similar to at least some of those in the Bill of Rights. The Court's discussion of the meaning of the Due Process Clause in the *Twining* case was the most generous concession it had yet made since the adoption of the Fourteenth Amendment in 1868 to contentions that the amendment applied to the states at least some of the rights in the Bill of Rights. As such, the *Twining* decision was an open invitation by the Court for the continuation of such arguments in future cases coming before it.[17]

Despite the promise of the *Twining* case, the Court had not taken any further steps in that direction before it was confronted by a series of free-expression cases arising from the federal government's suppression of dissent from U.S. participation in World War I. In the war cases, the Court more than ever before was constrained to authoritatively and systematically decide the scope of protection afforded to freedom of expression under the First Amendment. The war produced some of the most draconian governmental suppression of civil liberties in our history, yet the Court's free-expression decisions uniformly sustained the actions of the government.[18]

The most promising development in the Court's otherwise dismal treatment of the war-related free-expression cases was the formulation by Justice Oliver Wendell Holmes of the "clear and present danger" doctrine. This doctrine first emerged when the Court, in an opinion by Holmes, unanimously affirmed the convictions of members of the Socialist party for conspiring to mail leaflets to draft-eligible men urging them to resist induction into the military and to assert their rights. The government obtained the convictions under the Espionage Act of 1917, which in part prohibited obstructions of the war effort. In *Schenck* v. *United States* in 1919, the Court was required to determine whether the convictions violated the defendants' right to free expression under the First Amendment.[19]

Speaking for the Court in upholding the convictions, Justice Holmes conceded that "it well may be that the prohibition of laws abridging the freedom of speech is not confined to previous restraints, although to prevent them may have been the main purpose, as intimated in Patterson v. Colorado." "We admit that in many places and in ordinary times the defendants, in saying all that was said in the circular, would have been within their constitutional rights," he added. "But the character of every act depends upon the circumstances in which it is done." The most stringent protection of free speech, Holmes continued, "would not protect a man in falsely shouting fire in a theater, and causing a panic." "The question in every case is whether the words used are used in such circumstances and are of such a nature," he concluded, "as to create a clear and present danger that they will bring about the substantive evils that Congress has the right to prevent. It is a question of proximity and degree."[20]

Although the Court unanimously approved a serious governmental intrusion upon freedom of expression in the *Schenck* case, Holmes's opinion appeared to go beyond previous interpretations of free expression by first acknowledging, albeit grudgingly, that the First Amendment might protect expression more broadly than simply by prohibiting prior restraints. In addition, his opinion suggested that any subsequent punishments of expression must be based upon a showing by the government that the expression had created a "clear and present danger" of unlawful conduct or other antisocial acts before it could be legitimately subjected to punishment. This clear and present danger test thus appeared to afford a greater scope for freedom of expression than the bad tendency test, which allowed the imposition of subsequent punishments of expression that only had the tendency to lead to unlawful or antisocial conduct at some indefinite, remote, future time.

If Holmes's comments were indeed advances in the scope of protection afforded free expression, the performance of the Court, and of Holmes himself, in subsequent cases cast doubt that they were in any way permanent ones. In 1918, Congress enacted the first sedition act in the history of the Republic since the Sedition Act of 1798, and the act of 1918 was if anything more restrictive of free expression than the earlier act. The 1918 act made it a crime to "willfully utter, print, write, or publish any disloyal, profane, scurrilous or abusive language" about the form of government of the United States, the Constitution, military or naval forces, the flag, or the uniform of the army or navy or to use language intended to bring any of these things "into contempt, scorn, contumely, or disrepute." The act also forbade anyone to "willfully urge, write, or advocate any curtailment of production" of materials necessary for the war effort with the intent to cripple or hinder the United States in the prosecution of the war. The U.S. postmaster was authorized to stop mail delivery of any publications that, in his judgment, violated the provisions of the act.[21]

In 1919, the Supreme Court upheld the conviction and ten-year sentence given to Eugene V. Debs, the leader of the Socialist party, for a speech violating the Sedition Act. Justice Holmes again wrote for the Court, saying only that the First Amendment objections raised by Debs to the conviction had been "disposed of in Schenck v. United States." Holmes and the Court were thus silent on the applicability of the clear and present danger test to the circumstances of the *Debs* case.[22]

The *Debs* decision was announced in March, and in the following November the Court decided *Abrams* v. *United States*, which involved the convictions of five anarchists for distributing leaflets in violation of the Sedition Act. In an opinion by Justice John Clarke, the Court upheld the convictions, holding that the defendants' First Amendment objections to their convictions and to the validity of the Sedition Act, which had been "faintly urged," were fully answered by the *Schenck* and *Debs* cases. In the *Abrams* case, however, Justice Holmes, joined by Justice Louis Brandeis, dissented from the decision of the Court and expounded the most eloquent defense of freedom of expression yet heard from the Court. Holmes conceded that the government "constitutionally may punish speech that produces or is intended to produce a clear and imminent danger that it will bring about forthwith certain substantive evils that the United States constitutionally may seek to prevent." But the defendants in the *Abrams* case, he said, had as much right to publish the leaflets in question "as the government has to publish the Constitution of the United States now vainly invoked by them."[23] Holmes continued:

> Persecution for the expression of opinions seems to me perfectly logical. If you have no doubt of your premises or your power and want a certain result with all your heart you naturally express your wishes in law and wipe away all opposition. To allow opposition by speech seems to indicate that you think the speech impotent, as when a man says that he has squared the circle, or that you do not care whole-heartedly for the result, or that you doubt either your power or your premises. But when men have realized that time has upset many fighting faiths, they may come to believe even more than they believe the very foundations of their own conduct that the ultimate good desired is better reached by free trade in ideas,—that the best test of truth is the power of the thought to get itself accepted in the competition of the market; and that truth is the only ground upon which their wishes safely can be carried out. It is an experiment, as all life is an experiment. Every year, if not every day, we have to wager our salvation upon some prophecy based upon imperfect knowledge. While that experiment is part of our system I think that we should be eternally vigilant against attempts to check the expression of opinions that we loathe and believe to be fraught with death, unless they so imminently threaten immediate interference with the lawful and pressing purposes of the law that an immediate check is required to save the country.[24]

Gone from Holmes's dissent in the *Abrams* case was the assumption he had expressed in *Patterson* v. *Colorado* that constitutional guarantees of free expression only prohibited prior restraints. Gone too was the approval of subsequent punishment of expression that had a tendency to cause unlawful or antisocial acts at some remote time. Even subsequent punishment of expression, he had said in his *Abrams* dissent, could be justified only if the expression "imminently threaten[ed] immediate" unlawful or antisocial acts.

Despite the eloquence of the Holmes dissent in the *Abrams* case, it nevertheless reflected the views of only two members of the Supreme Court, and the majority of the Court clearly rejected the broad view of freedom of expression adopted by Holmes and Brandeis in favor of a much more restrictive and traditional interpretation. This view was reaffirmed by the Court's majority in 1925, when in *Gitlow* v. *New York* it upheld the conviction of Benjamin Gitlow for engaging in the advocacy of criminal anarchy in violation of the New York Criminal Anarchy Act. Rejecting an argument that the state was required to demonstrate that Gitlow's expression had created a clear and present danger of unlawful action occurring, Justice Edward T. Sanford instead affirmed Gitlow's conviction on the basis of the bad tendency test. Advocacy such as Gitlow's, Sanford said, might concededly create only a "single revolutionary spark," but that spark might later "burst into a sweeping and destructive conflagration."[25]

Justices Holmes and Brandeis again dissented, arguing that in order to restrict freedom of expression, the government must show that advocacy of illegal action had created a clear and present danger that such illegal action might occur. Again, their dissent was to no avail. *Gitlow* v. *New York* was thus another in a growing body of cases that narrowly construed the scope of free expression, but it nonetheless constituted a breakthrough as far as the potential expansion of free expression on another front.

The argument on behalf of Gitlow had been based on the contention that the Due Process Clause of the Fourteenth Amendment guaranteed freedom of speech and freedom of the press and that Gitlow's rights in that regard had been violated by the state of New York. While rejecting the proposition that Gitlow's rights had been violated, Justice Sanford during the course of his opinion in the *Gitlow* case conceded that for "present purposes, we may and do assume that freedom of speech and of the press—which are protected by the 1st Amendment from abridgment by Congress—are among the fundamental rights and 'liberties' protected by the due process clause of the 14th Amendment from impairment by the states."[26]

A giant step had thus been taken by the Court beyond its concession in the *Twining* case in 1908 that the Due Process Clause might guarantee against abridgment by the states of rights similar to some of those in the Bill of Rights. The Court had now "assumed" in the *Gitlow* case that the Fourteenth Amendment prohibited the states from violating freedom of the press and freedom of speech. As the decade of the 1930s approached, however, the question remained whether the assumption in the *Gitlow* case had been adopted by the Court only for the purpose of disposing of that case, or whether the Court's assumption was in fact a reality, so that freedom of speech and freedom of the press had become permanent barriers to encroachment upon civil liberties by the states. The 1930s would therefore prove to be a watershed in U.S. constitutional development as it related to the protection of freedom of expression against deprivation by the states.

Assurance that the Court would have the opportunity to decide whether its assumption in the *Gitlow* case was in fact reality was provided by litigation that had begun in California and Minnesota during the late 1920s—litigation based on arguments that freedom of speech and freedom of the press were indeed protected from deprivation by the states under the Due Process Clause of the Fourteenth Amendment. In California, Yetta Stromberg, a member of the Communist party, had been prosecuted for displaying a red flag in violation of the state's law prohibiting such displays. When the California courts upheld Stromberg's conviction, *Stromberg* v. *California* was appealed to the U.S. Supreme Court on the ground that displaying a flag was a form of expression protected by the Fourteenth Amendment.[27]

In Minnesota, freedom of the press was invoked by J. M. Near in his fight against a state court injunction prohibiting him from publishing his weekly newspaper, the *Saturday Press*. In the *Saturday Press*, Near and his partner, Howard Guilford, charged that Minneapolis was under the domination of gangsters who were engaged in gambling and controlling vice within the city and that the mayor, chief of police, and other officials were under the influence of gangster elements. The gangsters in question were Jewish, Near and Guilford alleged, and in denouncing them the *Saturday Press* displayed a decidedly anti-Semitic character.[28]

The Minnesota legislature in 1925, reacting to attacks on politicians by what were regarded as scandal sheets, enacted what came to be called the Minnesota gag law. The gag law authorized local county attorneys to seek from the state courts permanent injunctions against publications that were "obscene, lewd or lascivious" or that were "malicious, scandalous or defamatory," and it was under the latter provision of the law that J. M. Near's *Saturday Press* was permanently enjoined by a state court. It was this Minnesota gag law that served as the model for the gag legislation proposed by Huey Long's forces in the Louisiana legislature of 1930, and there were fears in the press that if the Minnesota law were upheld, it would be copied by other states as well.

Following the issuance of the permanent injunction against the publication of the *Saturday Press*, J. M. Near appealed his case to the Minnesota Supreme Court, but that court in 1928 sustained the gag law and the injunction against Near, rejecting his claim of freedom of the press. Publication of scandalous material such as that contained in the *Saturday Press*, the Minnesota Supreme Court said, tended to provoke assaults and the commission of crime, and such publications served no valid public purpose. The Minnesota legislature, the court held, could prohibit such publications in order to protect the public welfare without offending constitutional guarantees of freedom of the press.[29]

Following the decision of the Minnesota Supreme Court, J. M. Near lacked funds to pursue his case further, and he therefore contacted the American Civil Liberties Union (ACLU) in New York, seeking its assistance in pursuing a further appeal to the U.S. Supreme Court. The ACLU concluded that the Minnesota gag law was indeed a serious threat to the maintenance of a free press and agreed to take the *Near* case to the Supreme Court. While the ACLU and Near were negotiating regarding what Minnesota attorney should be employed for the appeal, however, representatives of the *Chicago Tribune* contacted Near and persuaded him to allow the appeal of his case to be financed by the *Tribune* and its publisher, Colonel Robert R. McCormick, instead of the ACLU. Near finally agreed to this arrangement, and *Tribune* attorneys conducted the appeal in *Near* v. *Minnesota* to the U.S. Supreme Court.[30]

A political reactionary, Robert McCormick appeared at first blush to be an unlikely champion of civil liberties issues such as freedom of the press, but he and the *Chicago Tribune* had been sued for libel by the city of Chicago and its mayor for publishing allegedly libelous articles and editorials exposing corruption in the city. The Illinois Supreme Court had ruled in favor of McCormick and the *Tribune* in 1923, holding that citizens were free to criticize government and that libel against governments was contrary to the basic principles of free expression in U.S. law.[31] Since that ruling, Robert McCormick had become an adamant defender of the freedom of the press, and in 1928 he persuaded the American Newspaper Publishers' Association (ANPA) to create a Committee on Freedom of the Press to monitor any threats to press freedom that might arise. Under the militant leadership of Robert McCormick, the committee involved the ANPA in free-press issues as never before. Because of McCormick's prodding, the association adopted a resolution condemning the Minnesota gag law and became the official sponsor of the litigation in *Near* v. *Minnesota*, contributing five thousand dollars to finance the case. The *Chicago Tribune* and McCormick furnished most of the money for the appeal, which amounted ultimately to over thirty-five thousand dollars.[32]

As the 1920s came to a close, the status of freedom of expression in U.S. constitutional law had therefore seen relatively little development beyond traditional concepts defining that freedom. Free expression was still largely regarded by the courts as primarily a prohibition against prior restraints, and subsequent punishment of expression was judged according to the narrow "bad tendency" test that rationalized most such punishments. As the litigation in *Near* v. *Minnesota* and *Stromberg* v. *California* approached the Supreme Court early in the new decade, however, there was the possibility at least that the Court might use those cases to explicitly hold that freedom of the press and freedom of speech were indeed guaranteed by the Due Process Clause of the Fourteenth Amendment from impairment by the states—a holding that would nationalize the federal Constitution's First Amendment guarantee of free expression. In the meantime, events in Louisiana during the 1930s would furnish the Supreme Court with an opportunity to expand the constitutional right of freedom of the press beyond the boundaries that had previously cabined that basic right, as Huey P. Long finally made good on the threats that he had initiated against the press in 1930.

NOTES

1. *Editor & Publisher* 63 (June 21, 1930): 5.
2. Ibid., 63 (June 28, 1930): 8.
3. Ibid., 63 (June 21, 1930): 5.
4. Ibid., p. 32.
5. Quoted in Ibid., pp. 5, 6; *Baton Rouge Morning Advocate*, June 22, 1930, p. 4.
6. *Editor & Publisher* 63 (June 21, 1930): 6. A detailed description of the negotiations between Long and the New Orleans newspapers regarding the safeguarding of the expenditures of bridge and highway bond monies may be found in the *New Orleans Item*, June 4, 1930, p. 8.
7. *Editor & Publisher* 63 (June 21, 1930): 5.
8. Ibid., 63 (June 28, 1930): 8; 63 (Sept. 13, 1930): 48.
9. Ibid., 63 (June 28, 1930): 8.
10. Robert Allen Rutland, *The Birth of the Bill of Rights* (New York: Collier Books, 1962), p. 212.
11. *Barron* v. *Baltimore*, 7 Pet. 243, 249–50 (1833).
12. Anthony Lewis, *Make No Law* (New York: Random House, 1991), p. 59.
13. Ibid., pp. 53–54.
14. Marvin Meyers, ed., *The Mind of the Founder* (New York: Bobbs-Merrill, 1973), pp. 341–42. On the status of freedom of expression during the founding period, see Leonard Levy, *Emergence of a Free Press* (New York: Oxford University Press, 1985); on the operation of the Sedition Act, see James Morton Smith, *Freedom's Fetters* (Ithaca, N.Y.: Cornell University Press, 1956); see also Stanley Elkins and Eric McKitrick, *The Age of Federalism* (New York: Oxford University Press, 1993), pp. 691–726.
15. *Hurtado* v. *California*, 110 U.S. 516 (1884); *Chicago, Burlington & Quincy Railway Co.* v. *Chicago*, 166 U.S. 226 (1897).
16. *Maxwell* v. *Dow*, 176 U.S. 581 (1900); *Patterson* v. *Colorado*, 205 U.S. 454, 462 (1907).
17. *Twining* v. *New Jersey*, 211 U.S. 78, 99–106 (1908).
18. On the climate of opinion relative to civil liberties during and after World War I, see Julian F. Jaffe, *Crusade against Radicalism* (Port Washington, N.Y.: Kennikat Press, 1972); and Paul L. Murphy, *The Meaning of Freedom of Speech* (Westport, Conn.: Greenwood Press, 1972).
19. *Schenck* v. *United States*, 249 U.S. 47 (1919).
20. 249 U.S. 47, 51–52.
21. Quoted in Richard Polenberg, *Fighting Faiths: The Abrams Case, the Supreme Court, and Free Speech* (New York: Viking, 1987), p. 34.
22. *Debs* v. *United States*, 249 U.S. 211, 215 (1919).
23. *Abrams* v. *United States*, 250 U.S. 616, 627–29 (1919).
24. 250 U.S. 616, 630.
25. *Gitlow* v. *New York*, 268 U.S. 652, 669–70 (1925).
26. 268 U.S. 652, 665–66.
27. See Richard C. Cortner, *The Supreme Court and the Second Bill of Rights* (Madison: University of Wisconsin Press, 1981), pp. 73–81.
28. Ibid., pp. 66–73.

29. *State ex rel. Olson* v. *Guilford*, 174 Minn. 457, 463–64 (1928).

30. Cortner, *The Supreme Court and the Second Bill of Rights*, pp. 66–73.

31. *City of Chicago* v. *Tribune Co.*, 307 Ill. 595 (1923).

32. Cortner, *The Supreme Court and the Second Bill of Rights*, pp. 66–73; see also Fred Friendly, *Minnesota Rag* (New York: Random House, 1981); *Chicago Tribune*, June 2, 1931, p. 1.

Chapter 2

The Kingfish and the "Lying Newspapers" of Louisiana

> Can any sensible man or woman fail to see that the daily newspapers are straining and struggling every minute of the day to give . . . [them] LIES instead of truth?
>
> —*Louisiana Progress*, April 24, 1930

> I will tell you now, there is not a man or concern in this state that knows that he is as much hated, as little respected and as little believed as these newspapers know they are.
>
> —Governor Huey P. Long, April 17, 1930

♦ After he won election as governor of Louisiana in 1928, Huey Long's relations with the state's leading newspapers suffered a steady deterioration, and by the early 1930s Long and his political organization faced an almost unified and implacable opposition from the Louisiana daily press. The opposition to the Kingfish was overwhelmingly centered in the urban press of the state, while the governor enjoyed some support from the smaller, rural weekly papers that had limited circulations. In an attempt to counter press opposition to him and his policies, Long established his own newspaper in 1930, the *Louisiana Progress*, which was described as "probably the most cheerfully venomous publication in the nation." Published in Meridian, Mississippi, the *Progress* was renamed the *American Progress* in 1933, reflecting Long's attempt to influence public opinion not only in Louisiana but also nationally as he sought to further his presidential ambitions.[1]

During the 1930s, the press in Louisiana numbered 163 publications, and included in that number were 120 weekly, mostly rural newspapers with an additional thirteen urban daily papers with substantial circulations in the cities of the state. Among the urban dailies, the *Shreveport Times* and the *Shreveport Journal* dominated northern Louisiana, along with two smaller dailies, the *Monroe News-Star* and the *Monroe Morning World*. The publisher of the *Shreveport Times* was Colonel Robert Ewing, who in 1930 also established the *Monroe Morning World* and purchased the *Monroe News-Star*. Robert Ewing was also the publisher of the *New Orleans States* and was therefore one of the most influential publishers in the state.[2]

Ewing was born in Mobile, Alabama, in 1859, the son of a wealthy cotton broker who had emigrated from Scotland. The Civil War destroyed the elder Ewing's business, and Robert was constrained at an early age to quit school and secure employment. He worked at several jobs, but eventually became an expert telegrapher with Western Union. As a leader of an unsuccessful strike against Western Union in the 1880s, Ewing was blacklisted and required to seek other employment. After pursuing business endeavors in Texas and St. Louis, he returned to Louisiana and became the manager of the *New Orleans Chronicle*, after which he was in rapid succession the telegraph editor, circulation manager, business manager, and finally proprietor of the *New Orleans States*. He acquired the *Shreveport Times* in 1908 and expanded his press empire to include the two Monroe papers in 1930. With Robert Ewing's death in 1931, his press holdings were passed on to his sons, with James associated with the *New Orleans States*, while John D. Ewing published the *Shreveport Times* and the youngest son, Wilson, was associated with the Monroe papers. The Ewing family thus continued to be a powerful force in Louisiana press circles.[3]

The dominant city in middle Louisiana was Alexandria, where the *Alexandria Daily Town Talk* was published by R. C. Jarreau. In the southern section of the state several urban papers were influential, but they were overshadowed by the New Orleans dailies. On the west, the *Lake Charles American Press* was published by Frank A. Smith, and further to the east the *Lafayette Daily Advertiser* was published by Thomas M. Callahan. The capital of the state, Baton Rouge, was dominated by two papers, the *Morning Advocate* and the *State-Times*. Both of the Baton Rouge papers were published by Charles P. Manship, who was a popular figure both in Baton Rouge and in the state's press circles. The Baton Rouge papers were usually referred to as the "Manship papers."

Charles Manship was born in 1881 in McComb, Mississippi, and educated at Millsaps College in Jackson, where he became a reporter for the *Jackson Daily News*. He moved from Mississippi to Baton Rouge in 1904 as a correspondent for the *New Orleans Times-Picayune*, and he later purchased the *State-Times* and, in 1925, established the *Morning Advocate*.[4]

New Orleans boasted four dailies including the Ewing-published *States*. The *New Orleans Item* and *Tribune* were published by James M. Thomson, but by far the leading daily in the city was the *Times-Picayune*. Leonard K. Nicholson was president of the Times-Picayune Company, while Esmond Phelps also possessed a financial interest in the newspaper.[5]

James McIlhaney Thomson was a native of West Virginia, where he was born at Summit Point in 1878. His father was a physician who wanted him to be a lawyer, and James received his college education at the Johns Hopkins University in Baltimore, graduating in 1897. Rather than pursuing a legal career, however, Thomson became a reporter for the *Washington Post* and he purchased the *Norfolk (Va.)Dispatch* in 1900. Ill health forced him to sell the *Dispatch*, and he left Virginia and came to New Orleans, where he purchased the *New Orleans Item* in 1909. Thomson established the *New Orleans Tribune* in 1924 to compete with the *Times-Picayune* as a morning daily. His right-hand man at the *Item* and *Tribune* was his editor in chief, Marshall Ballard. Ballard had received a degree in chemistry at Johns Hopkins, but began his newspaper career as a reporter for the *Baltimore Evening News* in 1897. Thomson had known Ballard at Johns Hopkins, and after Ballard became a reporter in Baltimore, Thomson hired him as editor of the *Norfolk Dispatch* in 1900 and subsequently brought him to New Orleans to edit the *Item* in 1909.[6]

Leonard K. Nicholson of the *Times-Picayune* was born in 1881 in New Orleans, the son of George Nicholson and Pearl Rivers. Rivers was the first woman owner of the *Daily Picayune*, the predecessor of the *Times-Picayune*. Leonard Nicholson became president of the Times-Picayune Company in 1918, succeeding Ashton Phelps, who was in failing health. Ashton's son, Esmond Phelps, was an influential figure not only in New Orleans press circles and the city's politics but also in state affairs. Born in 1889 and educated in private schools, Esmond received both his undergraduate and law degrees from Tulane University and entered the active practice of law in New Orleans in 1909. His firm became one of the leading law firms in the city, and his influence extended across the state's legal, press, and political circles.[7]

At the outset of Huey Long's political career, the opposition to him by these urban dailies was not as monolithic as it eventually became. Indeed, in his successful race for governor in 1928, Long was supported by the Ewing papers—the *Shreveport Times* and the *New Orleans States*—as Long and Robert Ewing formed a political alliance that resulted in Ewing's selection with the Kingfish's support to the Democratic national committee in 1928. The political alliance between the young governor and Ewing was nevertheless doomed to failure. Imperious in manner and sporting a white mustache that fairly bristled, giving him the appearance, some said, of an "angry schnauzer," the sixty-eight-year-old Ewing had apparently felt that he would serve as senior adviser to the thirty-four-year-old governor. Neither Robert Ewing nor Huey Long, however, possessed temperaments that would allow them to be dominated by others, with the result that relations between the two deteriorated rapidly after Long's election as governor and he rather pointedly began ignoring Ewing's advice.[8]

Apparently alluding to Ewing's schnauzer-like appearance or his clipped speaking style, Long adopted toward Ewing one of his favorite tactics against his critics or enemies—the practice of giving them humorous nicknames—and he was soon referring to Ewing as "Colonel Bow-wow." "Colonel Ewing got sore at the governor . . . when he found to his dismay, that he couldn't hold the governor under his pudgy thumb," the *Louisiana Progress* asserted, disparaging Ewing's *States* as the "darling old screech sheet of Camp Street—Col. Bow-wow's *Daily States*." Ewing especially resented the Kingfish's attacks on his son John, associate publisher of the *Shreveport Times*, and Long's insistence on referring to John as "Squirt Ewing." John Ewing, it was said, appeared "to hate [Long] with a deadly and unholy hatred." For his part, Colonel Ewing denounced the governor as a "cheap libeler of men whose shoes he is not fit to tie." Long, Ewing declared, was that "little chinkapin-headed misfit in the governor's chair."[9]

Although Long feigned a supreme indifference to published criticism of him or his policies in the press, in fact he was unusually sensitive to such criticism, displaying that sensitivity throughout his career. While he usually avoided physical confrontations to the extent of being labeled a coward by his enemies, as a young attorney in Shreveport Long attacked Adoph Franz, the editor of the *Shreveport Journal*, which had accused Long of drunkenness. "I'm tired of your lies," he said to Franz as he bloodied his mouth and fell wrestling with him into a gutter before bystanders separated the two men. Almost from the beginning of his term as governor, the Kingfish adopted the policy of refusing interviews with reporters from the Louisiana newspapers. Tiring of reporters importuning him for interviews, Long telephoned the city editor of the *New Orleans Item* and announced, "I'm getting damn tired of these reporters following me all the time. Have you got one man over there that's got any sense at all that I can talk with and I'll clear everything with this one man?" The city editor suggested *Item* reporter Charles Frampton, and consequently "Chick" Frampton became the only Louisiana reporter the Kingfish regularly communicated with from then on.[10]

Another incident early in his term as governor also vividly illustrated Long's unusual sensitivity to press criticism. Although he was born in rural Winn Parish near the town of Winnfield in northern Louisiana, he had established his law practice in Shreveport soon after being admitted to the bar. It was apparently galling to the Kingfish that the Shreveport newspapers in his home base were strongly opposed to him and his policies, at least after his final break with Robert Ewing. Shreveport, which was in Caddo Parish, needed to acquire land for an air base in an adjacent parish, and Shreveport leaders requested that Long seek legislation authorizing the land acquisition. Instead, the Kingfish demanded among other things that the local chamber of commerce publish a public apology for the shabby treatment shown him by Shreveport and that the city's newspapers agree to treat him with more respect, as a condition of his support for the legislation. Only after Shreveport and Caddo Parish surrendered to his demands, he maintained, would he lend his support for the needed legislation. His resentment of Shreveport and Caddo Parish continued, however, and when a request for another favor came to Long from Caddo Parish officials, he angrily refused and declared, "I will teach you to get off the sidewalk, take off your hat, and bow down damn low when Governor Long comes to town." He then, it was alleged, engaged in a tirade against his enemies in Shreveport, denouncing one as "goddamned nigger loving" and another as a "goddamned . . . sonofabitch," and referred to John Ewing of the *Shreveport Times* as that "goddamned shitass Ewing."[11]

At the first regular session of the legislature during his governorship, Huey Long compiled an impressive record of legislative success. He had campaigned in part on a promise to provide free textbooks to the state's schoolchildren at public expense, and the free-textbook measure was successfully enacted. When opponents argued that the free-textbook act violated the principle of separation of church and state because textbooks were furnished to both public and parochial school students, Long responded that the textbooks aided the children of the state in obtaining an education rather than being an aid to the religions operating parochial schools. Despite the contentions of the critics of the free-textbook measure, the U.S. Supreme Court upheld the constitutionality of the program in 1930.[12]

In addition to the free-textbook program, the legislature also authorized, at Long's urging, a bond issue to pay for an expanded highway program to pave hundreds of miles of state roads. When the Kingfish became governor, Louisiana, with pitifully few paved roads, relied primarily on a primitive system of dirt and gravel roads. As a result, during wet seasons the people traveling through the state were frequently mired in mud, and the highway program was intended to remedy this situation. The legislature at Long's behest also passed a severance tax on extractive industries in the state, a tax that would raise considerable revenue, especially from the pumping of oil. Finally, night schools were established to teach literacy to the state's large adult illiterate population. As a whole, the first legislative session under Governor Long had proven eminently successful for him and his program.[13]

When the Kingfish summoned the legislature back into a special session in March 1929, however, and announced that one of the principal measures to be enacted would be a license or manufacturer's tax of five cents a barrel on the refining of oil, the legislators rebelled against his leadership. The oil tax would have fallen principally on the Standard Oil Company, which operated a large refinery in Baton Rouge employing eight thousand people, and Standard Oil was regarded as something of a sacred cow by conservatives in Louisiana. Charges that Long was attempting to destroy one of the state's great industries were soon heard throughout the state, and in the legislature, instead of rather docilely following his leadership, members denounced the governor as a tyrant.[14]

The Manship papers of Baton Rouge, the *Morning Advocate* and the *State-Times,* had until now been less strident in their criticism of Long and his policies than many of the other state dailies and had reported the political scene with considerable neutrality. Charles Manship, however, believed the oil tax would have a devastating impact on the economy of Baton Rouge, with its heavy dependence on the large Standard Oil refinery located there, and the Manship papers pursued a course of vigorous opposition to the adoption of the Kingfish's oil tax, denouncing the measure in editorial after editorial.[15]

Maintaining that the prosperity of Louisiana was at stake, the *Morning Advocate* charged in a front-page editorial on March 19 that all the "years of planning and building and hoping on the part of a far-sighted citizenry have suddenly been jeopardized by the personal whim of a man thrown by chance into a position where he can exercise that whim to the detriment of an industry he conceives to be antagonistic to him." Long was seeking "personal vengeance" against Standard Oil, the *Advocate* said, and the "welfare of Louisiana must come first, ahead of Huey P. Long's whim." If the oil tax were adopted, the paper subsequently warned, two thousand workers would be thrown out of work. In yet another front-page editorial on March 20, the *Advocate* pointed out that the oil tax was opposed by every daily newspaper, every chamber of commerce, and every business executive in the state. "On the side advocating the tax, we find Huey P. Long. And who else? Why naturally, Huey P. Long's following of job-chasers and the small army of favorites who already have their heads shoulder deep in the public swillpail, and who have no desire to be nudged from the trough." "To us," the *Advocate* continued, "there seems little argument on this question, when one side is admittedly motivated by personal hate and a desire for revenge on fancied enemies and when the other side gathers its sole interest in the matter from a love of state and a joy in that state's prosperity, a desire to see all men well-employed, well-fed, able to afford the luxuries which this age offers." Every legislator should reexamine his oath of office, the *Advocate* advised, and then ask the question, "In that oath, did you swear allegiance to a man or to a state?"[16]

At this point an especially ugly event occurred, even for the commonly rough-and-tumble politics of Louisiana. The managing editor of the *Baton Rouge State-Times*, C. P. Liter, encountered Governor Long in the state capitol on the night of March 20. Liter asked the governor if anything of importance was occurring, and they had a general conversation for several minutes. Then the Kingfish bluntly informed Liter, "Tell Manship that if he don't lay off me, I am going to have to publish a list of names of the people who are fighting me who have relatives in the insane asylum." The editorial that had appeared that day in the *Morning Advocate* had gone too far, the governor said, and if Manship failed to tone down his criticism Long would broadcast on the radio the names of people in the mental hospital. Charles Manship's brother, Douglas, had been shell-shocked during service in World War I and was receiving treatment for his condition in the East Louisiana Hospital. After the managing editor's encounter with Long, Charles Manship himself happened upon the Kingfish in the lobby of the capitol, and Long shouted, "Did you get the message I sent you?" Upon receiving a negative response, the governor said, "Well, I sent it to you by Liter." Long warned Manship to "cut out those spite editorials or I'll give out a statement that'll hurt you." When Manship and Liter met later in the evening, Liter informed Manship that the governor had threatened him, but was reluctant to tell Manship the nature of the threat. Only after Manship pressed him did Liter reveal the specifics.[17]

Manship responded to the governor's threat by immediately publishing in the *State-Times* a front-page editorial addressed to the members of the legislature and titled, "This, Gentlemen, is the Way Your Governor Fights." After detailing the threat Long had made against him, Manship stated that he had "a brother, named Douglas Manship. He is in the East Louisiana Hospital." Douglas had left the hospital that day for a visit with him, Manship continued, and in "a few weeks, we hope he will be returned to us well and strong, thanks to the work of Dr. Perkins and his staff." "It is hardly necessary to comment to the intelligent people of Louisiana on such political tactics," Manship concluded. "I might say, however, that my brother Douglas, whom Governor Long has brought into the discussion, is about the same age as the Governor. He was in France in 1918 wearing the uniform of a United States soldier while Governor Long was campaigning for office."[18]

"Not in many years," the *New Orleans States* reported regarding the impact of the Manship affair, "has the state capital been as profoundly shocked as it was this morning." The Kingfish nevertheless made good on his threat against Manship during an address on radio station KWKH in Shreveport. Owned by a wealthy supporter of the Kingfish, William K. Henderson, station KWKH could be heard at night throughout Louisiana, and in his address Long asserted that "Charley Manship is fighting me and I am taking care of his brother in the insane asylum." Given Manship's personal popularity not only in Baton Rouge but in press circles throughout the state, Long's attack on him outraged the state press and "aroused the indignation of every newspaper man in the state." The Manship affair thus deepened the alienation of the press from the Kingfish even further. On March 22, 1929, the day following the appearance of the Manship editorial in the *State-Times*, the *Shreveport Journal* in Long's home base demanded his impeachment—a demand that would soon be acted on by the legislature.[19]

The Kingfish had also failed miserably in his attempt to intimidate Charles Manship, and the Baton Rouge papers continued to hammer away at the proposed oil tax. Long's oil tax had aroused a "public clamor in the state such as had rarely, if ever, been witnessed before," the *Morning Advocate* declared on March 21. The tax was "unfair, unreasonable, uncalled for and unnecessary." "We call upon you, Governor Long, to admit honestly and publicly that you have made an error in suggesting this monstrous tax," the *Advocate* said. "In the face of an overwhelming public opposition, you have no other course. . . . For jobs and offers of jobs have failed, and the Long alignment is ruptured and split before the spear-head of an awakened public interest which intends to defend the state's payrolls to the last ditch."[20]

Governor Long's attack on the Manships also prompted immediate counterattacks by the anti-Long forces in the legislature. Charles Manship's claim that his brother had been shell-shocked during World War I made the governor especially vulnerable to attack, since he had himself avoided military service during the war. At his request, Long had received a deferment from his draft board as a man with dependents, since he and his wife had their first child in 1917. But he had unsuccessfully sought even further protection from the draft by claiming he was entitled to a deferment as a state official because he was a notary public. Reacting to the Manship affair, Representative J. Y. Sanders declared in the legislature that "Charles Manship is an honored citizen of East Baton

Rouge parish. His brother, Douglas Manship, is a personal friend of mine—I served with him in the United States army in France. Douglas Manship is a lovable fellow, and I am proud to call him my friend. I have known Douglas Manship for years, and I have never known him to do anything to increase another's sorrow, nor have I ever known him to make an idle jest of another's suffering."[21]

"I have never known a more humiliating moment in my life," Sanders continued, "than when I read of Governor Long's attack on the World War veteran, torn in mind and body, who has been a patient in one of the state's institutions." "I can think of no deeper humiliation for any Louisianian than to conceive that we have as the governor of the state," he concluded, "a man who would attempt to intimidate a political foe by pressing down the crown of suffering on his brow—a governor who seeks to hold up to idle scorn a veteran of the World War, a victim of disease."[22]

Within days following the Manship affair, it became clear to Governor Long and his legislative leaders that they could no longer command a working majority in the legislature, and they decided it would be best to simply end the special session by adjournment. The anti-Long forces in the legislature, on the other hand, were opposed to adjournment, since they were increasingly convinced that they could end Longism in Louisiana once and for all by impeaching the Kingfish. When a Long leader offered a motion to adjourn the house of representatives, and the electronic voting device used by the house malfunctioned and incorrectly reported a majority in favor of adjournment, bedlam broke out on the floor. An anti-Long member was cut on the head in the ensuing melee while fistfights broke out throughout the floor of the house. The events of that day would always be referred to as "Bloody Monday." Finally, calm was restored and the house overwhelmingly voted approval for an adjournment until the following day.[23]

The *Morning Advocate* accused the Kingfish and his supporters of tampering with the voting machine in the house of representatives, and on March 26 it declared that after "the performance of last night [Bloody Monday] there is but one thing left for the Louisiana legislature to do. That one and overwhelming duty is the impeachment of Governor Long." "Calmly and deliberately, but with a determination that should not be shaken, the Louisiana legislature should move forward with its impeachment of Governor Long," the *Advocate* said. "Governor Long's tyranny over Louisiana should end. Free men—decent men, who respect themselves and love their state can do no less."[24]

When it reconvened the day following Bloody Monday, the anti-Long forces in the house of representatives introduced a resolution providing for the impeachment of Governor Long for "high crimes and misdemeanors in office, incompetency, corruption, favoritism, oppression in office, [and] gross misconduct." During the first week of April, the house began considering impeachment charges against the Kingfish. The first accusation against the governor was that he had made "an attempt to intimidate Charles P. Manship and threatened to make known the infirmities of a member of said Manship's family as a punishment." The impeachment count on the Manship affair was offered on the floor of the house by Representative George K. Perrault of St. Landry Parish, who declared that he could not believe "that any man here, be he lawyer or be he layman, can deep down in his heart approve the act of Governor Long in placing before the people of the world the misfortune of Douglas Manship." In doing so, he said, the governor was "guilty of this reprehensible thing, of this brutal thing." "He is governor of the state. It is his duty to uphold its dignity, to enforce its laws," Perrault continued. "It is difficult to believe that so ruthless, so heartless a character should occupy the high office of governor of this state. And it is your duty to do your utmost to see that he does not much longer hold it." By the mere fact that Long continued to hold the office of governor, he concluded, "the honest and decent citizenry of this state has been brought into disgrace and shame."[25]

The house approved the Manship impeachment charge by a vote of fifty-eight to forty on April 5, and it subsequently approved seven other impeachment charges against the Kingfish. The house had originally considered a wide variety of impeachment charges, including allegations that the governor had used abusive language to citizens, carried a concealed weapon, and fondled a New Orleans nightclub stripper, but in addition to the Manship charge it finally approved seven additional charges. Long, it alleged, had attempted to bribe members of the legislature; taken money for a governors' conference that he had not accounted for; illegally interfered with the state colony and training school and dismissed one of its officials; spent money earmarked for maintenance of the governor's mansion for other purposes; used state money to purchase his private law library; paid a construction firm for defective road culverts; and, in a final, catchall charge, compelled appointees to sign undated resignations, insulted citizens, discharged a college president, appointed a corrupt parole officer, and demonstrated incompetence and temperamental unfitness for his office.[26]

In the hundred-member house of representatives, only a majority vote was needed to approve impeachment charges against Governor Long, but in the senate, which would sit as a court of impeachment to try Long on the charges preferred by the house, a two-thirds majority was required to convict—twenty-six votes out of a total of thirty-nine senators. The Kingfish therefore needed only fourteen votes for an acquittal in the senate on all charges. In the fight over impeachment, the anti-Long and the Kingfish's forces resorted to bare-knuckle, no-holds-barred tactics, with intimidation, cajolery, job offers, and, as a last resort, bribery being used by both sides. The governor also resorted to one of his favorite tactics to rally public opinion to his side, the use of political circulars, and in them he asserted that he was being impeached simply because he had dared to attempt to tax Standard Oil. "I would rather go down to a thousand impeachments than to admit that I am the governor of the state that does not dare to call the Standard Oil Company to account so that we can educate our children and care for [the] destitute, sick and afflicted," he declared. "If this state is still to be ruled by the power of the money of this corporation," Long concluded, "I am too weak for its governor." Nine hundred thousand copies of political circulars supporting Long were delivered during the impeachment battle in April–May 1929.[27]

The governor also toured the state, making speech after speech as he sought to rally his supporters to his cause, and the newspapers were a frequent target of his denunciation. Addressing a large crowd in New Orleans, Long charged that "you can never tell when those newspapers are sincere. They ain't an honest bone in their body. They don't mind telling an untruth." The newspapers of Louisiana had sold out to the Standard Oil Company, he claimed. "The Standard Oil Company's money is filling the columns of the newspapers," he asserted. "They are carrying more advertisements now from the Standard Oil Company than they did this time last year. Every time they write a line, the Standard Oil Company pours in another $1000."[28]

The Kingfish defended himself against the impeachment charges and especially denounced the charge that he had threatened Charles Manship. "Among the charges that the *Times-Picayune* urges is that I have threatened to tell about Charlie Manship having a crazy brother," he said. "Let me tell you about the case. It is not a case that would be an impeachable offense, but let me tell you the facts about the case." Manship was a millionaire who owned both Baton Rouge papers, he pointed out, and he "had a brother who went crazy. What did he do about it? Did he put him in the jail cells to wait until someone died [making room in the state asylum] like your brother would have done? Did he lock him in a back room of a house and put a guard over him like you would do with your brother or mine?" "No," Long answered, "he put him in a hospital the next day, and they started to cure him."[29]

One hundred people were waiting to be admitted to the mental hospital, the governor charged, but Charles Manship had secured the admittance of his brother ahead of those less fortunate people. "I met Manship and told him I wanted to appeal to him as a man not to attack me personally and call me false names when he knew his brother was put in the insane asylum over hundreds of other people, and that he ought to be loyal enough at least not to attack me when I am trying to take care of the other man's brother," Long claimed. "Manship said: 'You are right, I won't attack you again,' but as a result of that he comes out with that damnable infernal lie, and the truth ain't in him, and he knows it." Douglas Manship was being treated in a state hospital, the Kingfish maintained, "and they say I made a terrible offense because they say the insanity of this young man, the brother of Manship, is due to shell shock in the World War. That ain't so—it is due to a venereal disease, the records show."[30]

A constant theme of Long's defense against impeachment was that the newspapers had been bought by Standard Oil, and while his enemies were cowards, he charged, they "didn't cowardize the newspapers, they bought them." There "never was a lower down, more unscrupulous set of scoundrels than there are in newspaper offices today," he declared. The newspapers were "dirty, low down lying sheets." Charles Manship was a "dirty liar," the governor maintained, and he attacked other newspaper publishers as well. He referred to Colonel Robert Ewing of the *New Orleans States* and *Shreveport Times* as "Colonel Bow-wow" and asserted he would label John Ewing, editor of the *Shreveport Times*, a jackass except he had nothing against jackasses. John Ewing was a young squirt, Long said, but he could not be called a scoundrel because Ewing was not enough of a man for that label.[31]

Speaking to a crowd in a high school in Alexandria, the Kingfish charged that the *Alexandria Daily Town Talk* had been bought by the Standard Oil Company, adding that that "bird Jarreau's buying him a limousine, I hear." R. C. Jarreau, publisher of the *Town Talk*, was in the audience, and he called the governor a liar. Most of the audience failed to hear Jarreau's remark, and Long proceeded with his speech and repeated that the *Town Talk* had sold out to Standard Oil, asking the crowd if it had "ever known the *Town Talk* to take a stand on anything before now?" This time, Jarreau rose from his seat and shouted for all to hear, "That's another lie." The crowd became unruly at that point, interrupting the governor's speech for five minutes while some of Long's supporters shouted, "Throw him out." After glaring speechless at Jarreau, the Kingfish assured the crowd that he could take care of the "cowardly" newspapers. The "truth ain't in the newspapers," he asserted, "and it ain't in you, sir," pointing to Jarreau. The *Town Talk*, along with the *New Orleans Times-Picayune*, *States*, and *Item* were all Standard Oil papers, the governor maintained: "I say that and I mean it."[32]

Long charged in another speech that the state's farmers had produced $180 million in crops in 1928, while Standard Oil had profits of $216 million from just one refinery in the state, yet the farmers paid forty times more in taxes than Standard Oil. "But you won't see this in the newspapers," he said. "They can't and won't tell the truth." Reverting to the Manship affair, the governor accused Charles Manship of filing an affidavit swearing that his brother could not pay for his treatment in the mental hospital while it was well known Charles Manship was a millionaire. Again denying that Douglas Manship was suffering from shell shock, Long asked his audience, "Did you ever hear of shell shock causing syphilis? That's what he's crazy with." Charles Manship should not mind having his brother called crazy, Long said, since from what was being printed in the newspapers during the impeachment fight the people had become convinced that all newspaper men were crazy.[33]

A glimpse into the rough tactics engaged in by both sides in the impeachment fight is offered by the anti-Long forces' attempt to convince Representative Lester Lautenschlaeger, who was also the backfield coach of Tulane University's football team, to support impeachment. Esmond Phelps, part owner of the *New Orleans Times-Picayune,* volunteered his services to the anti-Long forces. Phelps was also chairman of the board of administrators at Tulane, and he lobbied Lautenschlaeger to vote for impeachment, but Lautenschlaeger maintained that he would take a neutral stance until he had seen the evidence against the governor. "Unless we can count on you now your position at Tulane is at stake," Phelps threatened, and within hours Lautenschlaeger received a telegram dismissing him as a Tulane coach. Threats by the other coaches to resign in protest apparently were all that saved Lautenschlaeger's job at Tulane.[34]

The state senate convened as a court of impeachment on May 14 to a packed audience that expected the trial of Governor Long to last for six weeks. The state chief justice presided, and the Kingfish appeared wearing an immaculate white suit and smoking a cigar. The attorneys for the governor demurred to seven of the eight charges against him, arguing that under the terms of the call for the special legislative session, the legislature could not legally have met after April 6, and those seven charges had been adopted after that date. The senate narrowly rejected the demurrer on May 15, but the vote on the Manship charge, which Long's supporters argued was the only legally adopted charge against the governor because it had been adopted on April 6, was twenty-one to eighteen in favor of dismissal. On the following day, the impeachment proceedings came to an unexpected end when the Long forces introduced a motion that listed fifteen senators as being pledged to vote against the remaining charges because they had been adopted after the April 6 date. This list of fifteen senators, which became famous in Louisiana politics as the "Round Robin," made it plain that a two-thirds majority was impossible on any impeachment count. To the incredulity of his opponents, the Kingfish had won the fight of his political life, and when a motion to adjourn the impeachment proceedings permanently was offered, there was no opposition to its adoption.[35]

Reflecting the disappointment felt generally by the anti-Long forces, the *New Orleans Times-Picayune* maintained in a front-page editorial that the Kingfish was "temperamentally and otherwise unfit to hold the office." Pointing out that it had twice called for his removal from office during the impeachment fight, the paper decried the fact that the charges against the governor had not been tried on their merits and declared its support for "any properly organized movement to compel Governor Long to vacate his office." "It is not a pleasant business, nor one that adds to the peace and happiness of the people, either at home or abroad, but we feel that there is enough red-blooded manhood and high-minded womanhood in our state which wants to see the thing settled on the merits, to justify the additional efforts that must be made to terminate the matter as it should be," the *Times-Picayune* continued. "We, therefore, favor the recall." Efforts to recall Governor Long after impeachment failed, however, also came to nothing.[36]

As a result of the impeachment fight, what had been a wide division between supporters and opponents of Huey Long in Louisiana became a chasm. To the anti-Long forces, which included almost all of the daily press, Long was a clownish figure, a country rube, or a redneck radical demagogue, lacking in dignity, who had shattered the veneer of gentility that had previously characterized politics in the state. He had proven that he would play politics not by the traditional rules but by his own set of rough-and-tumble, give-no-quarter rules of vindictiveness as far as his opponents were concerned. The anti-Long forces longed for a return to the Louisiana that existed before the rise of the Kingfish as a political force; they favored a state government that intruded minimally in the business and economic affairs of the state—one that kept the tax rate low and maintained a climate favorable to business and industry. Long's plan of raising taxes and of financing the roads and bridges program by increasing the state's bonded indebtedness was therefore anathema to those who opposed him. Not only was his plan a profligate squandering of the state's treasury, they felt, but it also furnished a slush fund to feed the Kingfish's political machine.

The Kingfish's penchant for publicity-attracting comic antics confirmed the belief of his opponents that he was hopelessly lacking in the essential dignity and gentlemanly qualities that should characterize Louisiana's governor. Two incidents during 1930 that attracted national attention to Louisiana and Long's clownish antics confirmed these beliefs in the eyes of his enemies. One involved Long's comic campaign to educate the public on the proper preparation of potlikker, the residue left after vegetables and greens are boiled and a favorite of rural southerners. To the amusement of the national press, the Kingfish humorously described how potlikker should be properly prepared and consumed by dipping corn pone into the potlikker. The impression that Louisiana had an eccentric clown for a governor could only have been discomforting to the dignified, conservative elements in the state.[37]

The second incident had potentially more serious repercussions, but was again embarrassing to the state. The German cruiser *Emden*, on a goodwill tour of the United States, docked at New Orleans in March 1930. The commander of the *Emden* decided to pay a courtesy call on the governor of Louisiana and learned that, as was frequently the case, Long was residing at the Roosevelt Hotel in New Orleans. On a Sunday morning, the German commander presented himself in full-dress uniform at the Roosevelt and was taken to the governor's suite. Long appeared from a bedroom in green pajamas, a red and blue robe, and blue slippers. Although the German commander and the Kingfish had an apparently amicable conversation, the German consul later protested that Long's appearance at the interview was an insult to his country and demanded an apology. The incident was only smoothed over by an official visit by Governor Long, properly attired, to the German ship on the following day. But the green pajamas incident was thereafter used by the Kingfish's opponents as a vivid illustration of his utter lack of dignity and fitness for his office. These beliefs were only reinforced when the governor subsequently received Major General Frank McCoy, commander of the U.S. Fourth Army, clad only in his underwear. The *States-Times*, however, congratulated the general for his narrow escape, since Long had previously received a delegation from Baton Rouge in the nude.[38]

Although never the subject of public discussion in the press, another embarrassing aspect of Huey Long's behavior was his relationship with Alice Lee Grosjean. Alice Grosjean was a native of Shreveport and her grandfather, Victor Grosjean, was the editor and publisher of the *Shreveport Caucasian*. Despite her apparent innate intelligence, Alice quit school at the age of fifteen and married James Terrell, but the couple later separated and were divorced in 1928. Long hired the teenaged Grosjean as his secretary when he was serving on the Louisiana Public Service Commission, and she became an important member of the Kingfish's entourage, working in his unsuccessful campaign for governor in 1924 and in his victorious campaign in 1928. Among Long's intimates, Alice Grosjean was also considered to be his mistress. Upon his election as governor, Long blithely installed Grosjean in the governor's mansion in Baton Rouge, whereupon his wife, Rose McConnell

Long, promptly moved out and returned with their children to Shreveport. Apparently as an inducement for Rose to return, Grosjean was then installed in the Heidelberg Hotel, where the governor also maintained a suite and spent most nights. When this pattern of behavior continued, Rose Long again returned to Shreveport and subsequently appeared only occasionally in Baton Rouge. Although the Kingfish later acquired a home in New Orleans where he installed his family, when not in the capital, he lived not at home but mostly in the Roosevelt Hotel in the Crescent City.[39]

Despite the close call he had experienced with the impeachment attempt, Governor Long soon proposed for enactment by the 1930 session of the legislature measures that would renovate the New Orleans docks to restore that city as a great port and build new roads around the city and a new bridge across the Mississippi. In addition, he proposed a new $68 million bond issue to pave three thousand miles of roads and build bridges in other parts of the state and, finally, he proposed a bond issue to build a new high-rise state capitol building. With the onset of the Depression in the fall of 1929, these increased state expenditures, he argued, would provide sorely needed jobs and a stimulus to the state's economy.[40]

In an attempt to defuse the otherwise predictable opposition of the New Orleans dailies to his ambitious program, the Kingfish met with their publishers as well as New Orleans business leaders in an attempt to negotiate a compromise acceptable to all sides. An independent commission of prominent citizens that would have the power to control the disbursement of the $68 million in highway funds, free of the governor's control, was temporarily agreed to but was subsequently repudiated by Long. He had had conferences with the publishers of the New Orleans dailies, the governor later admitted. "We had a conference, all right. They told me what to do and I told them where to go. They won't run this state while I am governor."[41]

With the collapse of the negotiations regarding the independent citizens' commission, the state's daily press began a full-throated editorial outcry against the Long program. "We think the professional, business and industrial interests of Louisiana have become convinced that Huey Long is a brigand, having no respect for the constitution, the law or obligations of honor. We know he is," the *Shreveport Times* observed in an editorial typical of those that began appearing in the dailies. Recognizing that the daily press would now constitute a powerful obstacle to his program and the realization of his ambitions, the Kingfish responded with the publication on March 27, 1930, of his own newspaper, the *Louisiana Progress*. A primary purpose of the *Progress* was indicated by Long in a radio address that was reprinted in the first issue of his paper. "I don't know who is going to oppose my road program, but the daily newspapers fought the last highway project," Long said. "If the daily papers had their way there wouldn't be any free school books, paved roads or night classes for illiterates in Louisiana. These daily newspapers have been against every progressive step in this state and the only way for the people of Louisiana to get ahead is stomp them flat."[42]

From the beginning, it was clear that a principal mission of the *Louisiana Progress* was to "stomp flat" the Louisiana dailies, and this overriding mission was attempted in its columns not only by slashing criticism of the dailies themselves in order to discredit them in the eyes of the public but also by caustic personal attacks on the individuals associated with their publication. Each week, the *Progress* announced in an early issue, it pledged to "correct the lies published in the daily press of the state during the preceding week. These daily newspapers admit that they will print any kind of a lie to keep the constructive work of the state administration from continuing. These daily newspapers are against paved roads, free school books, night schools for adult illiterates and all other Long policies while Governor Long is doing the work."[43]

In early April, Colonel Robert Ewing's *New Orleans States* editorially bemoaned the fact that such a low character as Huey Long should be governor of Louisiana, and it nostalgically expressed a longing for a return to the political convention system of nominating political candidates. The convention system had resulted in the nomination of candidates of high caliber, it maintained, while the current political primary system had resulted in the nomination of such disasters as Long. The *Progress* immediately denounced the *States* for seeking to deprive the people of their right to vote in primaries for candidates of their choice, observing that the "editorial announcement of the *States* may be taken as the policy of all the daily newspapers as it is generally known that at this time the politics of these daily newspapers is one and the same." The newspapers "have been told by the people time after time and by the governor of the state that what they want is one thing and that what the people want is another," the *Progress* said. The support of the dailies "was more harmful to a candidate than good," it continued. "These once mighty influences are understood to have investigated conditions and their editorial pronouncement against the people being allowed to vote at all Democratic primaries is taken to mean that they understood that they cannot match arms with the governor of the state in any election before the people at this time."[44]

The Kingfish's proposal of the $68 million paved roads program required an amendment to the state constitution that would have to be approved in a public referendum. Prior to the 1930 legislative session,

Long stumped the state to drum up popular support for the program, charging that the newspapers were "trying to keep you people from having a chance to vote on this law." He challenged the press to allow a vote on the amendment authorizing the road program and promised to run for the U.S. Senate at the same time. If he failed to be elected to the Senate and the road program were not approved, he pledged to resign from the governorship. "I will tell you now," the Kingfish told his audiences around the state, "there is not a man or concern in this state that knows that he is as much hated, as little respected and as little believed as these newspapers know they are." "It's horrible for one to know he is a no good, the people know he is a no good, that he will not tell the truth, that he doesn't deserve to be considered honest or decent, but that is a fact with these newspapers," he said. "And, yet, admitting that the people do not believe them, that they are no good, they are trying to keep the people from having a chance to vote on their own laws." The newspapers knew that if the people could vote on the highway program they would overwhelmingly approve it, Long maintained. "You cannot pay any attention to what the daily newspapers may say I have said in these speeches. They will say anything on the living earth and then will devote columns pretending to answer something that they say I have said even when I have never said anything of the kind or maybe when I have said the contrary."[45]

When the dailies criticized the Kingfish for publishing the *Louisiana Progress* in Meridian, Mississippi, rather than in Louisiana, the *Progress* responded by attacking the "four oracles of New Orleans—the pompous *Times-Picayune*, the slip-shod *States*, the smart-aleck *Item* and the baby-faced *Tribune*." "Ignorant as they all are it is to be expected," the Long paper said, "that these four would fall like buzzards upon any newspaper in this state that is dedicated to fearless publication of truth. They don't know what truth is." The dailies were "hypocritical, double-crossing polecats," the *Progress* continued. "They won't print the truth in New Orleans, Shreveport and Monroe. They won't print the truth because it's killing them." All of the New Orleans dailies operated on a nonunion basis, it charged, while the Meridian print shop where the *Progress* was printed was unionized. "When the day comes that the printing industry of the State of Louisiana is not dominated by the four New Orleans newspapers who are guzzling like bleary eyed hogs from a trough filled with malice, lies and hypocrisy," it said, "then the *Louisiana Progress* will be published in Louisiana."[46]

The New Orleans dailies were united by their fear of Governor Long, the *Progress* subsequently charged, and they had consciously decided to oppose any program he proposed regardless of how beneficial it might be for the people of the state. The dailies were opposing the constitutional amendment to authorize the highway program, it claimed, because "they know that the people are with Governor Long. They know that the people of this state have passed the stage when they believe what is misrepresented in the . . . lie merchants of New Orleans and the little lie-peddlers of Shreveport, Monroe and Baton Rouge." The New Orleans papers "fear the truth as the devil is reputed to fear holy water," the *Progress* continued. "Can any sensible man or woman fail to see that the daily newspapers are straining and struggling every minute of the day to give . . . [them] LIES instead of truth?" By May, the *Progress* claimed a circulation of 125,000 copies weekly, with 30,000 copies sold weekly in New Orleans. It now had "the New Orleans newspapers on the run and groggy," and it promised to continue to expose those papers "in all their deceit, crookedness, treachery and hypocrisy."[47]

The 1930 legislative session convened in mid-May, and Governor Long presented his program in an address to the legislators in Baton Rouge. The *Progress* printed the governor's address in its May 15 edition and also published a page-one cartoon depicting the *New Orleans Item, States, Times-Picayune, Monroe Morning World, Shreveport Times, Alexandria Daily Town Talk,* and *Baton Rouge State-Times* as figures assaulting a character labeled "the Truth," who complained that its assailants were threatening to "chase me out of the State of Louisiana." With the convening of the legislature, the *Progress* predicted editorially, the "great lying handicap is on and it bids to be a close race between the *Item,* the *States* and the *Times-Picayune.* These three shallow organs, each with a peculiar genius and ability for lying, have gone through the warming up process and are ready for their greatest work." The *Progress* believed that the *Item* would win the "Lie Handicap" with the *Times-Picayune* a close second. Although the *Times-Picayune* "could lie better than any," it said, its best brains had been diverted from their usual task of "concocting the brand of lies upon which the reputation of the paper has been founded."[48]

With considerable glee, the *Louisiana Progress* regularly singled out for personal abuse the individuals associated with the publication of the New Orleans dailies, with Esmond Phelps of the *Times-Picayune* a frequent and favorite target. The *Times-Picayune* had upbraided the Kingfish for putting favorably disposed legislators on the state payroll, allowing them to draw double salaries as legislators as well as state employees. The Kingfish discovered, however, that Esmond Phelps's brother-in-law, Arthur B. Hammond, had been retained as an attorney for both the state dock board and the levee board at a total salary of over seven hundred dollars a month, and the governor promptly dismissed Hammond from both positions. "Times-Pic Dictator's Kin Pried from 2 Swill Tubs," the *Progress* headlined the story. "Governor Long, catching the spirit of the Pic's two-job propaganda, examines payrolls and finds that Mussolini of the *Times-Picayune* has his relative modestly taking state pay in New Orleans with both hands at the same time." Arthur Hammond, the *Progress* observed, had been discovered "luxuriously reclining, fed with the amber ladle of the levee board and at the same time sitting at the pie counter of the port." Esmond Phelps, it claimed, had become "maddened" by the governor's treatment of his brother-in-law, and "the political dictator of the *Times-Picayune* now sets the *Times-Picayune* liars of all denominations to work. It makes no difference what happens, what is not done, or what is done, they must get up some lie to offset the good impression the constructive work of the state administration is making." As a member of the board of administrators of Tulane University, Phelps was subsequently accused by the *Progress* of securing a job for a crony, fired from the dock board by the Kingfish, with the Tulane Educational Fund. "Esmond has apparently seen the futility of getting jobs for his yes-men on public payrolls and now has changed tactics," the *Progress* observed. Phelps was "politicizing Tulane University," where "the distinguished political framer of the *Times-Picayune* gets slop for his swill tub."[49]

Although Esmond Phelps had only a limited financial interest in the *Times-Picayune* and was on friendly terms with Alvin P. Howard, a major stockholder of the paper, the *Progress* nevertheless identified Phelps as the real power behind the *Times-Picayune* and subsequently alleged that a personal feud had developed between Phelps and Howard over who would issue orders to Leonard Nicholson, the paper's president. Howard, the Long paper asserted, had asked Phelps to sell his interest in the *Times-Picayune* to avoid embarrassing the paper because of the Arthur Hammond incident. Alvin Howard and Esmond Phelps, the *Progress* reported in May, "today were still sneaking around with bared knives behind their backs waiting for the chance to spring a coup and gain control of the *Times-Picayune*." Howard, it claimed, glowered at individuals he met in the street who questioned his control of Leonard Nicholson and the *Times-Picayune's* editorial policies, and when he overheard someone suggest that Phelps was the real power behind the throne at the paper, Howard was observed "muttering incoherently."[50]

Another favorite target of the *Progress* was Marshall Ballard, the editor of the *New Orleans Item*, which the Long paper referred to as the "Lie-to-em." Ballard was well known for his caustic editorials, and his attacks on the Kingfish were a constant source of irritation to the governor. In 1924, the wife of James Thomson, the publisher of the *Item*, was a candidate for Congress, and Ballard of course wrote editorials supporting Genevieve Thomson and attacking her opponent. Colonel Ewing of the *New Orleans States*, however, supported Genevieve Thomson's opponent, and as the contest heated up, Ewing published a cartoon attacking Ballard that depicted the *Item* editor as a narcotics addict, smoking what appeared to be an opium pipe and with hypodermic needles protruding from his arm. The *Louisiana Progress* gleefully reprinted this cartoon in May 1930, explaining that "Colonel Ewing pictured Mr. Ballard as in the above picture to explain to the people why Mr. Ballard wrote so many amazing things in the *Item*, and so we pass it on today as a possible explanation as to why one finds the same editorial condition in the *Item* as existed in 1924." *Progress* cartoons subsequently portrayed the New Orleans papers either as disreputable appearing characters or as a multiheaded snake. The *Item* character was always depicted with hypodermic needles protruding from its arms, neck, or head, sometimes with bats and snakes hovering above, and Marshall Ballard was usually referred to as the "hop-needle part." Should the *Item* win the "Lie Handicap" during the 1930 legislative session, the *Progress* reported, "the *Picayune* owners will protest on the grounds that the *Item* horse was full of hop."[51]

The publishers of the New Orleans dailies were "weird old ducks" who had made their fortunes in the publishing business, the *Progress* charged. "What matter if their pudgy, softening hulks are blockading all progressive movement in the state?" They had met their match in Governor Long, it maintained, and the "once powerful New Orleans press, makers of governors, dictators of politics, mighty Machiavellis of the broken promise and double-cross are now one with the gnarled impotence of the 1910 automobile." The New Orleans publishers had "lost honor, respect, truth and the power to think straight," the *Progress* asserted, and it was now common knowledge that the surest way to pass a law or start a successful movement was to "first earn the hostility of the *Times-Picayune*, the [*Item*] and the . . . *States*. When Bow-wow barks it is a victory signed. When Ballard berates the game has been won. When Phelps deplores the gong sounds."[52]

In addition to Ballard, Phelps, and Nicholson, others associated with the state's dailies also drew fire from the *Progress*. In a speech in Baton Rouge that was reprinted by the *Progress*, Governor Long referred to Charles Manship and told his audience that "I feel I must pay due homage to Charley." "Some people seem to be afraid of Charley Manship," he continued. "Let me tell you there never was a bigger coward on the Lord's green earth than that fellow." Manship had even used his own brother in his attacks on him, the Kingfish claimed. "I pleaded with him that he, above all men, should not attack me when I was trying to get money for hospitals and asylums. He doesn't want the new capitol, he didn't want the [new governor's] mansion, and he doesn't want me in Baton Rouge. Well, let him try to put me out. Just let him try." The local Baton Rouge merchants had made Manship successful with their newspaper advertising, the governor charged, but Manship was now betraying them by filling his papers with the ads of chain stores that were competing unfairly with local merchants.[53]

The bravado with which the *Progress* assured its readers of the impotence of the state's daily press was belied by the fate of the Kingfish's program in the legislature. The constitutional amendment authorizing the $68 million bond issue for paved roads, which the *Times-Picayune* deemed the "road bonds racket," encountered immediate difficulty at the hands of the legislators, and in May the New Orleans Old Regular Democratic organization, led by New Orleans mayor T. Semmes Walmsley, announced it would oppose the paved roads amendment. The defection of the New Orleans delegation in the legislature made it highly unlikely that Long could muster the two-thirds majorities in both houses necessary for the passage of the roads amendment. Infuriated by this turn of events, he retaliated against New Orleans by attempting to cut off the city's ability to borrow money or collect taxes.[54]

The Kingfish also organized a rally of his supporters in New Orleans, and at the rally he charged that New Orleans had overextended its credit and that there were serious shortages in the city's finances, shortages he had exposed by ordering a state audit. "Col. Bow-wow called it an act of tyranny, bordering on revolution," Long said, again launching a slashing attack on the city's dailies. "Old Dr. *Times-Picayune*—the widow woman of the press—objected in a big streamer and the hop-needle part protested. These newspapers will do anything. They write the facts as they want them and then they write editorials on the facts they have decided on." Although there had been a time when "the *Picayune*, *States* and *Item* could pretty well run things as they pleased, that time is past," he continued. "I fought, bled and died with some of that gang until I became governor. And then I decided I would BE governor. Then it was that that crowd of renegades, pilferers and blackmailers found out they had struck one man who they could neither run nor ruin!"[55]

"The newspapers have not only aided in the pilfering of the treasury for the Walmsley family, but also for their own families," the Kingfish charged. "They've stopped at nothing at printing every form of lie." Esmond Phelps of the *Times-Picayune* "carries that little Nicholson around in his hip pocket," he maintained, and he renewed the allegation that Phelps's brother-in-law, Arthur Hammond, had been drawing salaries from both the dock board and the levee board, salaries that amounted to six thousand dollars a year. "I could hire better lawyers than Hammond at fifty dollars a month," Long asserted. "I take full responsibility for cutting Hammond away from teat No. 1 and teat No. 2." The New Orleans dailies had also been storing their newsprint in the warehouses of the dock board, he charged, paying much less than storage in private warehouses would have cost until he had ordered their newsprint out of the dock board's warehouses.[56]

The New Orleans press had been bought off by advertising money from the big interests, the governor continued. "Those papers don't care what happens to the city. They're out for what they can get. It's like a burglar who knows how to blow a safe but couldn't open one with the combination." "Those full-vested prevaricators are shrewd. They know how to keep money once they get it," he conceded. "Esmond Phelps never spent a dime for a shoe shine in his life. He uses Shinola and if he has none rubs his shoes on his pants' leg." Phelps, the Kingfish also asserted, had obtained a job with Tulane University for a henchman Long had fired from the dock board. "Talk about a gang like that! A self-respecting polecat couldn't sleep with them." The New Orleans ring and its daily papers "would rather have no town at all than to have their powers taken away," Long concluded. "But their day is almost done. . . . Let's be a free people. Fear no one. Fear no papers. To hell with the newspapers."[57]

Among supporters of the Kingfish, Esmond Phelps would thereafter be referred to derisively as "Shinola Phelps," and by dismissing Arthur Hammond, Long was able to strike out against Hammond's wife, Hilda Phelps Hammond, who was one of the Kingfish's most vociferous opponents. Mrs. Hammond was the sister of Esmond Phelps, and she had adopted as a mission in life the goal of driving the Kingfish from public life in Louisiana, organizing a committee of aristocratic women for that purpose. During the 1930s, she was a frequent witness and lobbyist in an effort to persuade the U.S. Senate to unseat Long and Louisiana senator John Overton because of alleged election fraud on their part.[58]

Despite the withering attack upon them by the Kingfish, the New Orleans dailies rallied to the defense of the city, which they said was plunged into a financial crisis by the governor's actions, and Mayor Walmsley charged that the governor was "insane." "The time has come when men with red blood in their veins, who are not ashamed to call themselves men, who are willing to revolt at the oppression of this tyrant, [will] . . . let him know once and for all that the State of Louisiana will unshackle itself, that the people of New Orleans will not cower at the crack of his whip, and will resist oppression from such a brute," the mayor declared.[59]

In June, the Kingfish retaliated further against the daily press by having introduced in the legislature a 15 percent tax on the gross receipts the papers obtained from the sale of advertising and a bill authorizing injunctions against papers found to be malicious, scandalous, or defamatory. Referring to the governor as "his erratic excellency," the *Times-Picayune* nevertheless continued along with the rest of the daily press to oppose the road program because it would make available an enormous amount of money to the Kingfish without any independent control of how it was disbursed. "It is this newspaper's belief," the *Times-Picayune* said, that "Governor Long will tolerate no safeguards [regarding the expenditure of highway money] that he cannot evade or override."[60]

On June 17, the paved roads constitutional amendment fell seven votes short of the two-thirds majority needed for its passage in the house of representatives. Having anticipated the defeat of the amendment, the Kingfish on June 11 had had his legislative leaders introduce a bill authorizing a constitutional convention that could adopt the $68 million roads program—a bill that needed the approval of only simple majorities in both houses. "All the schemes and designs of a handful of petty politicians, ward bosses and their lying newspapers are doomed to failure," the *Louisiana Progress* declared in support of the constitutional convention bill. "The demons of hell have been thrown into a frenzy."[61]

The daily press, however, warned its readers time and again that a constitutional convention controlled by Long would be more dangerous than any measure he had yet proposed, since a convention dominated by the governor could fundamentally alter the very fabric of the state's government. The *Shreveport Times* thus attacked the "wild reign of the demon despot, Huey P. Long." "God forbid," it declared regarding the proposed constitutional convention, "that this mad scheme of the demonical despot who has held the state up to the ridicule of the nation and scared away investment capital, be put over." The *Times-Picayune* warned that a constitutional convention would not be limited to the approval of the paved roads program and that "other possibilities of personal profit and advantage to be derived from a constitutional convention are not overlooked, we may be sure, by our imperial-minded and imperious excellency."[62]

Limitations currently in place, the *Times-Picayune* continued, preventing the Kingfish from doing as he pleased could be eliminated from the constitution by the convention. The limitations on taxation could be eliminated, it warned, and the amount of road bonds could be doubled or even trebled. The one-term limitation on the office of governor could be abolished, with the result that "the days of the dictatorship could be extended for any period deemed desirable, permitting his imperial excellency to reign and mete out rewards and punishments until the last penny of the bond money was spent and Louisiana's credit had been milked dry. Wouldn't that be lovely—for Governor Long?"[63]

The *Louisiana Progress* meanwhile continued to assure its readers that Governor Long, through the constitutional convention and the required public approval of any changes it might make in the constitution, was determined to allow the people to vote on the paved roads program. The governor, it declared, would see to it that "your constitutional rights are not relegated to the swill troughs of newspaper hokum" and that "no newspapers or cheap grafting politicians are going to deprive you of your fundamental rights as citizens." But the dailies maintained a steady drumbeat of opposition to the constitutional convention proposal, which the *Times-Picayune* labeled the "constitutional convention racket" and a "fantastic and costly absurdity" for which "there is no need, no popular demand, and not even a shadow of justification or excuse." The prospect of a Long-dominated constitutional convention pleased the governor, it charged, and "thrills and fills him with ardent imaginings of more power, more taxes, more bonds, more money for his spending under a constitution emasculated to his fancy and misshapen to suit his ends."[64]

Responding to criticisms that a convention would necessarily be unlimited in the changes it could propose in the constitution, Long supporters in the legislature restricted the convention measure to authorize the consideration of only the roads program, flood control, and pardons and paroles. The press, however, pointed out that any convention could ignore any such legislatively imposed limitations and the constitution would then be exposed to complete revision. "With all the taxation safeguards imperilled, all restrictions upon executive power subject to destruction, our judicial and legislative systems themselves exposed to change," the *Times-Picayune* again warned, "Louisiana's business and industry would inevitably suffer greatly."[65]

With the Kingfish, as the press reported, "using the virtual unlimited power of his office," the house of representatives approved the constitutional convention proposal on June 25 by a fourteen-vote margin, and the "raid upon the organic law" could then be prevented only by the state senate. By law, however, the legislative session was required to end on July 10, and in order to pass the constitutional convention proposal the Long forces in the senate were forced to attempt to suspend the rules to bring the proposal before the body out of order. But aided by the anti-Long Lieutenant Governor Paul Cyr, who presided over the senate, the opponents of the convention measure were able to block all efforts to suspend the senate's rules, and the legislature adjourned on July 10 without authorizing the constitutional convention. Indeed, almost no significant legislation had been enacted during the session, and among those measures dying with the legislature's adjournment were the road program, the proposal for a new capitol, and the taxation and injunction bills aimed at punishing the press.[66]

Although he had survived the impeachment attempt in 1929, the Kingfish had now witnessed his enemies, including the press, successfully block his program in the 1930 legislative session, and his domination of the legislature appeared to be at an end. "The Old New Orleans Ring and their lying newspapers," reinforced by other Long enemies, the *Louisiana Progress* charged, had blocked the paved roads program from being considered by a constitutional convention through the use of "hoodlum tactics." The *Times-Picayune*, on the other hand, applauded the legislative session's "chief and almost its only constructive achievement," the defeat of "Governor Long's twin rackets—his $68,000,000 road bond scheme and his project, flimsily disguised, for an unlimited constitutional convention." To the legislators in both houses who had accomplished those results, it said, "the gratitude and perpetual esteem of Louisiana's people are due."[67]

During the legislative session, the *Louisiana Progress* asserted, the "New Orleans dailies and other ring-dominated sheets throughout the state were ordered to open up their mud batteries and all responded with a unanimity worthy of a worthy cause." "Never before in the history of the state," it maintained, "has a public official been hounded, abused, vilified and lied about as has been Gov. Long." Stung by defeat, Huey Long was now confronted with the necessity of resurrecting his political fortunes, so badly mauled during the legislative session, and in a typically swift and dramatic fashion he would proceed to do so during the summer and fall of 1930.[68]

NOTES

1. T. Harry Williams, *Huey Long* (New York: Knopf, 1969), pp. 455–60; William Ivy Hair, *The Kingfish and His Realm* (Baton Rouge: Louisiana State University Press, 1991), p. 197; Glen Jeansonne, *Messiah of the Masses: Huey P. Long and the Great Depression* (New York: Harper Collins, 1993), p. 86.

2. Record, *Grosjean* v. *American Press Co.*, 297 U.S. 233 (1936), p. 3 (afterwards cited as Record); *New Orleans Times-Picayune*, April 28, 1931, p. 1.

3. *New Orleans Times-Picayune*, Aug. 28, 1931, pp. 1, 2; see also John Wilds, *Afternoon Story: A Century of the New Orleans States-Item* (Baton Rouge: Louisiana State University Press, 1976), chap. 10, "Robert Ewing: The Last of the Swashbucklers," pp. 183–203.

4. *New Orleans Times-Picayune*, Jan. 28, 1947, p. 1; Jan. 29, 1947, p. 10; *New York Times*, Jan. 28, 1947, p. 24.

5. Record, pp. 1–3.

6. Wilds, *Afternoon Story*, chap. 11, "The Rise and Fall of Jim Thomson," pp. 204–27; *New Orleans Times-Picayune*, March 25, 1953, pp. 1, 2.

7. *New Orleans Times-Picayune*, Oct. 19, 1950, p. 1; Thomas Ewing Dabney, *One Hundred Great Years: The Story of the Times-Picayune from Its Founding to 1940* (Baton Rouge: Louisiana State University Press, 1944), p. 305.

8. Williams, *Long*, pp. 342–45; Jeansonne, *Messiah of the Masses*, p. 43.

9. Ibid., pp. 224, 342–43; Hair, *The Kingfish*, pp. 153, 175, 195; *Louisiana Progress*, May 15, 1930, p. 4; May 22, 1930, pp. 1, 5.

10. Williams, *Long*, p. 455; Hair, *The Kingfish*, p. 145.

11. Williams, *Long*, pp. 329–32, 345, 378; Hair, *The Kingfish*, pp. 173–74; 176–77.

12. *Cochran* v. *Board of Education*, 281 U.S. 370 (1930).

13. Williams, *Long*, pp. 280–311.

14. Ibid., pp. 343–50; *New Orleans Times-Picayune*, March 15, 1929, pp. 1, 3; March 17, 1929, p. 1; March 19, 1929, p. 10; March 22, 1929, p. 12; *Baton Rouge Morning Advocate*, March 15, 1929, p. 1; March 17, 1929, p. 1.

15. Williams, *Long*, p. 351.

16. *Baton Rouge Morning Advocate*, March 19, 1929, p. 1; March 20, 1929, p. 1. Similar editorials also appeared in the *Baton Rouge State-Times*, March 18, 1929, p. 1; March 19, 1929, pp. 1, 6; March 20, 1929, pp. 1, 6.

17. *New Orleans States*, March 21, 1929, pp. 1, 6; *New Orleans Times-Picayune*, April 4, 1929, pp. 1, 4.

18. *Baton Rouge State-Times*, March 21, 1929, p. 1; *New Orleans States*, March 21, 1929, pp. 1, 4; Hair, *The Kingfish*, p. 178.

19. *New Orleans States*, March 21, 1929, p. 1; March 22, 1929, p. 1; April 6, 1929, p. 1; Hair, *The Kingfish*, pp. 151, 154; *Editor & Publisher* 63 (Sept. 13, 1930): 1, 48.

20. *Baton Rouge Morning Advocate*, March 21, 1920, p. 1.

21. Hair, *The Kingfish*, p. 83; *New Orleans Times-Picayune*, March 23, 1929, p. 3.

22. *New Orleans Times-Picayune*, March 23, 1929, p. 3.

23. Williams, *Long*, pp. 356–61.

24. *Baton Rouge Morning Advocate*, March 26, 1929, p. 1.

25. *New Orleans States*, March 26, 1929, p. 13; April 6, 1929, pp. 1, 2.

26. Williams, *Long*, pp. 364, 380.

27. Ibid., pp. 365, 369–95.

28. *New Orleans Times-Picayune*, May 2, 1929, pp. 1, 3.

29. Ibid.

30. Ibid.

31. Ibid., May 5, 1929, pp. 1, 21.

32. Ibid., May 12, 1929, pp. 1, 6.

33. Ibid., May 5, 1929, pp. 1, 21; May 12, 1929, p. 6.

34. Williams, *Long*, p. 388.

35. Ibid., pp. 400–405; *New Orleans Times-Picayune*, May 16, 1929, pp. 1, 3.

36. *New Orleans Times-Picayune*, May 17, 1929, p. 1.

37. Williams, *Long*, pp. 437–39.

38. Ibid., pp. 430–32; Hair, *The Kingfish*, p. 193.

39. Hair, *The Kingfish*, pp. 126–27, 168, 203–4.

40. Ibid., pp. 193–94.

41. *New Orleans Item*, June 4, 1930, p. 8; Sept. 4, 1930, pp. 1, 21; *New Orleans Times-Picayune*, July 4, 1930, p. 8; Williams, *Long*, pp. 440–41; *Louisiana Progress*, April 24, 1930, p. 8.

42. *Shreveport Times*, June 21, 1930, p. 4; *Louisiana Progress*, March 27, 1930, p. 1.

43. *Louisiana Progress*, April 10, 1930, p. 1.

44. Ibid., pp. 1, 8.

45. Ibid., April 17, 1930, pp. 1, 8.

46. Ibid., p. 4.

47. Ibid., April 24, 1930, p. 4; May 8, 1930, p. 8.

48. Ibid., May 15, 1930, pp. 1, 4.

49. Ibid., April 3, 1930, pp. 1, 8; April 10, 1930, p. 1; May 22, 1930, pp. 1, 5.

50. Ibid., April 10, 1930, pp. 1, 4; May 3, 1930, p. 1, 8.

51. Ibid., May 8, 1930, p. 4; May 15, 1930, p. 4; May 29, 1930, pp. 1, 4; June 12, 1930, p. 5; June 19, 1930, p. 1; June 26, 1930, pp. 1, 8.

52. Ibid., July 3, 1930, p. 4.

53. Ibid., April 17, 1930, p. 5.

54. *New Orleans Times-Picayune*, May 18, 1930, p. 1; May 19, 1930, p. 1; May 20, 1930, p. 1; May 26, 1930, p. 1; July 3, 1930, p. 12.

55. *Louisiana Progress*, June 12, 1930, pp. 1, 5; *New Orleans Item*, June 3, 1930, pp. 1, 4–5.

56. *New Orleans Item*, June 3, 1930, pp. 1, 4–5.

57. Ibid.

58. For Hilda Hammond's description of her efforts in this regard, see Hilda Phelps Hammond, *Let Freedom Ring* (New York: Farrar & Rinehart, 1936); Hair, *The Kingfish*, pp. 283–84.

59. *New Orleans Item*, June 8, 1930, p. 1.

60. *New Orleans Times-Picayune*, May 30, 1930, p. 10.

61. *Louisiana Progress*, June 19, 1930, p. 1; *New Orleans Times-Picayune*, June 12, 1930, p. 8; June 18, 1930, p. 18; Williams, *Long*, pp. 449–52.

62. *Shreveport Times*, June 22, 1930, p. 4; *New Orleans Times-Picayune*, June 12, 1930, p. 8.

63. *New Orleans Times-Picayune*, June 12, 1930, p. 8.

64. *Louisiana Progress*, July 10, 1930, p. 4; *New Orleans Times-Picayune*, June 13, 1930, p. 8.

65. *New Orleans Times-Picayune*, June 16, 1930, p. 8; June 18, 1930, p. 1; June 20, 1930, p. 12.

66. Ibid., June 26, 1930, pp. 1, 10; July 11, 1930, pp. 1, 3; Williams, *Long*, pp. 452–53.

67. *Louisiana Progress*, July 17, 1930, p. 1; *New Orleans Times-Picayune*, July 12, 1930, p. 6.

68. *Louisiana Progress*, July 24, 1930, p. 4.

Chapter 3

The Kingfish Goes National

> [Huey Long is] the liar, crook, petty larceny thief and scoundrel, who is now governor of Louisiana and seeks to perpetuate his evil power by not only controlling the governorship but by representing this great state in the United States Senate, which would be a disgrace and dishonor.
>
> —*New Orleans States*, August 1930

> You are being asked to help send to the United States Senate a man without a scintilla of respect for worthy womanhood, a reprobate of the first water, a man possessing neither culture nor refinement, a man whose every public and private act is offensive to good taste—a blasphemer, a ruffian and a cad.
>
> —*Shreveport Times*, September 7, 1930

♦ As his opponents blocked his program by delaying tactics in the waning days of the 1930 legislative session, Huey Long reluctantly admitted to his inner circle, "I'm licked." He undoubtedly commanded a majority in both houses of the legislature in 1930, but his opposition in Louisiana remained formidable and capable of summoning sufficient strength to prevent the enactment of his ambitious program. Following the legislative session of 1930, it was therefore clear that the Kingfish needed to strengthen his grip on the political process in the state even further and to reduce, if not eliminate, the power of his enemies in order to realize his political ambitions. On July 15, the means by which he chose to attempt to accomplish those goals became clear, when Long announced that he would be a candidate for the U.S. Senate in the September 9 Democratic primary, opposing the incumbent, Senator Joseph Ransdell. "I am now, as I have always been, the servant of the people of this state, the high and the low, and I have not been nor will I ever be bossed or ruled by Ring politicians, bosses or newspapers," Long said, announcing his Senate candidacy, "but at all times I stand ready to do the will of the people and to carry out what I find to be for their betterment and progress."[1]

His platform, Long announced, would be the program just defeated in the legislature, especially the roads program, and if he won it would demonstrate that the people were solidly behind both him and his program. The term of Senator Ransdell would expire in March 1931, after the election, but Long's term as governor would not expire until over a year later, in May 1932. Since the lieutenant governor, Paul Cyr, was an adamant anti-Longite, Governor Long could not risk resigning the governorship and turning the office over to an avowed enemy. If he were elected U.S. senator and served out his term as governor, however, Louisiana's Senate seat would be vacant for more than a year. Long pointed out, however, that the Senate would adjourn after a brief session in December 1931, and he could take his seat in that body the following May and would therefore miss only a short session of the Senate. Besides, he humorously noted, the four months his seat was vacant would mean it was no more vacant than it had been with Ransdell serving.[2]

That the daily newspapers would continue to be principal targets during the Kingfish's Senate campaign was indicated by the issue of the *Louisiana Progress* that announced his Senate candidacy with a banner headline. The same issue contained a cartoon in which the New Orleans papers were portrayed as a three-headed snake with the word "lies" covering its body. A cartoon in the following week's issue of the *Progress* repeated the three-headed snake portrayal of the New Orleans dailies along with the caption, "A 1929–30 Development: This quaint hybrid was generated from three species whose most marked common characteristic was an incurable weakness for fiction." Another *Progress* cartoon portrayed the New Orleans dailies as disreputable, with the character representing the *Item,* called "Hop," depicted with five hypodermic needles in its arm, while the *States* character was labeled "Colonel Bob" and the *Times-Picayune* character was called that "snake-in-the-grass, that bald-headed old hypocrite from Lafayette square."[3]

As the campaign moved on, the *Progress* charged that massive amounts of money were being spent by "plutocrats" to defeat the Kingfish. "The lying newspapers of the state have their coffers full of glistening talents. Col. Bow-wow of the infamous . . . *States* seems to have been purchased outright. His front page is covered with slimy innuendo and downright lies directed at Huey P. Long," the *Progress* asserted. "Predatory plutocracy will find out on September 9 that dirty, filthy, sweat-stained, blood-stained gold cannot balk the will of the people."[4]

While the daily press was unified in its opposition to Long's Senate aspirations, he garnered the endorsement of several of the state's weekly newspapers, including the *Rapides News* in Cheneyville, the *Donaldsonville Chief*, the *Bogalusa News*, and the *Thibodaux Commercial Journal*. As each of these papers enlisted in the Kingfish's cause, their endorsements were trumpeted by the *Progress*, which pointed out that "as everyone knows, the weekly press of the state is close to the wishes of the people of the state, speaking its mind independently of the clique of the rule-or-ruin publishers of the New Orleans dailies, who do not represent any of the people, not even the people of New Orleans."[5]

Opening his Senate campaign during August at St. Martinville under the Evangeline Oak, the Kingfish for his part continued his attacks on the state's press. Senator Ransdell, he charged, had tied himself politically to the old New Orleans ring and the "three lying newspapers. Senator Ransdell believes that the three lying New Orleans newspapers should run this state." He also subsequently attacked John Ewing of the *Shreveport Times* as a "contemptible little squirt," while Ewing charged that Long was an "impeached thief and scoundrel."[6]

Newspaper reporters, Long maintained during the campaign, were "lying low down skunks," and the New Orleans dailies were "public thieves. I don't see why they have anybody in Angola [the site of the state penitentiary] as long as the papers are out. If there is any man in the penitentiary as guilty I don't know it." The "rings, the lying newspapers and Wall Street," he claimed, had combined in an attempt to defeat him in the Senate race. The *Times-Picayune*, *States*, *Item*, and *Tribune*, the Kingfish charged, were "thieves, crooks, liars and rascals" who were "lower than the darkest Africa." The "Phelps-Nicholson bunch that runs the *Times-Picayune*, and the hop-needle Marshall Ballard, the king of the dope fiends," he again asserted, "robbed the dock board." The New Orleans dailies had stored their newsprint in the public warehouses of the dock board, he claimed, until he had ordered the newsprint out of the warehouses, saving the state thousands of dollars. "Whenever you take a hundred thousand dollars out of the filthy hide of these low-down, low-livered newspapers, you hit them where they live," he boasted. There was not a "burglar or safeblower in Angola that can hold a candle to any publisher of a New Orleans paper," the Kingfish continued to maintain. The newspaper publishers were "thieves," "robbers," "burglars," "hounds," "blackmailers," "pilferers," "skunks" and "mulcters."[7]

The newspapers returned the Kingfish's fire in kind during the Senate campaign. Indeed, Clarke Salmon, the managing editor of the *New*

Orleans Item, later acknowledged that the campaign was perhaps "one of the bitterest fought struggles between the press and an official ever witnessed in this country." "No name has been too vile for Long to apply to the press," Salmon said, "and no term too strong for the press to apply to him."[8]

The state's leading paper, the *Times-Picayune,* frequently ran front-page editorials urging his defeat. The governor, these editorials suggested, was mentally unbalanced and unfit to serve the state in the Senate. An August 29 editorial referred to the Kingfish as "His erratic and foul-mouthed excellency," and a front-page editorial on September 3 noted that as the Senate campaign was nearing its end, "Governor Long's erratic and neurotic tendencies are more clearly and unmistakably revealed." Long suffered from "megalomania," the editorial declared, and his election to the Senate would be to "the shame and discredit of Louisiana," since he was an "ambitious and unbalanced dictator" with "half-mad ambitions and schemes." In a subsequent editorial, titled "Czarism and Terrorism in Louisiana," the *Times-Picayune* charged the governor with attempting "to set up a personal despotism as irresponsible and oppressive as those in other lands." The day before the election, the paper asked the state's citizens, "Will you vote to accept this unbalanced egomaniac as your dictator?"[9]

Colonel Robert Ewing's *New Orleans States* confessed the error of its ways when it had supported Long in the governor's race in 1928, and it left no doubt of the current depth of contempt in which it now held the Kingfish. Huey Long, the *States* said, was "the liar, crook, petty larceny thief and scoundrel, who is now governor of Louisiana and seeks to perpetuate his evil power by not only controlling the governorship but by representing this great state in the United States Senate, which would be a disgrace and dishonor." Long, it maintained, was the "prince of liars" possessing a "perfidious, vicious and putrid character."[10]

Charles Manship and his Baton Rouge papers charged that Long had threatened to make grass grow on Third Street, the capital city's principal business thoroughfare. The *Morning Advocate* in a series of front-page editorials urged its readers to turn out for a Ransdell rally to be held in Baton Rouge in order to signal "to the world the immense and solidified local public opinion on decency in public office and the righteous uprising of feeling against the effrontery of a repudiated governor who seeks still higher office after proving himself wholly unfit for the office he now holds by accident." The choice in the Senate campaign, the Manship paper maintained, was between "honesty and distinguished service as opposed to graft, corruption and debauchery of public office." Huey Long was a "conscienceless and therefore dangerous official," the *Advocate* declared. "Let no one in Baton Rouge who has the future of the city at heart be found in the Huey Long voting column. . . . A vote for the spiteful and vengeance-bent governor is a vote against the welfare of the city."[11]

Any vote for the "imposter Long," the *Advocate* continued, was a vote for the continuation of "debauchery and graft and corruption in public and private affairs." The people must choose between "honesty and virtue in private and public life" and the "complete prostitution of every basic tenet of Christian life in America," it warned. The Kingfish was that "hypocrite Long, corrupt in all things, the bribe-taker and bribe-giver, the draft dodger, the unfaithful official." More was at stake in the Senate campaign than just a seat in the U.S. Senate, the *Advocate* declared: "Louisiana's honor is at stake!" If anyone in Baton Rouge voted for Long in the Senate election, it predicted, the "finger of scorn will be pointed at them for years to come. They will live under the odium of having joined the enemies of their home city and of having been willing to aid in its destruction."[12]

James Thomson, Marshall Ballard, and the *New Orleans Item* frequently reprinted editorial comments regarding the Louisiana Senate race that were appearing in out-of-state newspapers to indicate to their readers what an embarrassment the election of Long to the Senate would be to the state. A typical editorial reprinted in the *Item* appeared originally in the *New York Sun* attacking the antinewspaper legislation Long had supported in the 1930 legislative session. "Wild and fantastic legislative schemes are not unknown in other parts of the United States, but it is hard to think of one more wildly fantastic than this," the *Sun* said. The advertising tax on newspapers, if passed, would have threatened financial ruin for even the most prosperous newspapers, it pointed out. "In almost any other state a proposal of the kind put forward by Long would be laughed out of consideration. Experience indicates it may be no laughing matter in Louisiana."[13]

Summarizing the opinions of Governor Long expressed in the out-of-state editorials it had been reprinting, the *Item* noted that they "range from mild amazement and contempt to profound disgust." "We don't know of any state in the Union that ever was subjected to such injurious and continuous mal-advertisement, all over the country, as Louisiana has been under the shameful empire of Long," the *Item* observed. Louisiana under the Kingfish, it charged, had been subjected to "a despotic rule that strikes again and again at business and industry by crazy and vengeful misuse of legislation and of executive government." Responding to the *Item*, Long charged that Marshall Ballard had himself written the editorials critical of him for the out-of-state papers, but Ballard replied that such a charge was "Mr. Long's pitiful little fraud."

The *Louisiana Progress*, however, pointed out that Ballard and the *Item* had only recently denounced Senator Ransdell as a man whose principal virtues were "inertia, fatuity and sterility," but now were supporting him for reelection. "What is this our Mighty Ballard feeds on," the *Progress* asked, "to cause him to make a liar of himself?"[14]

Perhaps none of the Louisiana dailies were more strident in their denunciations of Long during the Senate campaign than John Ewing's *Shreveport Times* in the Kingfish's adopted home town. If he were elected a U.S. senator, the *Times* said, and he displayed the same lack of dignity, sense of moral ethics, and respect for the law "he has displayed since his induction into office at Baton Rouge, Louisiana and the whole nation would feel shame and endure disgrace to the saturation point." As a senator, the *Times* claimed, "if he chooses, he will receive the entire diplomatic corps in green pajamas." Given the contempt with which Governor Long had treated the interests of Shreveport and Caddo Parish, it was difficult to understand how anyone living there would vote for Long, the Ewing paper maintained. "No other governor has carried into the executive office such vengefulness, such vindictiveness, such bitterness of spirit as that exhibited by Governor Long in his relations with Caddo." The governor, it said, had "kicked the material interests of Caddo Parish into the gutter."[15]

Despite the bitterness and invective that characterized the relations between Long and the Louisiana daily press, the newspapers never commented openly on the relationship between the governor and Alice Lee Grosjean or asserted that she was his mistress. The *Shreveport Times*, however, appears to have come as close to doing so as any of the state's dailies in a front-page editorial on September 7. Addressed to the women of Louisiana, the editorial asked, "Which will the women of Louisiana choose—the clean man or the soiled one?" Long lived "apart from his family and occupies free quarters in a chain hotel," the *Times* observed. "So there is presented to the good women of Louisiana the candidacy of a man who not only vilely curses defenseless members of their sex, but is wholly lacking in those domestic virtues which make for happiness in the American home." "You are being asked to help send to the United States Senate," it warned, "a man without a scintilla of respect for worthy womanhood, a reprobate of the first water, a man possessing neither culture nor refinement, a man whose every public and private act is offensive to good taste—a blasphemer, a ruffian and a cad."[16]

As the Senate campaign approached its conclusion, the Ewing paper broadly implied that Long was also a bolshevik. If his program for the country were adopted, it said, the result would be "anarchy and riot." The Kingfish was demagogically appealing to the common people who envied those who were better off, the *Times* charged, and if the "demagogue be of the Long stripe, he tells his hearers that the newspapers, whose favor he once courted with all assiduity, are the 'tools and hirelings' of the people's common enemy—Money."[17]

In the closing days of the Senate campaign, in an obvious attempt to produce damaging information regarding the Kingfish, anti-Long Attorney General Percy Saint opened an investigation in Baton Rouge of the state highway commission. Summoned as a key witness in the probe was Samuel Irby, who had reportedly been high in the confidence of the Long organization, serving as chief test chemist for the highway commission before resigning to become a business manager for the *Louisiana Progress*. Irby was also the uncle by marriage of Alice Grosjean, and Grosjean had resided with the Irbys in Shreveport, Baton Rouge, and New Orleans. Irby's testimony in the attorney general's investigation of the highway commission, it was reported, sent a "buzz of excited political speculation throughout the state," and following Irby's testimony Attorney General Saint indicated that he would request a grand jury to be convened.[18]

After his appearance in the attorney general's inquiry, Irby charged that Governor Long and O. K. Allen, the chairman of the highway commission, had slandered him by telling his wife that he had beaten a woman and shot up a room while drunk at the Heidelberg Hotel in Baton Rouge, and Irby threatened the governor and Allen with a slander suit. Irby flew from New Orleans to Shreveport on September 3 and was joined there by James Terrell, Alice Grosjean's ex-husband. Terrell had said he was in Shreveport to file suit against the Kingfish for breaking up his marriage, but Irby and Terrell meanwhile reportedly got drunk in a hotel. Since the highway program was a key issue in the campaign, the Long camp recognized the damage charges of corruption in the highway commission would do. Fearing also that Irby and Terrell might reveal that Alice Grosjean was the governor's mistress, the Kingfish ordered the state police to take both into custody and seclude them in hideouts on the Gulf coast. When the men disappeared from Shreveport, U.S. District Judge Wayne Borah issued a writ of habeas corpus at Attorney General Saint's request requiring Long to produce the two allegedly kidnapped men.[19]

"What is it that Long and his secret constabulary are trying to hide by these methods?" the *New Orleans Item* demanded after headlining the reputed kidnapping of Irby and Terrell. Under the Long regime, the *Item* said, it had previously predicted "the destruction of private rights and liberties of individual men and women. That prediction is now confirmed by the abduction of Irby and Terrell." The Kingfish was a "lawless tyrant," it declared. "Shall Louisiana remain free? Or will the free men and women of Louisiana reduce themselves to slavery enforced by the midnight Cossacks of its would-be Czar?"[20]

When a U.S. marshal appeared at Long's suite at the Roosevelt Hotel to serve the writ of habeas corpus issued by Judge Borah, William Wiegand, an *Item* reporter, slipped into the room with the marshal. When the Kingfish noticed Wiegand and discovered who he was, he called him a "sonofabitch," whereupon Wiegand punched the governor. After the Kingfish's bodyguards seized Wiegand, the governor also struck him. The Wiegand–Long slugging incident was subsequently characterized by Clarke Salmon of the *Item* as an "amazing chapter of violence" involving Governor Long, a "notorious baiter of newspaper men who have opposed his efforts to twist the established form of government into a privately controlled despotism."[21]

Meanwhile, Sam Irby reappeared publicly and at the Kingfish's urging participated in a radio broadcast in which he stated that he had made charges of corruption in the highway commission as a means of entrapping Long's enemies. He denied being kidnapped, saying that he had voluntarily gone fishing on the coast. With Irby denying the kidnapping, Judge Borah subsequently dismissed the writ of habeas corpus he had previously issued in the case. The *Item*, however, charged that Irby's denial of his kidnapping was a transparent cover story concocted by the Kingfish, and on the day before the election the paper declared to the state's voters, "The issue between Freedom and Despotism, between Decency and Indecency" was "in your hands." Citizens, the *Item* urged, should vote for the "defeat of Long and the defeat of Russianism in Louisiana."[22]

Despite the adamant opposition of the press, on September 9 Huey Long won the Democratic primary for the U.S. Senate by a majority of over thirty thousand votes. Since there was no Republican candidate in the general election, the Kingfish was now for practical purposes a United States senator. He had carried the vote outside New Orleans overwhelmingly, and even in New Orleans he came within four thousand votes of securing a majority against his opponent.[23]

A jubilant *Louisiana Progress* declared that the election returns proved that the people could not be deceived by a press "employing the tactics of blackmail and bribery, resorting to malicious character assassination, publishing lies and refusing to give their readers a fair and impartial account of news happenings in the State of Louisiana." "The Old New Orleans Ring and their Lying Newspapers," the *Progress* announced, "lie today caked in the mud they dumped into the senatorial contest." "The unsuccessful campaign to defeat . . . [Long] with lies, venom, treachery, stealth, hi-jacking, coercion, intimidation, bribery, felonious assault, frenzy and every other wicked endeavor known to man," the Long paper asserted, "will go down in Louisiana history as the foulest this state has ever known."[24]

Long's show of strength in New Orleans during the election led the Old Regular Democratic organization to capitulate to him and agree to support his legislative program, which had been blocked in the 1930 legislative session. One week following his victory in the Democratic primary, the Kingfish summoned the legislature into a special session and in short order secured the passage of a $75 million bond issue for roads and bridges, a $5 million bond issue for the building of a new capitol, a new bridge across the Mississippi at New Orleans, and other measures he had advocated.[25]

Having established his preeminence in Louisiana public life, the Kingfish boldly appointed Alice Lee Grosjean as secretary of state when the incumbent secretary, James Bailey, died suddenly in October. In appointing the twenty-four-year-old Grosjean, the *Louisiana Progress* said, with perhaps an unintentional double meaning, Governor Long had selected "a person who, with the exception of himself, is probably the best posted individual on affairs of state in Louisiana." Grosjean was "exceedingly brilliant" with a "remarkable skill in diplomatically handling matters of great political importance," the *Progress* gushed. "No person in Louisiana has a better understanding of the affairs of the administration than Miss Grosjean." As the only woman to hold such high state office in the country at the time, Grosjean would serve the remaining two years of Bailey's term and subsequently be appointed state supervisor of public accounts by the Kingfish's handpicked successor as governor.[26]

Before he could take his seat in the U.S. Senate, the Kingfish had to insure his continuing control of the state with the election of a slate of officers, from the governor down, who would be unquestionably amenable to his control and direction. With this goal in mind, Long selected Oscar Kelly Allen (always called "O. K." in Louisiana) to be the next governor, John Fournet to be lieutenant governor, and Gaston Louis Porterie to be attorney general in the reconstructed state government.

As the election approached in January 1932, the *Louisiana Progress*, which had become a monthly after the 1930 Senate campaign, again attacked the state's daily press. It printed a cartoon depicting Esmond Phelps, the "dictator" of the *Times-Picayune*, shining his shoes with Shinola, and it once again warned voters to be "on your guard for these newspapers from this time on. They will lie, lie, lie to suit their case." The opponents of the Kingfish's O. K. Allen ticket were a "cold-blooded, thieving set," the *Progress* charged, "that is trying to manipulate certain lying newspapers to get back into power." The warnings of the *Progress* proved to be unneeded, however, when the Allen ticket carried fifty-four of the state's sixty-four parishes, including New Orleans, on January 19.[27]

In 1932 the *New Orleans Item* and *Tribune* broke ranks with the other papers of that city and supported the Long organization and the Allen ticket, over the bitter opposition of Marshall Ballard. The *Tribune* was in a circulation battle with the *Times-Picayune*, and the *Tribune's* publisher, James Thomson, felt an alliance with Long would aid his paper in that fight. State employees who had previously been required to subscribe to Long's *Louisiana Progress* were then required to subscribe to the *Item-Tribune*, while the *Progress* ceased publication. Although the alliance with the Kingfish temporarily boosted the circulation of the Thomson papers, it damaged their credibility with the public. That credibility was further damaged when Charles "Chick" Frampton, an *Item* and *Tribune* reporter, accepted a position with the Louisiana attorney general's office in 1932 at three hundred dollars per month.[28]

With their worst fears now realized, the gloom of the rest of the state's daily press was nevertheless lightened somewhat by the announcement in June 1931 of the U.S. Supreme Court's decision in *Near* v. *Minnesota* invalidating the Minnesota injunction-gag law that the Kingfish had sought to have copied into the law of Louisiana in 1930.[29] Writing for a bare majority of five of the justices, Chief Justice Charles Evans Hughes answered the question that had gone unanswered since the *Gitlow* case in 1925. He held that freedom of the press was in fact guaranteed against impairment by the states under the Due Process Clause of the Fourteenth Amendment. "It is no longer open to doubt that the liberty of the press and of speech is within the liberty safeguarded by the due process clause of the 14th Amendment from invasion by state action," Hughes said. "It was found impossible to conclude that this essential personal liberty of the citizen was left unprotected by the general guaranty of fundamental rights of person and property."[30]

By authorizing a permanent injunction to be issued against a newspaper, the chief justice ruled, the Minnesota gag imposed an invalid prior restraint upon publication in violation of the Constitution. Citing Blackstone's *Commentaries*, Hughes pointed out that the primary purpose of constitutional guarantees of freedom of the press was to prohibit previous restraints of publication, and since the Minnesota law authorized such restraints it was "of the essence of censorship." "The fact that for approximately one hundred and fifty years there has been almost an entire absence of attempts to impose previous restraints upon publications relating to the malfeasance of public officers," he noted, "is significant of the deep-seated conviction that such restraints would violate constitutional right." The growing complexity of government, with the resulting proliferation of opportunities for malfeasance and corruption by public officials, Hughes said, "emphasizes the primary need of a vigilant and courageous press, especially in great cities."[31]

Justice Pierce Butler, joined by Justices Van Devanter, Sutherland, and McReynolds, vigorously dissented from the Court's decision invalidating the Minnesota law. With the Court's decision a few weeks earlier in *Stromberg* v. *California*, however, which invalidated the California red-flag law as violative of freedom of speech, it was now clear for the first time that the twin pillars of freedom of expression, freedom of speech and freedom of the press, were protected from abridgment by the states under the Fourteenth Amendment.[32] The reaction of the press throughout the country to the *Near* decision was jubilant. The *Chicago Tribune*, which had financed the case to the Court, declared *Near* v. *Minnesota* to be "the great charter of freedom of the American press." Colonel Robert McCormick had a passage from Chief Justice Hughes's opinion in the case—that referring to "the primary need of a vigilant and courageous press, especially in great cities"—reproduced in marble in the lobby of the *Tribune* building in Chicago.[33]

The Louisiana press joined the national press in celebrating the *Near* decision, and the *Times-Picayune* pointed out that the decision had been predicted by constitutional experts. "Surprise is occasioned, not by the . . . [decision], but by the close division of the high tribunal, four of the nine justices having joined in a dissenting opinion," the *Times-Picayune* said. The Court's decision would block the copying of the Minnesota gag law in other states that many had believed would happen, it continued. "That belief was justified, for copies or adaptations of the Minnesota gag law found their way into the legislative sessions of other states, including our own." "Happily the temptation to imitate Minnesota was resisted for the time being and pending final adjudication of the gag law's validity," the *Times-Picayune* said, and now at least the Louisiana press would be relieved of the threat of a gag law as proposed by Governor Long in 1930. "Now that the Minnesota law is ruled invalid, the drive to muzzle the press by this type legislation probably will be dropped even by those who welcomed it so avidly."[34]

Ironically, the most direct beneficiary of the Supreme Court's decision in *Near* v. *Minnesota*, J. M. Near, whose newspaper had been suppressed by the Minnesota law, was embittered by his experience despite his victory in the Supreme Court. Possessed of an acid tongue and a trigger temper, the somewhat paranoid Near claimed that the litigation in his case had taken much longer than he had been promised by the *Chicago Tribune* attorneys, leaving him largely unemployed in the interim. Colonel McCormick and the *Tribune*, he maintained, had righteously belittled his newspaper as a "scandal sheet" and reneged on a promise to finance the renewed publication of his paper after the litigation ended.

In a letter to the American Civil Liberties Union after the Supreme Court's decision in his case, Near complained of his treatment by the *Chicago Tribune* and McCormick and their failure to keep their promises to him. "If you have read, and I presume you have, the numerous editorials in the *Chicago Tribune*," he said, "you must have noticed in all of them, a thinly veiled whine for that 'great moral journal's' ever having taken up the fight for a 'scandal sheet.' That eternal whine almost drove me wild." If he had received the financial support promised him to resume publication of his paper, the *Saturday Press*, Near believed, it "was plainly evident that in the event of a favorable decision, the *Saturday Press*, with the raging controversy over its fight for life, the little paper could easily be made into a publication of national prominence and influence." As it was, he said, "I'm broke flat,—a wonderful record for a four year fight for the publishers of this entire country. I richly deserve all I've gotten," he continued, since he had foolishly believed the promises of McCormick and the *Tribune*.[35]

In October 1931, it was announced that a "freedom of the press" room would be dedicated at Thomas Jefferson's home, Monticello, and in honor of his role in *Near* v. *Minnesota*, Colonel Robert McCormick was selected to be the principal speaker at the dedication ceremonies. That McCormick would be so honored, while he remained unemployed and forgotten, infuriated J. M. Near, and he wrote the head of the Jefferson Memorial Foundation blasting McCormick for the treatment he had received during the *Near* litigation. Near charged that McCormick and the *Chicago Tribune* never missed an opportunity to portray the *Saturday Press* as a "scandal sheet" and to emphasize the "terrible character of the small rag" it had defended, while betraying the promises to him. "Mr. McCormick never missed an opportunity at banquet, convention or club, to glorify his action in rushing to the defense of a free press, free speech (with Herr Mc. strong on the latter) but you never heard McCormick speak of or his paper mention the sap who stood by his guns in the face of certain disaster—the same sap who is writing these lines." He was "damtired of hearing old McCormick's praises sung in every key and at every opportunity," Near continued, since he "never played fair with me a single instance." He had been largely unemployed since the *Near* litigation began, he said, since there "isn't anything to be had for an ass who hasn't any more sense than to put up a fight to free a press of an iron censorship—a press as cringing and docile as the American press—as a whole." "Am I bitter?" Near asked. "Show me a man who will go through what I've been through since November 23, 1927, who won't be bitter." McCormick, he concluded, was "the most blatant four-flusher the world ever produced." While his case was being litigated, Near had lived mostly in California, but he subsequently returned to Minneapolis and remained a marginal figure in publishing circles there until his death in the spring of 1936 at the age of sixty-two.[36]

With the decision in *Near* v. *Minnesota*, and its confirmation that freedom of the press was a guarantee of the Fourteenth Amendment, it was for the first time possible to challenge infringements of that freedom in any state of the Union under the federal Constitution. For that reason, it is difficult to overestimate the importance of the case to the protection of a free press. Two aspects of the case, however, remained troubling. The first was that the case was decided by the narrowest of margins in the Supreme Court, five to four, with the result that, as the American Newspaper Publishers' Association warned, in some future "acid test issue . . . the Butler dissenting opinion may possibly in time become the majority of the nation's high court."[37]

The second troubling aspect of the *Near* case was the fact that the Court had again treated freedom of the press as a guarantee that primarily prohibited prior restraints of publications. The result was that, however important the *Near* decision had been, the scope of freedom of the press as a constitutional guarantee had not been significantly expanded by the Court beyond its restricted, traditional meaning. It therefore remained to be seen if the Court in some future case would not only reject the views of the *Near* dissenters but would also advance the definition of freedom of the press beyond the confines of the restrictive meaning the Court had adopted in the *Near* case.

Having become a United States senator, Huey Long now had a new stage on which to perform and with which to attract national attention to himself. Long soon launched publicity-generating attacks on the leadership of the Senate, and although he had supported Franklin Roosevelt in the presidential election of 1932, by 1933 the Kingfish had broken with Roosevelt and the administration. His attacks on the Roosevelt administration drew further national attention to Long, as did the publication of his autobiography, *Every Man a King*, in the fall of 1933. The Long newspaper, which had resumed publication after the *New Orleans Item* had rejoined the anti-Long opposition, was also renamed the *American Progress* in an attempt to reach a much wider audience for the Kingfish's views, indicating his growing national political aspirations.[38]

In 1933, however, the national publicity he reveled in turned decidedly sour, and the Kingfish was particularly irritated by a highly critical article regarding him that appeared in *Collier's* in July. In a hearing before the Senate Banking and Commerce Committee, Long hotly cross-examined Thomas W. Lamont, of Wall Street's J. P. Morgan company, who admitted that *Collier's* was owned by a company that was a subsidiary of the Morgan company. Long then claimed he had been attacked by the magazine because he was advocating the redistribution of wealth. A "secret war" to discredit Senator Long had thus been uncovered, the newly renamed *American Progress* proclaimed, adding that the "campaign to discredit, and if possible destroy, Senator Huey P. Long is being pressed with a ferocity seldom equalled in our political history."[39]

The publicity associated with the Kingfish, however, turned to ridicule and he became the butt of jokes and derision across the country as he stumbled from one personal embarrassment and political blunder to another during the summer and fall of 1933. These incidents began with one of those bizarre occurrences that had become characteristic of his public career. Visiting in New York City, Long was invited to attend a charity event on August 26 at the Sands Point Bath and Country Club on Long Island. Never known to handle alcoholic beverages well, the Kingfish soon became intoxicated at the event and proceeded to behave in a thoroughly boorish and obnoxious manner. He insulted a black musician at the club by referring to him as a "shine" and a "coon," and he seized a plate of food from a plump young woman with the comment, "You're too fat already. I'll eat this." Around four in the morning, Long went to the men's restroom, but he emerged with a cut over his left eye. Companions rushed him from the club to his hotel, and he soon entrained for Milwaukee, where he was scheduled to deliver an address to the Veterans of Foreign Wars.[40]

While the Kingfish was in Milwaukee, the Sands Point incident received front-page coverage by the *New York Times*, which soon editorially labeled the assault on the senator as "The Battle of Long Island." "Who that loves his country can doubt that the hired bravoes of 'the interests' perpetrated this outrage upon a . . . [man] so wise and beloved?" the *Times* proclaimed. The Kingfish was meanwhile besieged by reporters in Milwaukee, and after initially refusing any comment, he issued a statement to the press. He had been attacked by three or four men in the bath club restroom, he claimed, and he maintained that his assailants were undoubtedly thugs hired by Wall Street's house of Morgan. "I have been repeatedly threatened," Long said. "Any number of warnings have been given, even by column writers, that such a thing would happen sooner or later. I was lucky to have escaped with such a trivial injury and am grateful."[41]

The Kingfish never filed an official complaint with the police regarding the Sands Point incident, and his assailant was never identified nor was the motive for the assault ever revealed. As the *New York Times* pointed out, the failure of "the gentleman who landed the blow heard 'round the world to identify himself and prove his right to whatever honors are due him, left the door wide open for impostors and a broad field for guesses." There is, however, consensus among the leading Long biographers regarding why he was attacked. His biographers agree that since Long was known to be sloppy in his bathroom habits, the most likely explanation was that he provoked the assault by urinating on his attacker while in the restroom of the Sands Point club.[42]

The Kingfish's explanation that he had been attacked by thugs hired by Wall Street met with almost universal disbelief, and the Sands Point incident soon became a national joke and a source of ridicule directed at the senator. Various journals began to coin new names for Long, including Huey "Pee" Long, the "Pride of the Pelicans," "Hooey" Long, the "Crawfish," "Tin Can Napoleon," the "Catfish Caesar," the "Mud Pie Mussolini," and the "Hitler of the Bayous." He was offered a thousand dollars per night to appear as a freak attraction at Coney Island, while a rematch with his assailant at Chicago's Soldier Field was suggested, with the proceeds being donated to fighting political racketeers in Chicago and Louisiana. Comparing the Kingfish's attacker with contemporary professional boxers, the *New Orleans Times-Picayune* observed that neither "Tunney nor Dempsey, nor even Primo Canera, could have created such a national furor over one simple punch as did the anonymous but unsung hero who pasted Huey Long at the exclusive Sands Point Bath Club."[43]

Owen P. White, an editor of *Collier's* magazine, suggested that a medal be commissioned for Long's assailant, and although White offered the suggestion in jest, there was an immediate outpouring of contributions from the public for the medal. White consequently decided to proceed with the project, and the resulting medal depicted a kingfish, with Long's face as its head, the left eye blackened, receiving the impact of a clenched fist that also knocked off a small crown, with a background of wash basins with both faucets running. When the Kingfish's assailant failed to appear to claim the medal, it was presented to the American Numismatic Society's museum, where it was displayed with a Latin caption that when translated read, "Medal to the Unknown Hero who hit Huey Long, deposited in the Museum of the American Numismatic Society, by the American people." Hilda Phelps Hammond, Long's bitter enemy in Louisiana, announced that replicas of the medal would be distributed by her women's organization in a nationwide effort to oust Long and Louisiana Senator John Overton from the U.S. Senate.[44]

Although Long had avoided military service during World War I, the Louisiana chapter of the Veterans of Foreign Wars (VFW) had elected him an honorary member. One of the primary purposes of his appearance at the VFW national convention in Milwaukee was to invite the VFW to hold its next convention in New Orleans. When he appeared at the convention, however, he was besieged by photographers seeking pictures of his cut and blackened eye and by reporters asking for explanations of the attack on him at Sands Point. The Kingfish exploded in anger, and a contingent of VFW sergeants-at-arms escorted the photographers away from the senator. His damaged eye was covered with powder that streamed down his face as he perspired heavily, and glaring at the press table where the reporters were seated, he declared that "I drove all the skunks and polecats out of Louisiana. Now I see you're in Milwaukee. Get out—get out! You couldn't believe one of those newspaper men on oath. The man who has no more sense than to believe what they write ought to be bored with a hollow horn." "They did not come here for anything orderly," he continued. "They were sent here to create a scene with their hoodlumistic practices. The newspapers have learned a lesson in Louisiana. They never try anything there any more."[45]

Shouting and shaking his fists, Long then began a tirade against the press, asserting that there had been "an exodus of polecats in Louisiana, but when I picked up your Milwaukee newspapers I knew where all the polecats had gone. They drove the polecats out of Louisiana and they came up here and got jobs on newspapers." "In Louisiana we don't stand for polecats, thieves, rascals and other varmints, like skunks in the woods," he continued. "The newspapers of Louisiana have learned their lesson. They don't try anything like this down there. They don't dare!" A Fiji Islander, a Chinese man, and a Milwaukee publisher had engaged in an experiment to see who could stay in a room with a polecat the longest, the Kingfish told the convention. "The Fiji Islander went in and stayed fifteen minutes and then came out. The Chinaman stayed with the polecat fifteen minutes, and he had to come out. Then the Milwaukee newspaper owner went in the room and in five minutes the polecat came out." The senator then proceeded to lambaste the Roosevelt administration for an hour and a half, whereupon he abruptly left the convention.[46]

The officers of the VFW felt that the Kingfish's diatribe against the press was so offensive that they issued an apology to newspapermen. "The officers and members of the Veterans of Foreign Wars regret that an attack upon the Milwaukee press by Senator Huey P. Long of Louisiana should have interrupted temporarily an otherwise splendid reunion," the VFW said. "Senator Long's expressions of opinion represented his own views, not those of the V.F.W." Not only had he lost his composure in his anger at the press, but the Kingfish had forgotten in the heat of the moment the principal reason for his appearance at the VFW convention—the issuance of an invitation to the organization to hold its next convention in New Orleans.[47]

Long returned by train to New Orleans on August 30, where he was again confronted by a large group of reporters and photographers at the railroad station. He was immediately surrounded by his bodyguards, and as he was being ushered through the newspapermen, the Kingfish shouted, "Bust 'em up, boys! Hit 'em! Don't let them take my picture." After he arrived at his home in New Orleans, his spokesman issued only a one-line response to press inquiries. "Senator Long," it said, "isn't talking to newspapers any more." The usually safer environs of Louisiana, however, proved less hospitable to Long than usual, as he continued to blunder politically. Addressing a crowd at the South Louisiana State Fair at Donaldsonville, the Kingfish again attacked the popular Roosevelt administration and its recovery effort, but he was "hissed, booed and heckled." Surrounded as usual by bodyguards, he invited one of his hecklers to "come down here and I'll man-to-man with you." The reaction of the crowd was to laugh raucously and it "hissed and booed all the louder."[48]

Long was scheduled to speak next at the Washington Parish Fair at Franklinton, and apparently in response to the hostile reaction to his remarks at Donaldsonville, he toned down his criticism of the Roosevelt administration and referred to "my good friend President Roosevelt, with whom I do not always agree." Again, however, the crowd exploded in raucous laughter. Blundering further, the Kingfish asserted that "most men serving in the United States Army during the World War were dragged in by the hair of their heads." This comment enraged many veterans, and the commander of the Lafayette VFW post invited Long to repeat the remark at a meeting there, promising him the largest crowd in the city's history. The Kingfish, however, declined to respond to the invitation.[49]

The *American Progress* meanwhile attacked the coverage of the Sands Point incident in the national press and complained that the "slave newspapers" had begun a campaign of "lying about the *American Progress*. They got their orders from Wall Street and their editors were forced to carry them out." The campaign to discredit it, the *Progress* maintained, was an "attempt to try and stop our rapid growth. The *American Progress* is every day coming to be the most widely read and quoted journal in this country. Wall Street knows this and they are exerting every effort to try to stop us." Even the "moneyed press" was beginning to recognize the popular revulsion at "the effort sponsored by the J. P. Morgan and company editors to glorify the bandit assault made upon U.S. Senator Long when he went, on request, to a charity benefit function at Long Island," the *Progress* claimed. If the object of "the medal mountebanks was to inspire in the American public a supreme contempt for the conspicuous absence of ordinary brains and breeding on the part of the idle rich," it said, "the achievement of that objective has been the most notably successful of all."[50]

The ridicule heaped on the Kingfish following the Sands Point incident nevertheless soon began to produce predictions of the demise of his political career. After a Long-supported candidate for mayor of New Orleans was defeated, the *Providence News-Tribune* observed that "Louisiana seems well on the way to completing what some unknown fist in Long Island began, and the bell has begun to toll to mark the passing of Huey Long from the world of politics." For the rest of his term in the Senate, the *Boston Globe* predicted, Long would be "regarded as a joke, and a rather poor one at that," while the *New York Herald Tribune* added that it "is still too early to prepare for the political funeral, but surely one might begin to think about ordering the flowers." The *New York Times* also reported that many were predicting that the Kingfish's "next battle will be his Waterloo." "The most ominous sign," it added, "is that Huey Long is being laughed at."[51]

Hodding Carter, editor of the *Hammond (La.) Courier* and a usually astute observer of the state political scene, reported that a cartoonist for the *Times-Picayune* had depicted Long as a crawfish backing into mud. The cartoonist had "caught the nation's fancy with his cartoon of a crawfish backing away into slime," Carter said, "and rarely today is Huey designated by the name he gave himself, the 'Kingfish.' The crawfish started the laughter that has not been stilled since early summer." Carter noted that "laughter and ridicule" were proving more effective in diminishing Long's power in the state than the opposition of his bitterest enemies in the past, and when the Senator advocated new taxes during November, he had been greeted with rotten eggs hurled from the crowd. The Kingfish was also being damaged politically in Louisiana, Carter said, by the Roosevelt administration's decision to deny any federal patronage in the state to the Long organization and to award it instead to anti-Long forces.[52]

Huey Long, however, had shown rather consistently throughout his career that predictions of his political demise were a risky business, and he would do so again. During 1934, the Kingfish would demonstrate that his grip on the political process in Louisiana was as strong as ever, as he wielded his power to strike against his enemies in the press, creating another confrontation over freedom of the press both in Louisiana and the nation at large.

NOTES

1. T. Harry Williams, *Huey Long* (New York: Knopf, 1969), p. 452; *Louisiana Progress*, July 17, 1930, pp. 1, 2.
2. Williams, *Long*, pp. 460–61.
3. *Louisiana Progress*, July 17, 1930, p. 4; July 24, 1930, pp. 1, 4.

4. Ibid., Aug. 7, 1930, p. 4.
5. Ibid., July 31, 1930, p. 7; Aug. 7, 1930, p. 8; Oct. 2, 1930, p. 4.
6. *New Orleans Times-Picayune*, Aug. 20, 1930, p. 1.
7. Ibid., Aug. 3, 1930, pp. 1, 10; Aug. 23, 1930, p. 4; Sept. 2, 1930, p. 1; Sept. 4, 1930, p. 9.
8. *Editor & Publisher* 63 (Sept. 13, 1930): 5, 48.
9. *New Orleans Times-Picayune*, Aug. 29, 1930, p. 8; Sept. 3, 1930, p. 1; Sept. 7, 1930, p. 1; Sept. 8, 1930, p. 1.
10. Quoted in the *New Orleans Item*, Sept. 1, 1930, p. 1.
11. *Baton Rouge State-Times*, Aug. 15, 1930, p. 6; *Baton Rouge Morning Advocate*, Sept. 6, 1930, p. 1.
12. *Baton Rouge Morning Advocate*, Sept. 7, 1930, p. 1; Sept. 9, 1930, p. 1.
13. *New Orleans Item*, Sept. 3, 1930, p. 1.
14. Ibid., Sept. 4, 1930, p. 14; *Louisiana Progress*, Aug. 28, 1930, p. 1.
15. *Shreveport Times*, Sept. 2, 1930, p. 4; Sept. 4, 1930, p. 1.
16. Ibid., Sept. 7, 1930, p. 1.
17. Ibid., Sept. 8, 1930, p. 1.
18. *Baton Rouge Morning Advocate*, Sept. 4, 1930, p. 1.
19. Ibid., Sept. 5, 1930, p. 1; Sept. 6, 1930, p. 1; Sept. 7, 1930, p. 1; Williams, *Long*, pp. 471–77; William Ivy Hair, *The Kingfish and His Realm* (Baton Rouge: Louisiana State University Press, 1991), pp. 203–4.
20. *New Orleans Item*, Sept. 6, 1930, p. 1; Sept. 7, 1930, p. 1.
21. *Editor & Publisher* 63 (Sept. 13, 1930): 5.
22. Hair, *The Kingfish*, pp. 203–5; Williams, *Long*, pp. 471–77; *New Orleans Item*, Sept. 8, 1930, pp. 1, 8.
23. *Baton Rouge Morning Advocate*, Sept. 10, 1930, p. 1; Hair, *The Kingfish*, p. 204.
24. *Louisiana Progress*, Sept. 11, 1930, pp. 1, 4.
25. Hair, *The Kingfish*, p. 207.
26. *Louisiana Progress*, Oct. 16, 1930, p. 4.
27. Ibid., Jan. 12, 1932, pp. 1, 4; Williams, *Long*, p. 539.
28. John Wilds, *Afternoon Story: A Century of the New Orleans States-Item* (Baton Rouge: Louisiana State University Press, 1976), chap. 13, "Angling for the Kingfish," pp. 228–41.
29. *Near* v. *Minnesota*, 283 U.S. 697 (1931).
30. 283 U.S. 697, 707.
31. 283 U.S. 697, 713–20.
32. *Stromberg* v. *California*, 283 U.S. 359 (1931).
33. *Chicago Tribune*, June 2, 1931, p. 1; Fred Friendly, *Minnesota Rag* (New York: Random House, 1981), p. 161.
34. *New Orleans Times-Picayune*, June 3, 1931, p. 8.
35. J. M. Near to Forrest Bailey, June 23, 1931, American Civil Liberties Union (ACLU) Archives, vol. 346, Seeley Mudd Library, Princeton University.
36. *Chicago Tribune*, Oct. 20, 1931, p. 3; Oct. 21, 1931, p. 6; J. M. Near to Stuart G. Gibboney, Oct. 31, 1931, ACLU Archives, vol. 345; *New York Times*, April 19, 1936, sec. 2, p. 10.
37. Friendly, *Minnesota Rag*, p. 162.
38. Williams, *Long*, p. 645.
39. The article in question was Walter Davenport, "Catching up with Huey," *Collier's* 92 (July 1, 1933): 12, 45–46; *American Progress*, Aug. 24, 1933, pp. 1, 2.
40. Hair, *The Kingfish*, p. 258; *New York Times*, Aug. 29, 1933, p. 1.

41. *New York Times*, Aug. 29, 1933, pp. 1, 3; Aug. 30, 1933, p. 18.

42. Ibid., Aug. 31, 1933, p. 18; Williams, *Long*, pp. 651–52; Hair, *The Kingfish*, p. 258.

43. Hair, *The Kingfish*, pp. 258–59; *New York Times*, Aug. 31, 1933, p. 18; *Collier's*, Huey P. Long Scrapbooks, vol. 19, Hill Memorial Library, Louisiana State University, Baton Rouge; *New Orleans Times-Picayune*, Aug. 31, 1933, p. 9.

44. *New York Times*, Aug. 31, 1933, p. 18; Sept. 1, 1933, p. 3; Sept. 5, 1933, p. 19; Sept. 21, 1933, p. 21.

45. Ibid., Aug. 30, 1933, p. 21; *Chicago Tribune*, Aug. 30, 1933, p. 3; *New Orleans Times-Picayune*, Aug. 30, 1933, pp. 1, 11.

46. *New Orleans Times-Picayune*, Aug. 30, 1933, pp. 1, 11.

47. *New York Times*, Nov. 5, 1933, sec. 8, p. 2; *Chicago Tribune*, Aug. 30, 1933, p. 3.

48. *New York Times*, Nov. 5, 1933, sec. 8, p. 2; *New Orleans Times-Picayune*, Aug. 31, 1933, pp. 1, 9.

49. *New Orleans Times-Picayune*, Aug. 31, 1933, pp. 1, 9.

50. *American Progress*, Sept. 14, 1933, p. 1; Sept. 21, 1933, p. 1; Sept. 23, 1933, p. 3.

51. *Literary Digest* 117 (Feb. 3, 1936): 7; *New York Times*, Nov. 5, 1933, sec. 8, p. 2.

52. Hodding Carter, "Kingfish to Crawfish," *The New Republic* 77 (Jan. 24, 1934): 302–5.

Chapter 4

Guiding the Newspapers in the "Path of Rectitude": Censorship by Taxation

> Freedom of speech is one thing and freedom from taxation is another. I believe in freedom of speech, but it's got to be truthful speech, and lying newspapers should have to pay for their lying. I'm going to help these newspapers by hitting them in their pocketbooks; maybe then they'll try to clean up.
>
> —Senator Huey P. Long, July 2, 1934

> Freedom of the press will survive this assault in Louisiana just as surely as representative government, now chloroformed by the usurper, will be restored. But the rape of representative government, and the assault upon a free press just driven to success by the openly wielded lash of a dictator without principle, honest conviction or scruple constitute the blackest chapter in Louisiana's history.
>
> —*New Orleans Times-Picayune*, July 10, 1934

♦ Huey Long never concealed his ambition to be president of the United States. Soon after their marriage in 1913, Long explained to his wife the political career he planned to follow. He would first obtain election to a secondary state office and from there build a political base from which he could win election as governor. From the governorship, he continued, he would seek election as a U.S. senator and then he would ultimately be elected president. Long had been elected to the Louisiana Public Service Commission (the Railroad Commission until 1921) in 1918, to the governorship in 1928, and to the U.S. Senate in 1930, and had thus attained the first three of his goals. There remained only his election to the presidency.[1]

While governor of Louisiana, Long also made no secret of his presidential ambition, which he emphasized in one of those incidents that his enemies regarded as typically embarrassing to the state. Former president Calvin Coolidge and his wife paid a call in New Orleans in 1930, and an elaborate banquet was held in their honor. Governor Long not only appeared at the banquet thirty minutes late, but when photographers snapped a picture of the Coolidges and Huey, he remarked that it was a picture of the "ex-President of the United States, and the future one." He also told reporters that he had asked the Coolidges what condition the White House was in, and Mrs. Coolidge had said that it was not in very good shape. Alluding to the fact that he had torn down the old governor's mansion in Baton Rouge and built a new one, Long boasted that with the White House as well he would have "to go up there and tear it down and build another one."[2]

Long's presidential ambitions had matured sufficiently by February 1934 that he announced the formation of his own national political organization in a radio address to a nationwide audience. The organization's name, he said, was the Share Our Wealth Society and its slogan was "Every man a king." Its goal was the redistribution of the nation's wealth, which was to be accomplished by a federal tax policy that would limit family fortunes to five million dollars and limit yearly incomes to one million dollars. The revenues thus generated, he claimed, would provide old-age pensions, funds for college educations for worthy youths, and bonuses for veterans as well as guaranteeing every family five thousand dollars or enough to pay for a home, an automobile, a radio, and other conveniences. By 1935, the Share Our Wealth Society claimed a nationwide membership of over four million persons.[3]

In the meantime, Long intended to implement in Louisiana the program he hoped to provide the nation as president and at the same time solidify his political power in his home state. The legislature of 1932 had created a tax reform commission to study the restructuring of the state's tax system, and the commission reported its recommendations during the summer of 1933. The commission proposed a state income tax, a tax on oil produced in Louisiana, and taxes on natural gas, liquor, tobacco, lubricating oil, and the receipts of public utilities. To offset the impact of these new taxes on the state's poor, the commission also proposed a homestead exemption of two thousand dollars.[4]

While the Kingfish did not endorse all of the commission's recommendations, he did advocate the need for restructuring the state tax system and the establishment of some new taxes, especially an income tax. The senator and Governor O. K. Allen stumped the state during the summer and fall of 1933 attempting to sell the public on the need for new tax revenues. Although Long's endorsement of new taxes in a public meeting in Alexandria was greeted by a barrage of rotten eggs from the audience, Long and Allen claimed during the fall that in other meetings they had addressed throughout the state explaining the tax proposals, a show of hands by those attending had indicated that the new tax program was endorsed by a margin of approximately one hundred to one.[5]

The daily press of the state adamantly opposed any new taxes, arguing that the state administration was already profligately wasting millions of dollars and that new taxes would be ruinous for the state's business enterprises. The Long forces counterattacked in the columns of the Kingfish's paper, the *American Progress*, castigating the press for having opposed the progress that the state had made under the Long regime and again attacking the leading members of the press with personal derision. Ever since Senator Long had become the champion of the people's rights, the *Progress* said, he had been subjected to a campaign of lies in the press. "These attacks have come from the mouths and pens of men owned body and soul by the corporations who had been robbing the State of Louisiana for years."[6]

"The waters of popular opinion in Louisiana, which demanded something for the money they had been paying, rose in 1927–28," the senator himself added. "The bats, owls, polecats and other foul-smelling things that had controlled the politics of Louisiana for forty years ran to the highest hill." There were gathered such creatures, Long continued, as "Squirt" Ewing of the *Shreveport Times* and "Liverwurst" Nicholson, "Kinky" Howard (Alvin Howard, a principal owner of the *Times-Picayune*), and "Shinola" Phelps of the *New Orleans Times-Picayune*. "The lies and double lies published in the newspapers under the control of this element have never been equaled," the Kingfish declared, "even during the impeachment." Long's reference to the dark-complexioned Nicholson as "Liverwurst" and the curly-haired Howard as "Kinky" was evidence of his customary habit of attempting to demean opponents by accusing them of black ancestry.[7]

Taking note of the outpouring of negative comments and ridicule directed at Senator Long following the Sands Point incident, the *American Progress* asserted that Long "has been the target of vicious attacks levelled at him by the several newspapers of this country controlled directly or indirectly by Wall Street." As far as the Louisiana press was concerned, the *Progress* began to publish thinly veiled threats that unless the vigorous opposition of the state's newspapers to the tax program were curtailed, they themselves might well become the target of one of the new taxes.[8]

While the "bought out newspapers" and their "henchmen" had previously been clamoring for tax relief for the state, the *Progress* reported in October, "they are now lining up tooth and nail against the program sponsored by Senator Long, Governor Allen and the Louisiana Tax

Reform Commission for tax relief for the people of this state." Meanwhile, the corporations were supporting a sales tax as the best form of new taxation for the state. "Some newspapers have sensed that an effort might be made to tax their business," the *Progress* continued. "That is not yet included in the program to relieve the ordinary man of taxes, but many have said there is no good reason why the newspapers should not be made to pay something to help support the government." Most of the newspapers had long abandoned their primary function of providing the public with legitimate information, the *Progress* charged. On the contrary, they now existed "for the purpose of publishing advertisements and for spreading lies that may assist in propaganda against the welfare of the common man."[9]

The newspapers had opposed every measure designed to improve the lot of the common people of the state that had been advanced in recent years, the *Progress* asserted. They had "fought the eradication of illiteracy; they fought the paved highways; they fought the building of the new capitol; they fought to keep the oil interests from being taxed—all the time reaping large sums of money from these rich interests to use their columns to spread whatever lies might be necessary and helpful to keep the tax loaded on the back of the common man and to keep him from having anything which the rich element might be made to pay." Many members of the state legislature were prepared to offer amendments to the tax relief program that would impose taxes on the newspapers, the Long paper warned, but so far proposals for taxing the press had not been included in the tax program.[10]

The *American Progress* then proceeded to elaborate on the reasons why a newspaper tax would be eminently justified. The fairness of taxing the press was demonstrated by "the false statements they are already publishing in their efforts to defeat tax relief for the people," it argued. Since "the state is constantly caused to spend hundreds of thousands of dollars so that the truth may be known to the people because of the falsehoods published in some of the newspapers, the general view is that at least these papers should be made to pay enough money to pay for what is expended in having the truth made known to the people to correct falsehoods published in their columns."[11]

Another justification for taxing the press, the *Progress* argued, was the fact that the newspapers were constantly building up the reputations of certain public figures, lavishing flattery upon them and praising their greatness, all as a means of controlling the actions of these officials in violation of all ethical standards recognized by the profession of journalism. "Such practices are so frowned upon that there is no longer considered such a thing as ethics to such publications," it charged, "and in as much as they are mere propaganda sheets and advertising mediums for special interests, no fair reason is ascribed against their being taxed."[12]

Since the newspapers of the state had demonstrated such a total lack of respect for the truth and for the reporting of accurate information, the *Progress* warned the people against believing "anything appearing in the newspapers as to the tax program or as to what may be said at any meeting. These papers are not expected to report anything near the truth." The newspapers had already "resorted to manufacturing the same kind of lies unsuccessfully used by them during the past several years in their fights with Huey P. Long," the *Progress* continued. "In each instance, however, the truth has been presented to the people and these interests have been silenced." The battle in the legislature over the tax program would be bitterly fought, the Long paper predicted, and "bids fair to be a strip table affair with the little home owner with children to educate on one side of the board, opposed by the concentration of special privileges known to have run the affairs of Louisiana for scores of years."[13]

During the fall, the *American Progress* continued to suggest that there was increasing pressure by members of the legislature on Governor Allen and Senator Long to impose a tax on the newspapers and implied that the governor and senator were so far resisting that pressure. On October 26, the *Progress* reported that one member of the house of representatives had presented the arguments for a newspaper tax in an interview. "I have always felt that the newspaper interests should be made to pay the cost of government," the legislator purportedly said. "Take the *Times-Picayune* for instance. Everyone knows how that paper has black-jacked the corporations out of thousands of dollars by selling their editorial policies right and left." "Let somebody propose a tax on any product and immediately you see full page ads appearing in the *Times-Picayune* paid for by the corporations," he continued. "Simultaneously you will see the *Times-Picayune* begin lying and carrying on one of its usual blackmailing attacks on the proposed tax and the men who are its proponents."[14]

The legislator argued that when such a situation as he had described developed in the state, "whereby measures that would do good for the people are hampered by the sell-out policy of a bartered press . . . it is time for the people to do something about it." "The people and the state itself," he said, "frequently are forced to spend thousands of dollars in order to bring the truth to the people after papers like the *Times-Picayune* sell their columns outright."[15]

By November, the *American Progress* dropped the pretense that a newspaper tax was being pressed upon a reluctant Governor Allen and Senator Long. For the first time the *Progress* listed a newspaper tax as among the new taxes that would be sought from the legislature at its next session. "Will we have our taxes taken off by the men who have been reducing these taxes and placing them on big money," the *Progress* asked, "or will we let big money lie the people out of house and home? The people must again fight their own battle. Watch out for lying newspapers!"[16]

In the fall of 1933, the then deceased Robert Ewing's *New Orleans States* was acquired by the *Times-Picayune*. The event was portrayed in a *Progress* cartoon depicting Esmond Phelps, Alvin Howard, and Leonard Nicholson as pirates seizing the ship "*States*," which was grounded on the rocks, with its mast shattered and John "Squirt" Ewing and his brothers clinging to the deck. In November, the *Progress* gleefully reported that the *States* was losing money and costing the *Times-Picayune* ownership five hundred dollars a day. Esmond Phelps, the *Progress* said, owned an approximately 20 percent interest in the *Times-Picayune*, and as a result of the losses was near a nervous breakdown. His share of the losses, the *Progress* calculated, was one hundred dollars a day or the price "of 667 cans of Shinola." The owners of the *Times-Picayune* "are holding as an ace in the hole the prospect of getting a large chunk of corporation money that will be spent for shake-down advertising when the big companies begin fighting the Long–Allen–Tax Reform Commission program of tax relief," the Long paper asserted. It quoted a person allegedly familiar with the losses the *Times-Picayune* was incurring for the *States* as saying, "The guy I feel sorry for is Esmond Phelps. They tell me he is now wearing canvas sneakers so he don't have to buy Shinola anymore."[17]

Attacking and ridiculing those associated with the state's dailies continued to be a regular feature in the *Progress*. The publishers of the Shreveport papers were attacked for printing lies about the Long regime, lies that "were wired by these scoundrels to other states to get newspapers there to print falsehoods about the land where these snakes live and which they have tried to ruin." The *Times-Picayune* was accused of printing "lie No. 1,631,467," and Hilda Phelps Hammond, the Kingfish's perennial enemy whom the *Progress* christened "Hilda, the antique queen," was accused of drawing one hundred dollars a month in salary from the *Times-Picayune*.[18]

Having abandoned his alleged reluctance to endorse a newspaper tax, Senator Long in November strongly supported the tax and also renewed his slashing personal attacks on the newspapers and their publishers. Speaking at Marksville, the Kingfish attacked the *Times-Picayune*, the *Shreveport Times*, and the *Alexandria Daily Town Talk*. Those papers, he claimed, by playing "on the ignorance of the people, [have] kept you where you are. If we had some way to hang every man and newspaper that lies, the world would be better off today." "Take those lying *Times-Picayune, Shreveport Times* and *Alexandria Town Talk,*" he continued. "We are going to sock a tax on those damned rascals. Let them scoundrels pay for the privilege of lying." "If you tell a lie the judge can put you in jail and he ought to," the senator declared, "but newspapers get paid for lying. The freedom of the press lets those newspapers print any kind of lies. The big interests of Wall Street pay them for publishing lies."[19]

Taking its cue from the Kingfish, the *American Progress* also increased the virulence of its attacks on the Louisiana press. Personally attacking "Squirt" Ewing of the *Shreveport Times* and "Baby" Dolph Frantz, editor of the *Shreveport Journal*, the *Progress* charged that they "fought the free school books and lost. They fought the paved roads and lost. They fought the free bridges in Shreveport and everywhere and lost. They fight everything." "There isn't truth to be had from these lying elements, caught in one lie and they immediately tell ten more," it asserted. "They never correct their lies, they lie ten times more to cover up—and, in the end, THEY ALWAYS LOSE." "John (Squirt) Ewing," the *Progress* maintained, mishandled "the truth and uses the columns of his scurrilous newspaper to spread false propaganda." When the *Shreveport Times* published an item advocating the reduction of the disparity between great wealth and poverty in the country, the *Progress* gleefully noted the item, adding "How . . . the *Shreveport Times* ever let that little piece of Huey Long philosophy slip in the paper is a mystery. It is the first time in almost three years that a word of truth has ever been seen in the Ewing paper."[20]

The *New Orleans Times-Picayune* was also singled out for attack in the columns of the *Progress*. Referring to the paper's president as "Liverwurst" Nicholson, the *Progress* charged that in Louisiana "the newspaper that uses more venom, lies, fact-twisting and misrepresentation than any other in its fight against Huey Long is the *Times-Picayune*." "This newspaper is always getting caught in some lie or other," it claimed. "No one in Louisiana believes a word the *Times-Picayune* prints. Thousands of people refuse to even let the *Times-Picayune* in their homes." "Readers of the *American Progress* outside of Louisiana," it said, "probably would never believe that anywhere in the world are there newspapers as low as the *Times-Picayune*." When advertising revenues reportedly declined for the New Orleans papers, the *Progress* also reported that "coloring the news, suppression of the truth, political fanaticism and downright lying cost the New Orleans newspapers $75,000 during the months of November and December."[21]

Referring to the "lying *Times-Picayune*," the "thimble-rigging *States*," the "pettifogging *Item*," and the "hanky panky *Tribune*," the *American Progress* charged that the "editorials in these aforementioned black sheets are usually the result of a knavish mind bred on misrepresentation and developed on journalistic blackmail." Noting that the newspapers had been angrily attacking Senator Long, the *Progress* asked rhetorically why they were angry. They were angry, it maintained, because millions of dollars in "filthy lucre" had been paid to them by the special interests for their "prostitution" but without results. "They are mad because they have been unable to get more money for the results they have been unable to accomplish," the *Progress* maintained. "They are mad because they want to take the school books out of the hands of the little children and get money for themselves to do that. They are mad because they sit back night and day with the multi-millionaires scheming to build their fortunes bigger and rob the poor underfed children of the state of the last vestige of hope they have on earth, that Huey Long has devoted a life to giving them." "Corruption, prostitution, false statements, pledges to rob the children," the *Progress* declared, "are all part and parcel of the swag of the corrupt newspapers of the state, and the hope and aim of a filthy set."[22]

As the May 1934 session of the Louisiana legislature was about to convene, the anti-Long forces believed that the Kingfish's grip on the state and the legislature had considerably loosened, and they laid plans for wresting control of the legislature and even the state from Long's domination. Under their rather far-fetched strategy, Speaker of the House Allen Ellender was to be replaced with an anti-Long legislator, and if this were successful, they planned to remove Lieutenant Governor John Fournet and replace him with one of their men. Finally, if the first two steps were successful, they would impeach Governor O. K. Allen, who would be succeeded by the new, anti-Long lieutenant governor. Such an overly ambitious plan probably had little chance of success from the outset, but when the Kingfish got wind of it, he used patronage, favors, and even money to persuade a sufficient number of legislators to abandon any attempt at the plan. Having successfully defused the opposition's plans for a political coup, Long left Baton Rouge to attend the session of the U.S. Senate in Washington.[23]

Despite the defeat of their plan to obtain control of the legislature, the anti-Long forces remained formidable, and they were adamant in their opposition to the administration's proposals for new taxes. Their resistance was bolstered by unrelenting opposition to any new taxes by the daily press. The *Times-Picayune*, for example, ran an almost continuous stream of editorials opposing the new tax program and declared that it was the duty of all citizens in the state "to take action, singly and through their civic organizations against the menacing machine drive for more taxes and more wastes." The overwhelming majority of the people were against any new taxes, the paper asserted, and the "dictator himself, his governor and all his other lackeys know of this statewide feeling." If the administration persisted in pressing for the new taxes program, the *Times-Picayune* warned, "the battle over it will be raging furiously along a statewide front, with every member of the legislature forced to take an open stand for or against the 'more taxes' scheme and the dictatorship which is striving to force it down the throats of a resisting and wrathful citizenry."[24]

The unrelenting pressure of the daily press against the tax program led the house of representatives to pass a resolution on May 28 calling upon the press to cooperate with the legislature "to keep the peace" and to refrain from references to partisanship and factionalism. In turn, the legislators promised to assert their independence from any "would be dictator." On June 3, Representative William Pegues of DeSoto Parish offered a resolution that would have denied reporters access to the house because the newspapers were dealing in "personalities" of the members, but the house refused to approve the resolution.[25]

Meanwhile the bills that would implement the program of new taxes became stalled in committee in both the house and the senate, and on June 6 a mass meeting sponsored by the anti-Long opposition was held in Baton Rouge. One speaker at the meeting declared that Louisiana was "in one of the greatest crises of its history, and I don't exempt the reconstruction days," and other speakers called upon the people to revolt if the new taxes were imposed. Governor Allen counterattacked with a political circular warning that if "the people or their legislators can be fooled by the agents of big money and their lying, bought-out newspapers, they can be kept from having any tax relief at the present session of the legislature." "Every time a plan is on foot that would tax these big-moneyed interests so as to help the balance of the people," the governor charged, "their bought-out newspapers shout 'bloody murder!' They trump up a 'mass meeting' to holler against 'any more taxes' if the corporations are going to have to pay them. The old New Orleans ring, always under their thumb, do their loud hollering and yelling."[26]

The *Times-Picayune*, however, declared editorially that the " 'big shot' and his royal retinue may deride, but they must not mistake the public temper and spirit" that opposed any new taxes. The *Shreveport Times* reported regarding the tax bills that there was "little thought that they will reach the statute books." At another mass rally in Baton Rouge in mid-June, a resolution was adopted urging that "one man from each parish in the state be assembled here and now, and arrange for co-ordination of effort in enrolling men in each parish and community to conduct by whatever means that may be required, using force if necessary, to return governmental affairs to the people of the state."[27]

Toward the end of June, the legislature appeared to be in a state of near paralysis, as the tax bills continued to languish in committee and little of importance seemed to be occurring. Despite its undoubted grip on the politics of the state, the Long organization was exhibiting the glaring defect of not functioning properly, if at all, in the absence of its leader. Apparently recognizing this, Senator Long returned to Louisiana from Washington on June 21 and made a dramatic reappearance at the capitol in Baton Rouge.[28]

Time magazine reported that Long displaced Governor Allen in the governor's office in the capitol and immediately began to take action to break the deadlock in the legislature. "Senator Long may be mocked as a cheap demagog by the nation-at-large and his popularity with Louisiana voters may be on the wane," *Time* said, "but at Baton Rouge he is still an autocrat. In a fashion which would have won instinctive approval from Benito Mussolini, he began to get things done." One of the Kingfish's first moves was to remove as administration leaders in the house of representatives N. S. Hoffpauer of Acadia Parish and Arthur Provost of Iberia Parish. Having mismanaged a tax measure on the house floor, they were personally replaced by Long with Isom J. Guillory of St. Landry Parish.[29]

The Kingfish announced that, with regard to the tax program, "we are going to work out something satisfactory to everybody. That is, as satisfactory as possible." "The little man in this state has carried the burden of taxation long enough," he continued, "and now we are going to shift a big part of it off his shoulders and put it on the big money interests." "Of course," he added, "they are hollering bloody murder and will do everything to try to escape paying a share of the taxes."[30]

Despite the arrival of the Kingfish on the scene, the *New Orleans Item* reported on July 1 that opposition leaders had concluded that Long really did not want the new taxes passed, and they were considering supporting the tax bills so that the blame for the new taxes could be squarely fastened on the Long organization at the next election. But on July 2, Long arranged a meeting of the house committee on ways and means. When the committee convened it waited until the Kingfish and Governor Allen arrived, and Long immediately took charge of the committee's proceedings and orchestrated the approval of three tax measures. "The time is growing late for these bills to be put through," Long told the committee, and he humorously added, "I take it that you gentlemen of the committee will not be criticized if you report them out now. The newspapers have been criticizing us for delaying the bills, and I am sure that you will be praised if you report them out without further delay."[31]

Two of the proposals before the committee were a measure authorizing the imposition of an income tax and a bill taxing the New Orleans cotton exchange. The third bill would impose a 2 percent tax on the gross receipts from the sale of advertising by newspapers with weekly circulations of twenty thousand copies or more. The newspaper tax proposal before the committee, however, applied only to the New Orleans and Shreveport dailies, papers that had been the most vociferous in their denunciations of Long and his policies. Before the committee, the Kingfish pronounced the newspaper tax bill as "my own stuff" and humorously suggested that it was noncontroversial and had aroused no opposition. "There is no class of people who are as patriotic as the newspapers," he said with tongue in cheek. "They are civic leaders, some of them teach Sunday school classes and they are leaders in the church. They believe they should do what others want to do." The newspapers had campaigned for a state sales tax, Long noted, and "99.41 percent of the newspapers have been in favor of it," implying that the newspapers were willing to make a similar contribution to the state's revenues. "I think the tax is too small for the larger newspapers, but since there hasn't been any opposition to the tax so far, I am willing to leave it like it is—i.e., to apply to newspapers of 20,000 or more." "So long as we can have such cooperation," he continued, "I would not suggest any changes that might bring some opposition." The tax would not apply to small newspapers, Long pointed out, but only those with large weekly circulations. "Most of this advertising comes from out of state, from New York and every place," he said. "Every time you have a tax fight you find these large interests presenting full-page advertisements, so great is their interest in starting money into circulation, and the newspapers are always glad to do their share in being the first to start it."[32]

Hermann Moyse, a Baton Rouge attorney and a lobbyist representing the press, argued strongly before the ways and means committee against approval of the newspaper tax. He first pointed out that the proposed tax was on gross receipts derived from the sale of advertising and argued that a gross receipts tax was wrong in principle because it was unrelated to any profit or net income derived from the activity being taxed. Moyse also predicted that if this tax were approved by the legislature, it would later be extended to reach all newspapers in the state and not just those having weekly circulations of 20,000 copies or more. He pointed out that doctors were not subjected to a license tax and neither should newspapers, but Representative Isom Guillory of the committee argued that doctors were exempted from such taxes because of the charity work they did. "How many times have you been to a newspaper to try to get a free write-up of some kind, Mr. Guillory?"

Moyse responded. Like doctors, he contended, newspapers performed public service by liberally contributing space to the sponsorship of charitable and public welfare causes and should therefore be accorded the same exemption from taxation as doctors. "Did they support the good roads in 1930?" Senator Long inquired. "Some of them did," Moyse replied; "the *Item* . . . did, I believe." "Yes," the Kingfish said, "they supported it after they had been beaten down and had to support it." "I don't see why newspapers should be exempt from payment of license taxes," Representative Guillory observed, adding that "other businesses pay license taxes." "There is not a single state in the country that has a tax on newspaper advertising," Moyse answered. But Guillory suggested this was the case only because the press had used its power to prevent legislatures from adopting such taxes. "They haven't whipped you into line, have they, Mr. Guillory, or you, Mr. McGrath, and surely not you, have they, Senator Long?" Moyse asked. "Surely, you don't think newspapers could control such a situation, do you?"[33]

Representative Guillory said that as Moyse "well knew" the legislature was looking for alternative revenues to relieve the burden of the property tax on the average taxpayer. "We are looking for money," he emphasized. Moyse then asked the committee if it knew how much money the newspaper tax would raise in revenue, but there was no response. "The wholesale subject of freedom of the press is involved in this tax," he continued. "You are going to say that a man cannot speak without paying a tax of two percent. You are attempting to tax freedom of speech." "I will admit that this freedom is sometimes abused," Moyse added, "but when it is, you have your recourse." When one member of the committee inquired of Moyse as to whether the newspapers would leave the state if the tax were imposed, Moyse pointed out that the newspapers had sustained heavy losses in advertising revenues in recent years because of economic conditions. Representative Guillory in response said the losses the newspapers had suffered were no greater than the losses suffered by business generally because of the Depression.[34]

At this point, Senator Long cut off the discussion and curtly announced that "we've heard enough of this." "The tax goes on this advertising," and he rejected Moyse's objections to a gross receipts tax, suggesting that if the tax were on net income or profits derived from sales of advertising, the papers would manipulate their books to minimize their profits. A gross receipts tax would prevent this. The Kingfish then began a monologue attacking the newspapers for contributing virtually nothing toward their fair share of the cost of government. "The newspapers are the charmed free bull of this country," he declared. "They don't pay any tax on anything. They have newsprint on the free [tariff] list and they don't keep enough on hand to pay any taxes on that. They are the only outfit that pays no licenses. They enjoy public improvements like nobody else. They use everything on everything." He was very much surprised at the opposition to the newspaper tax, he claimed, and he had "a suggestion that will increase . . . [the newspapers'] business." Much of the public, Long pointed out, were dubious of what was said in many newspaper advertisements. "If a man knew when he was reading the news columns he was reading the truth, then he would believe the advertisements. I think we need to help the newspapers by making them tell the truth, but we'll give them a little time to see if they won't clean up their own houses before we do that."[35]

The Kingfish then returned to the theme that the papers received much in the way of government services but paid very little in return. They were using the mails for the distribution of their papers, he pointed out, while enjoying subsidized mail rates at the cost to the taxpayers of one hundred thousand dollars yearly. "There is only one way to give tax relief, and that is to tax those who are able to pay," he continued. Newspapers raised or lowered their advertising rates at will, with the *Times-Picayune*, "that just journal of righteousness and broadmindedness," varying its rates by as much as 15 percent. "If they put in the paper that a man stole a horse, and they can do it, because by the time a fellow files a suit and finally winds up with a judgment of $500, he won't have anything left," Long argued. "If they put in the paper that a man stole a horse, and the man came around to get it corrected, they would say that is 'political advertising' and would charge the extra rate."[36]

"Freedom of speech is one thing and freedom from taxation is another," the Kingfish asserted. "I believe in freedom of speech, but it's got to be truthful speech, and lying newspapers should have to pay for their lying. I'm going to help these newspapers by hitting them in their pocketbooks; maybe then they'll try to clean up." "The tax goes on this advertising, and it will be on gross advertising. We ain't going to give these newspapers any chance to juggle their books on the net basis," he concluded. "Come on and vote." Without further discussion, the ways and means committee then reported the newspaper tax out favorably by a vote of ten to three. With the newspaper tax, one committee member opined, the legislature would guide the newspapers "in the path of rectitude."[37]

On July 4, James Thomson, publisher of the *New Orleans Item* and *Tribune*, published a front-page open letter in the *Item* addressed to the speaker of the house and the president of the senate protesting the new tax. Under Thomson's direction, the *Item* and *Tribune* had changed positions and supported the Long regime in 1932, but in 1933 had again switched sides and begun to oppose Longism. Thomson pointed out that the tax was grossly discriminatory because it singled out for taxation one particular line of business. But he opposed the tax even more strongly because "it invites abuse of the taxing privilege to the destruction of the freedom of the press in Louisiana. If newspapers can be taxed two percent of their gross earnings, they can be taxed ten, fifteen, or twenty-five percent of their gross earnings." In other words, Thomson argued, "they can be taxed entirely out of business. They can be ruined or confiscated at pleasure by any political group temporarily dominating a legislature."[38]

The *Times-Picayune* also reacted with alarm to the proposed newspaper tax, pointing out that the ways and means committee under "the eye and direct order of the 'big shot' had reported the tax out favorably." "All the papers menaced by this levy on gross earnings stand opposed to the dictator and his royal rackets," the *Times-Picayune* maintained. "No paper which has not and does not oppose him is affected by the measure as he dictated it. No such tax is imposed anywhere else in the United States—nor has any such mulcting of a small group of newspapers singled out for punishment because of their stand on political issues and public questions ever been so much as proposed elsewhere." The sole and indisputable purpose of the tax, the *Times-Picayune* continued, was to punish the newspapers in the state that had taken an "open and fearless stand against the present dictatorship." The tax was a "deliberate attempt to punish, muzzle and destroy newspapers which, in fulfillment of their public duty, have exercised their God-given and constitutionally guaranteed right of free expression." The tax was, the paper warned, "the first step toward the destruction of the freedom of the press in this state, since the punitive tax later may be extended at the dictator's whim to strike other Louisiana newspapers whose utterances displease him."[39]

As for itself, the *Times-Picayune* declared, it would not bow down to the Kingfish, but would as in the past "maintain its tradition of free and plain speaking on public questions and issues despite this attempt to silence and destroy it by grossly oppressive and discriminatory taxation." But it warned the citizens of Louisiana that this was a thrust at a free and fearless press that "directly jeopardizes and menaces Louisiana's free press entire—and the public's right to be served by a free press." Whether the legislature would "blindly obey" the dictator remained to be seen, the *Times-Picayune* concluded, but it should be pointed out that this "direct and venomous attack upon America's prized and traditional guaranty of freedom of the press has had no parallel or precedent anywhere nor at any time in this nation's history."[40]

The *New Orleans States* also joined the chorus of condemnation of the newspaper tax and pointed out that it applied "to only two cities in the state, Shreveport and New Orleans, the newspapers of which happen to have had the courage to stand up, in the face of threats of such punitive legislation, and battle for the right of the people against the tyranny, oppression and frightful waste of the taxpayers' money that obtains under the reign of Longism." Denouncing the tax as unconstitutional and urging the legislature to reject it, the *States* vowed to continue its opposition to the Kingfish. The *States*, it said, "is too far advanced in its life to be intimidated by any such vengeful bill as that Mr. Long is trying to put over."[41]

The remainder of the Louisiana daily press generally repeated the warnings of the New Orleans papers, with Charles Manship in the *Baton Rouge Morning Advocate* declaring that if the principle contained in the newspaper tax bill were written into law by the legislature, "the guarantee of a free press, written in the Constitution of the United States, and traditional in American life, is at an end." The *Shreveport Times* pointed out that such an attempt by the Kingfish to punish the press was not unexpected. The senator wanted a press "which bends knee before him," the *Times* said, and nothing would "suit him better than to be able to dictate the contents and the editorial utterances of the newspapers." The question was, it said, whether the people of Louisiana wanted a free press that followed its own opinions or not. If the public wanted that "sort of press—and the Constitution of our country declares that a free press is essential to the preservation of liberty and democratic government—then this attempt of the senior senator to browbeat Louisiana's daily newspapers should arouse a storm of protest." No other state had a tax like the one the Kingfish was proposing, the *Times* pointed out, "or even contemplates using the authority of its government to give a politician power to suppress freedom or wreak vengeance on newspapers guilty of criticism." "The dangers inherent in the use of taxes to bludgeon the press are recognized in the other 47 states," it concluded, "and should be similarly recognized by the members of the Louisiana legislature, if they wish to promote the true welfare of their constituents."[42]

If there was any appreciation of the irony of its consideration of a measure to suppress freedom of the press by taxation on Independence Day, the Louisiana legislature gave scant indication of it. Never a model of decorum at best, the legislature was in a celebratory mood on July 4, and members marked the occasion by throwing firecrackers under one another's feet. Busy buttonholing and lobbying legislators as was his custom, Senator Long had one of the firecrackers land under his feet, and its explosion caused him to leap into the air and then to retreat from the floor in mock surrender.[43]

In addition to the newspaper tax, Long and the Allen administration were pressing for the passage of a measure that would repeal the state's poll tax. Although adopted in Louisiana and many other southern states as a method of discouraging blacks from voting, the poll tax had the additional effect of barring many poor whites from the polls as well. Long correctly perceived that poor whites were among his most ardent supporters, and he therefore backed the repeal of the tax as a means of strengthening the power of his organization at the ballot box. The repeal of the poll tax, along with the rest of the tax program, however, aroused a strong and vociferous opposition.[44]

The Kingfish and Governor Allen responded to the opposition their legislative program was attracting in a political circular in which they argued that this opposition was coming from "New Orleans Ringsters and Election Thugs" combined with the "Lying Newspapers and Big Money Interests." The opponents of the repeal of the poll tax, the circular charged, "feel and in their hearts believe that the government is made to be run by a select few. Many of them feel that the common run of mankind is just a little bit better than the common run of cattle." In the circular, Long and Allen also charged that the "lying newspapers are continuing a vicious campaign against giving the people a free right to vote." Although the newspaper tax had not yet passed the legislature, they claimed that they "managed to take care of that element here last week. A tax of 2% on what newspapers take in was placed upon them. That will help their lying some." The newspapers did not pay taxes as ordinary businesses were required to pay, the circular pointed out. "It is a system that these big Louisiana newspapers tell a lie every time they make a dollar. This should be called a tax on lying, 2 cents per lie."[45]

"We are out 100% to relieve the burdens of the poor and for a redistribution of wealth," Long and Allen declared. "We were laughed at when the fight started." Their goals would nonetheless be accomplished, they promised, and there will "be no starvation in the land of plenty when our program succeeds. We propose to fight until it does." They needed the support of the people, however, "to help us fight for their own rights and their own interest. Whoever tries to saddle them down with something that takes away from them their right to vote is standing in the way of a Democratic Government." The Long–Allen circular was distributed to the members of the legislature during its deliberations on the newspaper tax.[46]

The house of representatives took up consideration of the newspaper tax on July 5, with the Kingfish pacing up and down the aisles, giving orders to his supporters. Representative Rupert Payton protested the Kingfish's presence on the floor of the house, declaring that "we are treated to the rotten spectacle of his piscatorial majesty, the Crawfish, giving orders in this house, interrupting debate and otherwise disporting himself as anything but a gentleman. I am sick and tired of this and I think every other member is disgusted too."[47]

Representative Norman Bauer attacked the newspaper tax as "a spite bill pure and simple. It is a punitive measure and should receive no consideration at all!" The Kingfish was standing on the floor near Bauer when he made these remarks, and Long answered with a Bronx cheer. "I ask, Mr. Speaker, that Senator Long allow me to proceed," Bauer responded, and Speaker Allen Ellender rapped for order. Bauer was questioned by a Long supporter, who asked "what effect will this tax on advertising have on the freedom of the press?" "This tax is a continuous threat and is intended as such," Bauer said. "The only purpose of this tax is to warn every paper in the state, large and small, to 'line up' and stop criticizing the administration or they will suffer a similar fate." As presented in the house, the newspaper tax bill was drafted to apply only to the New Orleans and Shreveport newspapers, and Bauer pointed out that it thus "singles out four [actually six] newspapers simply because those newspapers have criticized the administration. Every member of this house knows this to be true." Passage of the bill would be used, he predicted, "to show the small papers what can be done to them if 'they don't get right.' "[48]

Bauer pointed out that while the bill's supporters argued that the imposition of the tax on newspapers would raise revenue that could be used to offset reduced property taxes on small homeowners, the administration in fact had not presented any information regarding how much revenue the tax would generate. "If we pass this newspaper tax, we are setting a dangerous precedent," he warned. "It is wrong in principle, and I hope the members of the house will not bow to the will of the dictator." Representative J. C. Buie of Franklin Parish asked whether Bauer thought the newspapers had been fair in their coverage of the administration. "I believe the newspapers have been a whole lot fairer than this administration deserves," Bauer replied. "Are the small papers of the state opposed to this tax?" another member asked Bauer. "All the small papers are opposed to it," he said, "because they know it is a club held over their heads. No one can deny this."[49]

Representative Lorris Wimberley of Bienville argued that the tax did not apply to "the little boy" and that as a consequence he did not "anticipate any opposition to this tax." "We are going to put it on, and we expect to collect it," he added. "The newspaper industry is a protected industry. It pays no license tax, and it ought to bear a share of the burden." Wimberley estimated that the tax would raise $250,000 yearly. "Why have only four [actually six] newspapers been singled out?" Representative Bauer asked, but there was no answer to his inquiry.[50]

Bauer again pointed out that the tax reform commission had made no effort to determine how much the newspaper tax would raise in revenue. Representative Goode Smith of East Baton Rouge Parish then asked the bill's supporters, "Why do you put this tax on the larger newspapers? Are the little papers broke?" Representative Wimberley responded that to his knowledge the small papers were not broke, but another opponent of the bill inquired how many other states levied such a tax on newspapers. "I don't know," Wimberley replied. "Don't you know that no other state in the Union has levied such a tax?" he was asked. "I am informed that is true," Wimberley finally conceded. Representative Joseph Fisher of Jefferson Parish insisted, however, that the tax was needed because the proceeds would go to homestead property tax relief, but Representative Bauer challenged that assertion. "I don't think it will help homesteads," he said. A vote was then held on the newspaper tax bill, and the house approved it with fifty-six members supporting it and thirty-eight opposed.[51]

A report in the *Monroe News-Star* furnished insight into the motives of at least some of the legislators who supported the newspaper tax and the stunted conception of freedom of the press they possessed. Just prior to the 1934 session of the legislature, a public meeting was held in Monroe at which local legislators were asked if they supported the proposals for new taxes being offered by the Long organization. Representative J. Porter Burgess refused to say that he was opposed to the new tax program. Subsequently, Burgess contacted the Monroe newspapers and asked them not to publish an account of the meeting, apparently fearing that his stance on the tax issue might arouse public opposition to him. The Monroe papers refused his request and ran the story. When the newspaper tax was being considered in the house, the *Monroe News-Star* contacted Representative Burgess and urged him to oppose the measure, but he declared that he was going to vote for it because "the Monroe papers were not his friends." "I am glad to do anything for my friends down here," he added, "but when the *World* and *News-Star* refused to keep out a story I asked them not to print several weeks ago, I knew they were not my friends." He concluded by saying he would vote for the newspaper tax.[52]

Burgess, the *News-Star* maintained, was typical of the members of the Long organization who supported the newspaper tax. By his own admission, the paper pointed out, he "had let it be known that the *Morning World* and *News-Star* could have purchased his aid in helping to defeat the advertising tax measure by suppressing a report of a meeting held in this city two months ago, at which time the representative curtly announced that he was 'against' those who favored 'no additional taxes' by the present legislative session." "For this failure in 'friendship,' " the *News-Star* declared, "Mr. Burgess felt free . . . to join the dictator in his punitive measures against the press."[53]

As passed by the house, the newspaper tax bill still applied only to the New Orleans and the Shreveport papers, but the Kingfish apparently came to realize that if the measure were enacted by the legislature in that form, it would be exceedingly vulnerable to attack under both the Louisiana and the federal constitutions. A great deal of latitude was customarily afforded legislatures by the courts in classifying subjects for taxation. Yet a tax that was imposed on certain newspapers with weekly circulations of twenty thousand copies or more, but not on other papers with the same or greater circulations, was too blatantly discriminatory to pass constitutional muster. To prevent the newspaper tax measure from being so discriminatory, the Kingfish recognized that it would require amendment while under consideration in the senate.

On July 6, the day following the approval of the newspaper tax in the house, the senate finance committee convened to consider the measure. As in the proceedings before the house ways and means committee, Senator Long was not only present but also dominated and orchestrated the senate proceedings. Addressing the committee chairman, the Kingfish curtly ordered, "Mr. Fredericks, you place in these amendments. We want to make a few changes to clarify the bill." The amendments were designed to make the newspaper tax applicable to all the newspapers in the state with weekly circulations of twenty thousand copies or more and not just the New Orleans and Shreveport papers. Senator W. Scott Heywood of Jefferson Davis Parish noted that the amendments would make the tax applicable to the *Lake Charles American Press*, among other papers, and he was opposed to them on that ground. The bill as amended, the Kingfish said, "will only get the papers in the cities." "How about the *Lake Charles American Press*?" Heywood asked. "It will get them," Long replied, adding that "they ought to pay the tax." "Well, I'm against it," Heywood said. Without further debate, the finance committee then approved the bill as amended by a vote of nine to two.[54]

Lake Charles is in Calcasieu Parish in southwestern Louisiana, and the *American Press* was the leading newspaper in that section of the state. The reason Senator Heywood objected to the newspaper tax being imposed on the *American Press* was undoubtedly because that paper's coverage of state politics and the Long regime had been largely neutral and without the fervent denunciations of Longism that characterized the remainder of the state's daily press. Indeed, a perusal of the *American Press* during the period reveals a newspaper that was almost deliberately bland in both its news columns and its editorial pages and that rarely took a strong editorial position on any issue. When the newspaper tax was finally passed by the legislature and was being denounced by the rest of the Louisiana dailies, for example, the *American Press* was editorially silent on the issue.[55]

Since the purpose of the newspaper tax was to punish his enemies in the press, the Kingfish himself recognized the unfairness of imposing the tax on the Lake Charles paper. "There was only one newspaper in the state that had not joined up with the gang opposing me," Long admitted in a subsequent speech, "and that was the *Lake Charles American Press*." "Well, we tried to find a way to exempt the *Lake Charles American Press* from the advertising tax," he explained, "but did not think we could do it, but we would have done it if we could." To have exempted the *American Press* from the tax would have opened the measure up to the same constitutional vulnerability that could have been raised against the bill as it had passed the house. Consequently the Kingfish had to make the Lake Charles paper subject to the tax.[56]

The newspaper tax did not come up for consideration in the senate until the early morning hours of Sunday, July 8. Some senators objected to working on the Sabbath, but the Kingfish insisted that the senate continue in session. "The Bible says if the ox gets stuck in the ditch to work Sunday to get him out," he lectured the complaining senators. "You members ought to follow the Bible's teachings and when the legislature is stuck in the ditch it's up to you to work on Sunday to get it out."[57]

The Kingfish paced the senate floor impatiently before it convened, and when that occurred, he rushed to Senator Coleman Lindsey of Webster Parish, the administration floor leader, and urged, "Why don't you bring those three [tax] bills up and pass 'em? That's all we want to pass." Introducing the newspaper tax on the floor, Senator Hugh Dore of Evangeline Parish remarked only, "This is the newspaper bill, that's all." Without further discussion the senate passed the newspaper tax and two additional tax measures in a period of twenty minutes. Long stood on the senate secretary's desk and carefully watched as the lights on the voting machine indicated how the senators were voting.[58]

The opposition of the daily press to the newspaper tax was strengthened when spokesmen for leading Protestant and Catholic publications in the state announced their opposition as well. In a telegram to Speaker Allen Ellender and Lieutenant Governor John Fournet, C. I. Harris, the managing editor of the *Church World*, the official Protestant publication for southern Louisiana that was endorsed by seventy-eight churches, entered his "solemn protest against this most unjust and un-American proposal." The newspaper tax was an attempt, Harris said, "to take away from the press of Louisiana the right of free speech and expression which is ours under the Constitution." The Rev. Peter Wynhoven, editor of the *Catholic World*, also denounced the measure and appealed to the legislature "to kill this vicious bill because it is un-American, striking at the constitutional right of free speech."[59]

On July 9 the house took up consideration of the newspaper tax measure as amended in the senate, and as he had during the initial debate on the bill, Representative Norman Bauer led the fight against it. When Representative Lorris Wimberley, a Long supporter, seemed uncertain what motion to offer regarding the newspaper tax, Bauer sarcastically observed, "I wish [Senator Long] would make up his mind so Mr. Wimberley will know what to do!"[60]

Bauer read the telegrams of Harris and Wynhoven opposing the bill and again pointed out that his prediction in the earlier debate that the tax would soon be applied to all of the press had now come to pass. "A few days ago," he said, "I pointed out that it was intended to be used as a club. I had no idea the club would descend so quickly." "When this bill reached the senate," Bauer continued, "a committee dominated by Senator Long amended it to include the smaller newspapers, just as I predicted eventually would happen. This was done to show even the smaller dailies and weeklies in the state what will happen if they 'don't behave.' " "The sole purpose of this tax is to be used as a club," he declared, "as I have said before. The $250,000 the administration says it will get from the advertising tax does not mean anything to the administration—it is just a club." "It is a warning to the smaller weeklies," he maintained, "that if they do not get in line, they will be clubbed out of existence." Present as always during the house debate, Senator Long responded to Bauer's charge that the tax menaced freedom of the press with nothing more that a "satisfied smile."[61]

Representative R. D. Jones of Washington Parish asked Bauer, "Do you believe this tax will close down the *Times-Picayune*?" "No, I do not," Bauer replied, but Jones persisted, "It will continue to print lies?" "Do you think it was fair to tax the New Orleans and Shreveport papers and exempt the rest?" another Long supporter asked Bauer. "I don't think it is fair to tax any of the newspapers," he replied. "Because under this administration that will be extended to your little parish papers too." When Bauer was asked, "Are you more interested in the newspapers than in homes and schools?" he responded, "I am not interested in the newspapers at all, but I am interested in ordinary decency, and in the vicious system of this administration in trying to throttle the right of free speech."[62]

Representative J. W. Ethridge of Grant Parish then charged that the *Times-Picayune* had opposed "good roads, bridges and bringing Louisiana State University up to A grade." But Representative Jack Williamson of Calcasieu Parish warned that the tax would fall on the *Lake Charles American Press*, placing it at a competitive disadvantage because the

Texas papers it competed with would not be subject to the tax. Representative Rupert Payton pointed out that if the newspaper tax, as the Kingfish described it, was to be a tax on lying, Long himself would be affected because he published the *American Progress* as a propaganda vehicle: if "every lie published in the *American Progress* were taxed money would flood the state's treasury."[63]

During the debate on the newspaper tax in the house, an incident occurred that would come to be regarded as epitomizing the power of the Kingfish and his domination of the Louisiana legislature. The opposition in the 1934 session had contended that the new taxes contained in the program would not, as the Long organization argued, fall exclusively on the "big interests," since any tax increases on them would ultimately be passed on to the people. This argument was renewed by Representative Joseph Hamiter during the house debate when he maintained that the newspaper tax would ultimately be passed on by the press to the public. Representative Isom Guillory, the floor leader handpicked by the Kingfish, answered Hamiter by saying, "Isn't it true that every tax is passed on to the consumer?" "Yes," Hamiter replied, "and that is exactly what I have been preaching in this legislature for the past six years." Guillory's question appeared to be a concession that the critics of the tax program had been correct in their arguments all along. When the exchange between Hamiter and Guillory occurred, the Kingfish harshly shouted across the house floor, "Sit down, Isom." Guillory immediately sat down and raised no further questions. With Long standing inside the rail on the house floor and shouting, "Vote yes, vote yes," the house passed the newspaper tax by a vote of fifty-six to thirty-six. The members supporting the tax largely represented the centers of the Kingfish's political strength: the rural parishes of northern Louisiana and a fewer additional parishes in the southern section of the state.[64]

The press immediately seized on the "Sit down, Isom" incident as a vivid illustration of the dictatorial power the Kingfish had come to possess over the legislature and the falsity of the claim that the tax program would fall on the "big interests" to the benefit of the common people of Louisiana. When Guillory admitted that all taxes were ultimately passed on to the consumer, the *Times-Picayune* said, "auditors gasped at this amazing acknowledgment of a truth that has been suppressed and denied by royal decree." Guillory had been silenced, it asserted, by a "wrathful dictator whose 'racket' had been thus unconsciously exposed by one of his own and favorite lackeys."[65]

"Occasionally in the weird march of events at Baton Rouge an illuminating incident occurs, throwing light upon the true nature of events," the *Shreveport Times* also observed. "The trick must be kept under cover.

The administration must preserve its little pretense that the levying of 'spite' taxes and ingenious 'lieu' taxes is destined to be beneficial to the people," it continued. "In a moment of excitement, Isom Guillory forgot to play his part. 'Sit down, Isom.' The three words tell the story." Also relating the "Sit down, Isom" incident, the *Alexandria Daily Town Talk* noted that if "there was any other evidence needed to demonstrate to the people of the state the utter servility of a large majority of the members of the legislature to the dictates of Huey Long, the above quotation is amply sufficient to prove that assertion."[66]

In addition to the newspaper advertising tax, the 1934 legislature enacted measures authorizing an income tax, repealing the poll tax, and imposing taxes on the New Orleans cotton exchange, liquor, chain stores, sulfur, and the gross receipts of utilities. In the closing days of the legislative session before adjournment on July 12, Representative Rupert Payton, an anti-Long leader, marched into the house chamber wearing a gilt paper crown, a lavender bathrobe with simulated ermine, and a stubby putty nose that made him resemble the Kingfish. Other members accompanied Payton while blowing tin horns and firing cap pistols and squirt guns. Mounting the rostrum of the house and adopting a speaking style that mimicked that of Senator Long, while making frequent references to "lying newspapers," Payton declared: "Newspapers, consider yourselves glared at. I'm here a-fightin' for the common peepul. I'm for the redistribution of potlikker, now controlled by J. P. Morgan and Standard Oil. I'm for the Share-the-Swag Society." When Representative Isom Guillory rose to speak to another member of the house, Payton shouted, "Sit down, Isom." He then proposed a bill that would confer the title of "Your Majesty" on every man and woman in the state and give every man a pair of green pajamas, a castle, a hotel suite, a queen, and an income of ninety thousand dollars yearly. The house immediately approved the measure overwhelmingly.[67]

However much fun might be poked at him, Long had once again routed his opponents and demonstrated his mastery of the Louisiana political scene, and the actions of the 1934 legislature made the Long organization even more formidable than before. Writing in the *New Orleans Item*, Hermann Deutsch observed that never "has there been a legislative session within the memory of this writer so completely dominated by the administration." "The administration lost not a single battle," he said. "It scored an unbroken series of victories, emerging in triumph from every fray. The opposition scored an absolute blank, and won not a single victory."[68]

The responsibility for collecting the new taxes imposed by the legislature lay with Supervisor of Public Accounts Alice Lee Grosjean, and for tax collection purposes, the legislature appropriated more than six hundred thousand dollars for the supervisor's budget. Noting that Alice Grosjean was the "political protege of Senator Huey P. Long," the *Shreveport Times* thus observed that the legislative appropriations for her office added "another fiscal jewel to her crown of authority." "The supervisor's office is regarded as the strongest link in the Long political chain," it continued. "With over $600,000 per year to spend during the next two years its value as a political asset will be greatly enhanced."[69]

While the Kingfish had consolidated his political grip on the state during the 1934 legislative session, his successful sponsorship of the newspaper advertising tax set off a firestorm of criticism and denunciation not only in the Louisiana press but in newspapers across the nation. The Louisiana daily press was of course appalled at what had occurred, and the *New Orleans Item* observed that while previous legislatures had been "dismal, discouraging, and dangerous" in their subservience to Long, the 1934 session had been "the most hopeless, harassing, and disquieting on record." In its servility to the Kingfish, it maintained, the legislature had been "a source of shame for a democratic society," and its performance had been an "exhibition in which the performers were leaping in the legislative landscape as briskly but as obscurely as trained fleas, or flopping about as obediently as circus seals." With its deplorable record of "extravagance, spoliation, and persecution," the *Item* concluded, the legislature's most "valuable and useful vote" had been for adjournment.[70]

The *New Orleans States* acknowledged the gratitude of the press to Representative Norman Bauer for his "courageous fight" against the newspaper tax, but agreed with the *Item*'s assessment of the legislative session. The scene in the house during the final vote on the newspaper tax "with Senator Long parading over the aisles of the house shouting to representatives to 'vote yes,' grabbing those who had not voted and telling them to vote," the *States* said, "would have reflected discredit on a negro republic in central America." "It is quite certain," it declared, "that they would not continue to bear in silence a flouting of constitutional government."[71]

The *New Orleans Times-Picayune*, joined by most of the other Louisiana dailies, remained defiant in the face of the newspaper tax while recognizing that a serious blow had been struck against freedom of the press. The tax was meant to punish newspapers that "have dared to oppose the demagogue dictator," it said, and Governor O. K. Allen, the "gubernatorial puppet of the 'big shot,' " was certain to sign the tax measure into law "regardless of any principle or conscientious scruple that may faintly survive in his own mind and heart." "With the temporary suppression of representative government in Louisiana, the first step thus is taken toward the destruction of freedom of the press within the 'big shot's' domain," the *Times-Picayune* declared. "Freedom of the press will survive this assault in Louisiana just as surely as representative government, now chloroformed by the usurper, will be restored. But the rape of representative government, and the assault upon a free press just driven to success by the openly wielded lash of a dictator without principle, honest conviction or scruple constitute the blackest chapter in Louisiana's history."[72]

Echoing the *Times-Picayune*, the *Monroe News-Star* observed that "Senator Huey P. Long has made good his threat to punish the newspapers for their failure to 'get right' with the state administration." "Thus Louisiana becomes the first state in the Union," it lamented, "to throw a halter around the press in an effort to stifle criticism of legislative authority." The newspaper tax, it maintained, was "one of the most bare-faced and contemptible attacks on the freedom of the press" yet seen, demonstrating that the "dictator has reached the ultimate in his defiance of the liberties of the people." Sounding a similar theme, the *New Orleans Item* warned that the newspaper tax, if carried to its logical conclusion, "would mean the end in practice not only of freedom of the American press, but virtually to freedom of speech as well."[73]

During August, the Louisiana Press Association condemned the newspaper tax as a threat to freedom of the press and urged the papers "directly affected by it to resist this legislation by every legal means at their command." The association also called on the national press to support the effort of the Louisiana press to resist the tax. *Editor & Publisher*, the voice of the American Newspaper Publishers' Association, immediately attacked the newspaper tax as well, and referring to the Kingfish, declared that it doubted "if Hitler, Goering and Goebbels have a lower estimate of a free and democratic press than this brazen, loud mouthed, smirking arriviste from Louisiana." "Given half a chance," it warned, "he would Hitlerize the state and nation."[74]

The record of the 1934 legislative session and Senator Long's role in it, on the other hand, were defended by the *American Progress* against what it characterized as the "greatest outpouring of wrath and spleen ever witnessed, in nearly every big newspaper throughout the land." "These newspapers have filled their front pages for two months with purple-faced ravings," the *Progress* said, "about Senator Huey P. Long and his 'domination' of the legislature." "When the legislature opened in May," it continued, "the Ringster-Corporation-Newspaper Combine of New Orleans had a scheme cooked up to regain their old-time right to pillage the state treasury and unload their taxes on the shoulders of the poor." Although the Long paper had adopted the slogan "A free press is the people's defense," it now defended the newspaper advertising tax. "These newspapers had been shouting loudest to have a sales tax of 2 percent put on every dollar the poor man gets and spends," the *Progress* claimed, "so it was felt that they should be glad to take a dose of their own medicine. They will pay only the same amount that they wanted the poor man to pay, and they can better afford it." The Kingfish himself also again defended the newspaper tax as a tax on lying, "at 2 cents a lie." In response, however, the *Hammond Courier*, which had just published a generally favorable article on Senator Long and Governor Allen, sent a check for twenty-five cents to the state treasury for the "twelve-and-a-half lies" it had published in the Long–Allen article.[75]

Editor & Publisher meanwhile continued to exhort the Louisiana newspapers to stand united in a fight against the newspaper tax and to challenge it in the courts. Demagogues in other states would soon adopt the Kingfish's tactics against the press, it warned, if his "assault is not met by united and militant press action." Long's attempt to regiment and intimidate the Louisiana press, it predicted, would begin "one of the fiercest battles that the roughneck demagogue has experienced." "An injunction should be sought to prevent the collection of the tax," *Editor & Publisher* advised. "The press and the nation must stand solidly with the Louisiana newspapers in this fight, for other brazen demagogues will follow any Long success." "Here is the challenge," it declared. "Meet it with the sure process of law if necessary carried to the U.S. Supreme Court!" A resort to the courts seemed logical since any attempt at redress regarding the newspaper tax was doomed to failure in the Long-dominated political process in Louisiana. But in the summer of 1934 it remained to be seen if the newspapers would follow *Editor & Publisher*'s advice and thereby open a new chapter in the battle between Huey Long and the Louisiana press.[76]

NOTES

1. T. Harry Williams, *Huey Long (New York: Knopf, 1969), p. 107.*
2. Ibid., pp. 429–30.
3. Ibid., pp. 642, 692–93, 701.
4. Ibid., pp. 662–63.
5. *American Progress*, Nov. 16, 1933, p. 1.
6. Ibid., Aug. 24, 1933, pp. 1, 4.
7. Ibid.; William Ivy Hair, *The Kingfish and His Realm* (Baton Rouge: Louisiana State University Press, 1991), p. 303; Glen Jeansonne, *Messiah of the Masses: Huey P. Long and the Great Depression* (New York: Harper Collins, 1993), p. 127.
8. *American Progress*, Sept. 14, 1933, p. 1.
9. Ibid., Oct. 19, 1933, pp. 1, 6.
10. Ibid.
11. Ibid.
12. Ibid.
13. Ibid.

14. Ibid., Oct. 26, 1933, pp. 1, 5.
15. Ibid.
16. Ibid., Nov. 2, 1933, p. 6.
17. Ibid., Sept. 21, 1933, p. 8.
18. Ibid., Nov. 9, 1933, p. 1; Aug. 7, 1934, p. 1.
19. Huey P. Long Scrapbooks, vol. 24, Hill Memorial Library, Louisiana State University, Baton Rouge.
20. *American Progress*, Nov. 9, 1933, p. 1; March 1, 1934, p. 2; March 8, 1934, p. 8.
21. Ibid., Nov. 23, 1933, pp. 1, 4; Feb. 22, 1934, p. 1; March 22, 1934, p. 4.
22. Ibid., Nov. 30, 1933, p. 2; May 29, 1934, p. 6.
23. Williams, *Long*, pp. 712–15.
24. *New Orleans Times-Picayune*, June 2, 1934, p. 8; June 5, 1934, p. 8.
25. Ibid., May 30, 1934, p. 3; June 3, 1934, p. 1; June 12, 1934, p. 1.
26. Ibid., June 7, 1934, p. 1; June 10, 1934, p. 9.
27. Ibid., June 13, 1934, p. 1; June 14, 1934, p. 10; *Shreveport Times*, July 1, 1934, p. 6.
28. *New Orleans Times-Picayune*, June 22, 1934, p. 1.
29. *Time* 24 (July 23, 1934): 14; *New Orleans Times-Picayune*, July 4, 1934, Long Scrapbooks, vol. 21.
30. *New Orleans Times-Picayune*, July 1, 1934, p. 1; July 2, 1934, p. 1.
31. *New Orleans Item-Tribune*, July 1, 1934, pp. 1, 4; *Baton Rouge Morning Advocate*, July 3, 1934, Long Scrapbooks, vol. 21.
32. *New Orleans Times-Picayune*, July 3, 1934, pp. 1, 10.
33. Ibid., p. 10.
34. Ibid., July 3, 1934, p. 10.
35. Ibid.
36. Ibid.
37. Ibid.; *Chicago Tribune*, July 4, 1934, p. 7; *New York Times*, July 4, 1934, p. 10; *Shreveport Times*, July 3, 1934, p. 3.
38. *New Orleans Item*, July 4, 1934, p. 1; Hair, *The Kingfish*, pp. 239, 265.
39. *New Orleans Times-Picayune*, July 4, 1934, p. 6.
40. Ibid.
41. *New Orleans States*, July 4, 1934, Long Scrapbooks, vol. 21.
42. *Baton Rouge Morning Advocate*, July 4, 1934, p. 4; *Shreveport Times*, July 4, 1934, p. 4; July 5, 1934, p. 4.
43. *Chicago Tribune*, July 5, 1934, p. 7.
44. Williams, *Long*, p. 720.
45. Record, *Grosjean* v. *American Press Co.*, 297 U.S. 233 (1936), pp. 42–44.
46. Ibid., p. 48.
47. *New Orleans Item-Tribune*, July 6, 1934, p. 1.
48. *New Orleans Times-Picayune*, July 6, 1934, p. 1.
49. Ibid.
50. Ibid.
51. Ibid., pp. 1, 9.
52. *Monroe News-Star*, July 9, 1934, pp. 1, 3.
53. Ibid., July 10, 1934, p. 4.
54. *New Orleans Times-Picayune*, July 7, 1934, p. 4.
55. The assessment is based on the author's perusal of the *Lake Charles American Press* during July 1934.
56. Record, *Grosjean* v. *American Press Co.*, 297 U.S. 233 (1936), p. 42.
57. *New Orleans Times-Picayune*, July 8, 1934, pp. 1, 16.

58. Ibid., pp. 1, 8.

59. Ibid., July 9, 1934, p. 9; July 10, 1934, p. 12.

60. *Shreveport Times*, July 10, 1934, p. 5.

61. *New Orleans Times-Picayune*, July 10, 1934, p. 12; *Baton Rouge Morning Advocate*, July 10, 1934, p. 1.

62. *New Orleans Times-Picayune*, July 10, 1934, p. 12; *New Orleans Item-Tribune*, July 9, 1934, p. 4.

63. *New Orleans Times-Picayune*, July 10, 1934, p. 12.

64. Ibid., July 10, 1934, pp. 1, 10. Compare the report of the house vote in the *New Orleans Times-Picayune*, July 9, 1934, p. 9, with V. O. Key, Jr., *Southern Politics* (New York: Vintage Books, 1949), p. 177.

65. *New Orleans Times-Picayune*, July 11, 1934, Long Scrapbooks, vol. 21.

66. *Shreveport Times*, July 10, 1934, p. 4; *Alexandria Daily Town Talk*, July 10, 1934, p. 4.

67. *Time* 24 (July 23, 1934): 14; *Baton Rouge Morning Advocate*, July 12, 1934, pp. 1, 2.

68. *New Orleans Item-Tribune*, July 15, 1934, p. 20.

69. *Shreveport Times*, July 11, 1934, pp. 1, 2; July 15, 1934, p. 8.

70. *New Orleans Item-Tribune*, July 12, 1934, p. 22.

71. *New Orleans States-Times*, July 10, 1934, p. 10.

72. *New Orleans Times-Picayune*, July 10, 1934, p. 10.

73. *Monroe News-Star*, July 10, 1934, p. 4; *New Orleans Item-Tribune*, July 10, 1934, p. 18.

74. *New Orleans Times-Picayune*, Aug. 5, 1934, p. 1; *Editor & Publisher* 67 (July 7, 1934): 20; 67 (July 14, 1934): 13.

75. *American Progress*, Aug. 7, 1934, p. 2; *Louisiana Progress*, March 27, 1930, p. 6; *New York Times*, Aug. 13, 1934, p. 5.

76. *Editor & Publisher* 67 (July 7, 1934): 20; 67 (Aug. 11, 1934): 26.

Chapter 5

The Press Counterattacks

A terrific howl has been set up by the lying New Orleans newspapers because they have been taxed 2 percent on their gross amount of advertising. "Bloody murder. Freedom of the press, persecution," they yell. Their big job has been lately in trying to make ignorant people believe that the freedom of the press has been jeopardized by a tax on advertising.

—*American Progress*, August 7, 1934

[E]very effort should be made to press the point on abridgment of freedom of the press, in the hope that the decision will turn favorably to the newspapers on this point. If it does, the newspapers are once and forever rid of the possibility of any license tax on them as newspapers.

—Eberhard Deutsch, August 1934

♦ During the months following the imposition of the newspaper advertising tax, Huey Long appeared to have become almost manic in his drive to monopolize control of Louisiana in his hands. In one of his continuing disputes over the political control of New Orleans, he not only defeated but crushed his opposition, revealing, as a sympathetic biographer said, "that he was approaching a point beyond which he would tolerate no opposition—from any quarter or any grounds." Commenting on events in Louisiana during 1934, Hodding Carter observed that nine months previously Long had appeared to be "politically finished." "Today, however," Carter added, "the bewildered belief of many is that Huey's grasp upon the destinies of this state is stronger than it ever was."[1]

Censorship by taxation was not enough for Long. He appeared determined to control the dissemination of information throughout the state to an even greater extent. He complemented the 1934 newspaper tax with legislation authorizing municipalities to impose a similar tax on publications with weekly circulations of twenty thousand copies or more. Even more chilling, however, was his successful sponsorship of legislation in 1935 creating a state printing board, appointed by the governor, with the power to approve which local, mostly weekly, newspapers could be the "official printers" of government notices and information the parishes, municipalities, and school boards were required by law to publish. Since most small weekly newspapers depended on the printing of this official information for their economic survival, the state printing board therefore held the power of life or death over the state's weeklies. The board could thereby insure their loyalty to the Long regime.[2]

As a result of the passage of the state printing board measure, several Louisiana weeklies abruptly stopped discussing political issues in their columns altogether. The *Hammond Vindicator*, another weekly that had previously been urging the people to revolt against the Kingfish, dropped that policy in order to obtain the approval of the state printing board to publish the legal printing of local governmental units. Long's grip on the sources of information in the state was also tightened by legislation creating a state board of censors, appointed by the governor, with the power to censor the contents of all motion pictures, including newsreels, exhibited in the state.[3]

With the printing board in a position to enforce the political conformity of the weekly press and the board of censors capable of deleting any coverage of events in Louisiana in newsreels that was not to his liking, the Kingfish would be in effective control of the dissemination of news in the state if the newspaper advertising tax were upheld by the courts. Once that happened, the advertising tax rates could then be increased to the point that the daily newspapers would have to hew to the Long political line or be forced into bankruptcy.

The Kingfish's utter contempt for freedom of the press was also revealed by an episode that occurred at Louisiana State University (LSU) during the fall of 1934. As governor, Long had greatly increased the appropriations for LSU and was especially proud of the university's band, which he had ordered to be expanded, and the football team. He wrote songs for the band and frequently served as its unofficial drum major, leading it in parades when the football team competed in other states. He insisted on sitting on the bench with the football team at games and personally selecting the team's coach. Long clearly regarded LSU as his personal creation and took a proprietary interest in its affairs.[4]

In November 1934, a mass rally presided over by the Kingfish was held on the LSU campus, at which it was declared that Abe Mickal, the star halfback on the football team, would be a state senator who would serve in a special legislative session to be held later in the month. The event involved only the usual clowning by Long, but an angry student wrote the student newspaper, the *Reveille*, protesting what he regarded as a mockery of the democratic process and an insult to the state senate. The editors of the *Reveille* viewed the letter as a legitimate expression of student opinion and decided to print it. But when Long learned of the *Reveille's* intention, he exploded in rage.[5]

Referring to the editor of the *Reveille*, Jesse Hardy Cutrer, Jr., Long fumed that if "that little ____ runs this letter tomorrow we are going to have a new editor. And as for that little ____ that wrote this—why he's not going to be in school." "That's my university and I'm not going to stand for any criticism from anybody out there," he declared. "I'll fire any student that dares to say a word against Huey Long. I'll fire a thousand. We've got ten thousand to take their places. That's my university, I built it, and I'm not going to stand for any students criticizing Huey Long." He had warned the president of the university not to allow Cutrer to become editor of the *Reveille*, the Kingfish continued. Cutrer's uncle, Long claimed, had sold his vote to support Long's impeachment for forty dollars. Jesse Cutrer was "rotten and his whole family are a bunch of dirty ____," the Kingfish declared.[6]

Long ordered guards to be posted at the *Reveille's* printshop and suppressed the publication of the offending letter. As a result, Cutrer and five *Reveille* staff members resigned in protest. Twenty-six students were subsequently suspended from the university for "gross disrespect" for signing a letter protesting the suppression of the student newspaper, and journalism students went on strike against censorship. Signs were hung by students on the *Reveille's* printshop door, saying "killed by suppression" and "Defunctus—By order of Huey, the State, the god."[7]

The Kingfish's callous censorship of the LSU student newspaper attracted nationwide press attention and condemnation. The *Times-Picayune* charged that "undertaking to gag the *Reveille*, its editors and student contributors is characteristic of dictatorship, as we see it in Nazi Germany and begin to recognize it here in Louisiana." U.S. Senator Elbert D. Thomas of Utah observed that Long had seriously damaged his chances of realizing his national political ambitions in the *Reveille* affair. Thomas had been a faculty member at the University of Utah for eighteen years, and he pointed out that the censorship of the *Reveille* had marked "a definite turn in Long's political career. When a man suppresses speech and the press, even if it be only a student publication, he marks himself as a non-believer in the great fundamentals of the American Constitution." "Huey wants to be president," Thomas continued. "But no man can gain the confidence of the American people who will openly suppress thought and break up printing presses." Long's action was also condemned by *The Nation* magazine, which named *Reveille* editors Jesse Cutrer and David McGuire to its 1934 "honor roll."[8]

Governor O. K. Allen had signed the newspaper advertising tax into law on July 12, 1934. Soon afterward, the *American Progress* derided the newspapers for denouncing the tax as a violation of freedom of the press. "A terrific howl has been set up by the lying New Orleans newspapers because they have been taxed 2 percent on their gross amount of advertising. 'Bloody murder. Freedom of the press, persecution,' they yell. Their big job has been lately in trying to make ignorant people believe that the freedom of the press has been jeopardized by a tax on advertising," the *Progress* disparagingly reported. "Anybody with as little brains as even Squirt John D. Ewing of Shreveport knows that there is nothing 'free' about advertising."[9]

To prove that the attacks on the advertising tax as a violation of freedom of the press were groundless, the *Progress* relied upon the rather pathetic person of Judge Gilbert Dupre of Opelousa. Elderly and deaf, Dupre was representative of many Louisiana political figures who had shifted from opposing the Kingfish to supporting him as the political winds in the state had changed. Even after Long's sweeping triumph in the Senate election of 1930, Dupre as a member of the house of representatives had continued to oppose the Long program. He had voted against the appropriation for the new capitol, and in retaliation the Kingfish had ordered a hole bored in the roof of the old capitol directly above Dupre's desk in the house so that rain would drip on the unfortunate representative. Although Dupre had at one time referred to Long as a "slimy person" who ought to be in "the asylum or penitentiary," he fell on hard times and subsequently became a paid columnist for the *American Progress*, in which he defended white supremacy.[10]

Dupre was now paraded forth by the *Progress* as a lawyer who was "considered one of the most capable barristers of the state." "Whether the papers should be taxed was debatable," Dupre was quoted as saying. "But to argue that taxing them was an assault on freedom of the press is rot pure and simple." Both the state and federal constitutions protected freedom of the press, he pointed out, and therefore the advertising tax was not invalid. Dupre's reasoning, such as it was, apparently was that so long as freedom of the press was constitutionally protected, no legislation could possibly violate it.[11]

Almost immediately after the advertising tax was signed into law by Governor Allen, the publishers of the affected papers began coordinating their plans to fight the tax. As he had when the newspapers were threatened by a Long-sponsored advertising tax and injunction-gag law in 1930, Charles Manship of the Baton Rouge papers assumed the leadership, and at his request the publishers of the affected papers convened for the purpose of planning what action should be taken. Manship was subsequently chosen by the publishers to be chairman of a committee representing the state's dailies to coordinate their efforts in the battle against the advertising tax.[12]

The first step they took was to retain attorneys to determine whether the advertising tax could be successfully challenged on constitutional grounds and, if so, what the best strategy would be to guide the attack in the courts. The Ewing newspapers in northern Louisiana, the *Shreveport Times*, the *Monroe News-Star*, and the *Monroe Morning World*, were joined by the publisher of the *Shreveport Journal* in retaining the services of John H. Tucker, who would thereafter represent the Star-World Publishing Co., the Times Publishing Co., and the Journal Publishing Co. In middle Louisiana the *Alexandria Daily Town Talk*, published by McCormick & Co., retained S. G. Thornton; in southern Louisiana the *Lafayette Daily Advertiser*, published by the Lafayette Advertiser-Gazette, retained J. J. Davidson; the Manship papers in Baton Rouge, the *Morning Advocate* and the *State-Times*, published by the Capital City Press, retained Ben B. Taylor; and the *Lake Charles American Press*, published by the American Press Co., retained Clement M. Moss. In New Orleans, the *Item* and the *Tribune*, published by the Item Co., were represented by Eberhard P. Deutsch, and the *Times-Picayune* and the *States*, published by the Times-Picayune Publishing Co., were represented by Esmond Phelps.[13]

The counsel for the Alexandria paper, the forty-year-old S. G. Thornton, had received his education at LSU and George Washington University, while James Joseph Davidson, a native of Lafayette, was thirty when he was retained to represent the Lafayette paper and had received his undergraduate education and his law degree from Tulane University. Born in East Feliciana Parish, Ben B. Taylor, the counsel for the Manship papers, was forty-nine and had received his undergraduate education at Centenary College in Shreveport and subsequently earned law degrees both at Tulane and the University of Michigan. The attorney for the Lake Charles paper, Clement Moss, was a native of Lake Charles who had earned his bachelor's degree at Virginia Military Institute and his master's and law degrees at Tulane. Moss served as a state senator from Lake Charles from 1932 to 1936 and had thus been present in the legislature when the advertising tax was adopted.[14]

Among the seven attorneys retained by the newspapers, Esmond Phelps, John Tucker, and Eberhard Deutsch were the most outstanding. In addition to having a financial interest in the *Times-Picayune*, Esmond

Phelps was a leader of the bar in Louisiana and his New Orleans firm, Spencer, Gidiere, Phelps & Dunbar, had become one of the leading law firms in the city. As the representative of the *Times-Picayune*, by far the largest of the papers affected by the advertising tax and the one with the greatest financial interest at risk, the forty-six-year-old Phelps would assume a leading role in the legal battle to come.

John Tucker, who represented the Ewing papers and the *Shreveport Journal*, had been born in Pine Bluff, Arkansas, in 1891, but his family subsequently moved to Louisiana. A graduate of Washington and Lee University with a law degree from Louisiana State University, Tucker had established his law practice in Shreveport. At the time of the litigation regarding the advertising tax, the forty-three-year-old Tucker was already recognized as an expert on Louisiana's civil code, and in 1938 he would be elected president of the Louisiana State Law Institute, charged with the responsibility of reforming the state legal code.[15]

Eberhard P. Deutsch had been born in Cincinnati, Ohio, in 1897. Having relocated to New Orleans, Deutsch obtained employment in the circulation department of the *Item* while he attended Loyola and Tulane University law schools at night. After receiving his law degree in 1925, he became the *Item*'s general counsel and in 1926 he joined with Robert E. Kerrigan to form the New Orleans firm of Deutsch, Kerrigan & Burke, which soon became one of the city's leading firms. In addition to representing the *New Orleans Item* and the *Tribune*, Deutsch also had close familial ties to the *Item*, since his brother, Hermann Deutsch, was a writer for that paper. The participation of the thirty-seven-year-old Eberhard Deutsch in the attack on the newspaper tax would ultimately prove crucial, since it was he who developed, over some opposition, the constitutional argument that would finally prevail in the litigation to come.[16]

Once the Louisiana dailies had decided to explore a court test of the advertising tax, Deutsch began to formulate a strategy by which the tax could be successfully attacked on constitutional grounds. By August, he had produced a paper titled "Memorandum and Discussion Relative to Validity of Act 23 of 1934 (Newspaper Advertising Tax) and Jurisdiction and Procedure to Set It Aside." This remarkable fifty-one-page document laid out the strategy and principal constitutional arguments that newspaper counsel would in fact follow almost to the letter in the subsequent legal attack on the newspaper tax.[17]

"There are two primary grounds on which the constitutionality of the entire [newspaper tax] act may be attacked," Deutsch reported in his memorandum. "The first involves the infringement of the freedom of the press effected by the passage and operation of the statute, as against the guaranties contained in both the federal and state constitutions. The second lies in the discriminatory features of the legislation, also in violation of both state and federal constitutional guaranties." Deutsch left no question regarding which constitutional ground he considered should be pressed by newspaper counsel as the principal line of attack. "The first, and most important, ground on which the invalidity of the legislation turns," he said, "is found in the underlying abridgment of the freedom of the press, involved in the passage, operation and effect of the act." On its face, he conceded, the advertising tax appeared to be a neutral license tax on the business of selling advertising, but, he argued, in "its background and between the lines, however, the statute is one formulated and passed for the unquestioned purpose of punishing an opposition press."[18]

Deutsch pointed out that the Bill of Rights in the federal Constitution was originally held to contain restrictions on the powers of the national government alone, but "recent decisions of the Supreme Court of the United States, notable among them the famous Minnesota freedom-of-the-press case, have universally held that freedom of the press is protected against state action by the 'due process clause' of the Fourteenth Amendment to the Constitution of the United States, just as it is protected against congressional action by the First Amendment." The 1931 decision of the Supreme Court in *Near* v. *Minnesota*, he continued, "is now the leading decision in the country, if not the world, on freedom of the press." The *Near* case dealt with restraint of the press by injunction and therefore did not deal directly with the issues confronting the Louisiana newspapers, he conceded, "but its general language is so enlightening on the general principle of the freedom of the press, that it cannot help but have an important bearing on the decision in the instant [Louisiana] case, since it holds, in effect, that any slight infringement, direct or indirect, of the freedom of the press will invalidate legislation." Quoting liberally from Chief Justice Hughes's opinion in the *Near* case, Deutsch maintained that there "can be no proper discussion of any point involving the freedom of the press without including the foregoing decision."[19]

Quoting Erskine May's *Constitutional History of England*, he pointed out that taxation had been a principal method of political control of the press in that country until the middle of the nineteenth century. Stamp taxes that affected the press had also been introduced into the American colonies, where they had been denounced as "taxes on knowledge" and met such bitter resistance by the Americans that they came to be considered one of the leading causes of the Revolution. The framers of the First Amendment, he argued, were well aware of the long struggle of the press in England to free itself from political control through taxation and had intended the Free Press Clause of the First Amendment to prohibit any such use of the taxing power in this country. "Act 23 of 1934 of Louisiana, therefore, insofar as it imposes a tax on advertising, is no novel attempt at restraint of freedom of the press," Deutsch argued. "This form of restraint was originally conceived as a political measure in 1712, from which time it continued for nearly a century and a half, until finally, in man's great struggle for liberty of thought and expression, the last vestige of oppressive medievalism passed out of existence with the repeal of the 'tax on knowledge' in 1853."[20]

U.S. Supreme Court justice Benjamin N. Cardozo, who was recognized as a leading legal scholar, strongly approved historical background as a method of interpreting constitutional and statutory provisions, Deutsch noted. "Can there be any clearer light on the freedom-of-the-press clauses of our constitutions, as applying to such a tax on advertising as is imposed by Louisiana Act 23 of 1934, than this history of constitutional provisions?" he asked. "Can it be said that the framers of our constitutions standing in the background of the Boston (stamp tax) Tea Party, were unfamiliar with that history?" "One must inevitably return to the conclusion," he continued, "that a tax on advertising in the press is one of the restraints against which constitutional guaranties of freedom of the press are aimed."[21]

Anyone familiar with political conditions in Louisiana under Huey Long was aware that the advertising tax had been adopted as a punitive measure against the metropolitan dailies for their opposition to the Long regime, Deutsch argued. There was no doubt, he said, "but that the legislation is a reprisal for editorial criticism of the dominant political faction in the state, and a threat of further reprisals by increased taxation, if the press fails to discontinue its free discussion of affairs." A difficulty that counsel for the newspapers would face, he believed, would be in convincing the courts to look beyond the appearance, which was that the advertising tax was merely another form of taxation that the state had the legitimate power to impose, to the reality that it was intended to restrict the freedom of the press to communicate views unacceptable to the Long regime.

On this point, Deutsch noted that the Supreme Court had in fact looked beyond appearances to the real purpose of an act of Congress in the child labor tax case, which had been decided by the Court in 1922. In the Child Labor Act of 1916, Congress attempted to regulate child labor, and to prohibit it altogether under certain ages, by prohibiting products manufactured by child labor in violation of congressional regulations from being transported in interstate commerce. The Court, however, had invalidated the Child Labor Act in 1918, holding that manufacturing was not interstate commerce, which Congress could regulate, but rather separate from it. According to the Court, Congress had not only exceeded its power under the Commerce Clause by attempting to regulate manufacturing and the use of child labor therein, but was also invading the reserved powers of the states under the Tenth Amendment.[22]

In response to the Court's decision, Congress enacted new legislation that imposed a stiff tax on any business employing child labor in violation of congressionally mandated regulations. The Child Labor Tax Act was then challenged before the Court in 1922. Although the child labor tax appeared on its face to be just another tax on business, its purpose was of course to require employers in manufacturing to conform to congressional regulations regarding child labor, a purpose the Court had held to be beyond the legitimate scope of congressional power. Speaking for the Court in the child labor tax case, Chief Justice Taft pointed out that "a court must be blind not to see that the so-called tax is imposed to stop the employment of children within the age limits prescribed. Its prohibitory and regulatory effect and purpose are palpable. All others can see and understand this. How can we properly shut our minds to it?"[23]

Only a few changes in Chief Justice Taft's language in the child labor tax case would be needed to make it equally applicable to the Louisiana advertising tax, Deutsch argued. Although the advertising tax was ostensibly merely a tax on the sale of advertising, its real underlying purpose was to punish the press and to deter it from continuing to criticize the Long regime, just as the child labor tax was meant to prevent employers from using child labor. "The foregoing language from the child labor tax case, if applied to the instant case," Deutsch therefore maintained, "should result in a decision by the Supreme Court of the United States, that the necessary operation and effect of the advertising tax bill are to abridge the freedom of the press, and accordingly, that the legislation is unconstitutional and invalid." This conclusion was bolstered, he continued, by Chief Justice John Marshall's statement in *McCulloch* v. *Maryland* in 1819 that "the power to tax is the power to destroy." If the legislature had the power to tax the press, Deutsch argued, "it has the undoubted *right to destroy* the press." "From all the foregoing," he wrote at the end of his free-press discussion, "we can only reach the conclusion that the court can very well hold the statute in question unconstitutional on the ground that it abridges the freedom of the press, and can find ample authority on the basis of which to reach such a conclusion."[24]

The advertising tax was vulnerable not only on free-press grounds, Deutsch pointed out; it could also be challenged on the basis of provisions in the Louisiana constitution requiring license taxes to be uniformly applicable to all members of a profession, trade, occupation, and so on, and not merely to some members of such groups. Because the advertising tax discriminated against some publications while being inapplicable to others, Deutsch noted that it could be challenged under the Equal Protection Clause of the Fourteenth Amendment, which prohibited the states from denying persons within their jurisdictions the equal protection of the laws. "We are quite firmly of the opinion," he said, "that even if all other defenses fail us, we should prevail in having the advertising tax statute declared unconstitutional in the matter of discrimination."[25]

The advertising tax would thus ultimately be held unconstitutional either because it violated freedom of the press or because it was discriminatory, Deutsch summed up. But he again emphasized his preference for attacking the tax principally on free-press grounds, since a holding by the courts that the tax was discriminatory could be overcome by legislation amending the tax to make it applicable to all publications in the state. It would be far "preferable for the press," he pointed out, "if a decision could be obtained from the courts, holding the statute invalid because of its abridgment of the freedom of the press. The other points [the discriminatory features] involve matters subject to legislative correction."[26]

"If the case turns on the freedom of the press, and if a decision is rendered holding the statute invalid because it abridges the freedom of the press," he continued, "it is hardly conceivable that the Constitution will ever be amended to permit an abridgment of freedom of the press, and even if the state constitution were so amended, it is certain that the Federal Constitution will not be amended to permit such legislation in Louisiana." "For this reason," Deutsch concluded, "every effort should be made to press the point on abridgment of freedom of the press, in the hope that the decision will turn favorably to the newspapers on this point. If it does, the newspapers are once and forever rid of the possibility of any license tax on them as newspapers."[27]

In the conferences of the counsel for the newspapers during the summer and fall of 1934, there were two key questions to be resolved. The first was what legal and constitutional arguments should be used against the newspaper tax and the likelihood of their success in the courts. The second was which court would offer the best chances of success to a challenge of the tax, assuming that was to be done. Despite the persuasiveness of the Deutsch memorandum, eventually the consensus among the newspaper attorneys was that the best line of attack against the newspaper tax was not the one he favored. They decided to contend that the tax unconstitutionally discriminated against the affected papers in violation of both the Louisiana and federal constitutions.

Indeed, their strongest argument, the attorneys concluded, could be based on the Louisiana constitution. Article 10, section 8 provided that if license taxes were to be imposed on any business, trade, occupation, vocation, or profession, they must apply to all persons or businesses engaged in the business, trade, profession, and so on being taxed. Since the newspaper tax affected only a few of the state's approximately 163 publications, it seemed clearly to be violative of this provision. A further argument could also be based on the federal Constitution and the Fourteenth Amendment's Equal Protection Clause. It could be contended that the Louisiana legislature, by singling out for taxation the advertising revenues of only a few of the state's 163 papers, had engaged in discriminatory treatment of the affected papers and therefore violated the Fourteenth Amendment by denying them the equal protection of the laws.

The difficulty with this argument was that it completely ignored the issue of the freedom of the press. Yet the Louisiana tax had been almost universally condemned both in the state and national press precisely because it was perceived as a direct threat to press freedom. The failure to raise the free-press issue in the attack on the newspaper tax consequently could prove embarrassing to the Louisiana newspapers and their counsel.

The attorneys, however, felt that a free-press-based attack would almost certainly be rejected by the courts. The courts did recognize that the constitutional guarantee of freedom of the press protected from governmental interference the gathering and dissemination of information by the press. The attorneys also knew that the guarantee nevertheless did not confer upon the press special exemptions from governmental regulations applicable to businesses generally, including taxes. Federal and state income taxes, for example, applied to all businesses generating income, including businesses whose activities involved the publication of newspapers, and this was not regarded as in any way violative of freedom of the press. Although there had been no U.S. Supreme Court decision on the relationship between freedom of the press and taxation, state taxes affecting the press had been challenged on five occasions in the lower state and federal courts, and on each occasion, the courts had sustained the validity of the tax in question.[28]

The attorneys also reasoned that the courts, including the U.S. Supreme Court, had in the past been reluctant to expand the concept of freedom of the press beyond an interpretation that it primarily prohibited governmentally imposed prior restraints on the press. A tax on the gross receipts of newspapers derived from the sale of advertising did not fit within the classic definition of a prior restraint. It did not impose any restrictions on the content of what was published prior to publication, but rather taxed gross receipts from the sale of advertising without attempting to control the contents of the accompanying materials published in newspapers.

Eberhard Deutsch dissented from the argument advanced by his fellow lawyers, as he had earlier indicated in his memorandum. While he readily conceded that an attack on the tax based on its discriminatory effect would probably be successful, he was nonetheless convinced that the tax should also be attacked on the additional ground that it violated freedom of the press. Deutsch maintained that he was certain that when the courts "understood what is attempted in this particular advertising tax, under these particular circumstances, they can be induced to condemn it and stop it." "The power to tax is the power to destroy," Deutsch argued, again quoting Chief Justice John Marshall's famous statement in *McCulloch* v. *Maryland*. "If you can select your newspapers for this process," Deutsch continued, "you can destroy them. No newspaper is safe against that sort of tyranny, and this can be shown." With the use of the state's taxing power as it was being used in Louisiana with the advertising tax, he argued, the result would be that the "public has lost its voice, and becomes terrified and dumb."[29]

While the other attorneys remained skeptical of the viability of a free-press argument in court, Deutsch was encouraged to engage in further research on the issue and to present the results at a later date. He consequently devoted a substantial amount of his time to intensive study of the history and development of freedom of the press in England and the United States. He contacted the American Newspaper Publishers' Association (ANPA) and requested staff assistance as well as aid from the members of the association and the law firms representing them. Elisha Hanson, the general counsel of the ANPA, cooperated with Deutsch in the research, and assistance was also furnished by the law firms representing the Hearst and Scripps-Howard papers as well as the *Chicago Tribune* and the *New York Herald Tribune*. Deutsch also enlisted the assistance of schools of journalism and libraries as far-flung as Washington, London, Paris, New York, Boston, and the Harvard Law School.[30]

From his research, Deutsch learned that the press had first been shackled in England through a system of censorship imposed by the prior restraint of requiring a license from the government and its approval of the contents to be published. Publication of material without a license and government approval was thus made illegal. The system of prior restraint and censorship of the press had been initiated by Henry VIII in 1538 and extended by act of Parliament in 1643. It was this licensing scheme that evoked John Milton's eloquent protest against censorship in his *Areopagitica—A Speech for the Liberty of Unlicensed Printing* in 1644.

The licensing-censorship system was abandoned in England when the act of Parliament authorizing it was not renewed in 1695, but new methods of preventing the free dissemination of information to the public were soon devised. The charge of seditious libel was used in the courts to suppress criticism of the government, and in 1712, at the request of Queen Anne, Parliament imposed a tax on all newspapers and on advertising for the purpose of suppressing the circulation of information, particularly to the masses. This use of taxation was later extended to the American colonies, and in 1765 stamps were delivered in America for the purpose of collecting taxes on newspapers there. The protest aroused by the stamp taxes, which were denounced as "taxes on knowledge," subsequently became one of the leading causes of the American Revolution. Despite this, after the Revolution, the Massachusetts legislature in 1785 imposed a stamp tax on newspapers and magazines and a like tax on advertising in 1786. The public condemnation of these taxes was so vigorous that both taxes were repealed in Massachusetts by 1788.

The framers of the First Amendment in 1789 were undoubtedly well aware of these recent events in Massachusetts, as well as the long history of struggle by the press in England against suppression by prior restraint and later by taxation. Eberhard Deutsch became convinced that the Louisiana newspaper tax was merely a contemporary revival of an ancient method of suppression of the dissemination of ideas and information through taxation. The Louisiana newspaper tax was even more threatening to a free press than the English taxing system had been, since the Louisiana tax was aimed not at all newspapers but only at select ones that had been conspicuous for their opposition to Huey Long and his organization. Deutsch was convinced that when these circumstances were presented to the courts, the Louisiana newspaper tax would be invalidated as a blatant violation of the freedom of the press.[31]

The results of Deutsch's research were sufficiently convincing to his colleagues to cause them to abandon their previous reluctance to include a free-press argument. The tax would be constitutionally attacked, newspaper counsel now agreed, on the grounds that it was discriminatory and denied equal protection of the laws and that it invaded the freedom of the press.

Although Eberhard Deutsch had prevailed on the free-press issue, there remained the question of what court should be selected as the forum for launching the attack on the newspaper tax. In his initial memorandum Deutsch had discussed methods that could be used in the federal or state courts, but he had indicated no preference regarding in what court litigation should be initiated. The tax could obviously be challenged in the state courts if the newspapers simply refused to pay the tax; in enforcement proceedings brought by the state, the constitutional objections to the tax could be raised and if they were sustained, that would be the end of the matter. The problem with this strategy, however, was that violations of the tax were punishable by fines of five hundred dollars and imprisonment for six months for each offense. If the attorneys for the newspapers proved to be wrong in their conclusion that the tax was constitutionally invalid, the newspapers and their agents would pay a rather high price for the error of their counsel.[32]

There was, however, another and even more compelling reason for the attorneys of the papers to avoid the state courts. In Louisiana, as in most of the states, the judges of the state courts were elected, including the seven members of the Louisiana Supreme Court, who were elected by districts into which the state was divided for that purpose. Most of the judges of the state trial courts had long since ceased opposing the Kingfish or had become dependent on the Long organization for their offices. Until 1934, the state supreme court had also generally divided four to three in favor of Long's policies that were challenged before it.[33]

At almost the same time that the Louisiana dailies were planning their litigation strategy, one pro-Long judge of the state supreme court retired and the term of another expired, requiring him to run for reelection. Long successfully supported the winning candidate for the retiring judge's seat, but the pro-Long judge seeking reelection, Winston Overton, died suddenly two days before the Democratic primary election. Overton's opponent in the primary was strongly anti-Long, but Louisiana law in such cases was clear. If a candidate died prior to a primary election and had been opposed by only one other candidate, the opposing candidate automatically became the nominee of the Democratic party and was thus insured victory in the subsequent general election. Despite the clear mandate of the law, the Kingfish blocked the state Democratic executive committee's attempt to certify Overton's opponent as the party's nominee and instead had the committee schedule a new primary election. In that election, the Kingfish persuaded Lieutenant Governor John Fournet to be a candidate for Overton's seat on the supreme court, and Fournet handily won.[34]

Through a blatant violation of the law, the Kingfish had therefore maintained a working majority in his favor on the Louisiana Supreme Court. It must have been obvious to newspaper counsel that because of Long's influence with the state judiciary, the avoidance of the state courts was the prudent course to pursue. Both the possibility of risking criminal penalties for violation of the tax law by the agents of the papers and the existence of a Kingfish-influenced state judiciary weighed heavily in the decision to seek another forum in which to test the constitutionality of the newspaper tax—and that forum was the federal courts.

From the outset, *Editor & Publisher* as the voice of the American Newspaper Publishers' Association had urged a test of the newspaper tax in the federal courts through a suit for an injunction to prohibit Louisiana officials from collecting the tax. "The matter," *Editor & Publisher* maintained, "belongs in the federal courts," and after evaluating the advantages of an injunction suit in the federal courts as an alternative to proceedings in the state courts, counsel for the newspapers agreed.[35]

Under the procedures then governing the conduct of litigation in the federal courts (procedures that were repealed in 1976), a suit for an injunction against state officers to prohibit the enforcement of a state law because of its violation of the federal Constitution could not be heard by a single U.S. district judge, as were most cases filed in the federal district courts. Rather, such a suit was required to be heard by a special three-judge district court, with one of the judges being a judge of the U.S. court of appeals for the circuit in which the lawsuit arose. The decisions of the three-judge district courts were appealable directly to the U.S. Supreme Court and therefore bypassed the U.S. courts of appeals that normally heard appeals of district court cases prior to their reaching the Supreme Court.

The procedure requiring three-judge courts to hear constitutional challenges of state laws was adopted by Congress in 1910. In 1908, the Supreme Court had ruled that state officers could be enjoined by the federal courts from enforcing policies that violated the Constitution, despite the provision of the Eleventh Amendment of the Constitution that prohibits suits against the states in the federal courts. At the time, the federal courts were frequently issuing injunctions prohibiting state officials from enforcing state policies, particularly against the railroads, that were enthusiastically supported by the public. The result was that there was vehement denunciation of the Supreme Court's 1908 decision by both the public and state officials.[36]

In response, Congress enacted the requirement of a three-judge district court to hear such suits, based on the rationale that a decision of a federal court to invalidate a state law was of such importance that it should not be left to the judgment of a U.S. district judge alone. Given the importance of such cases, Congress also provided for direct appeals from the decisions of the three-judge courts to the Supreme Court, bypassing the courts of appeals, since the speedy resolution of the issues in these cases was deemed to be in the public interest. Because the federal courts had frequently enjoined state officers from enforcing state laws without giving notice to the affected state officers, Congress additionally provided that when a suit seeking an injunction against a state statute was filed in the district court, five days' notice should be given by the court to the governor and attorney general of the state before any further proceedings in the case occurred.[37]

When lawsuits requiring the convening of three-judge district courts arose in any state, it was common practice for the chief judge of the U.S. court of appeals for the circuit in which the state was located to designate, if possible, three federal judges who hailed from that state. If this customary practice were followed in the suit contemplated by the attorneys for the Louisiana newspapers, they could anticipate a three-judge court that would not be in the least infected with Longism, as was the Louisiana judiciary.

The contemplated lawsuit would seek an injunction against Supervisor of Public Accounts Alice Lee Grosjean. The federal court having jurisdiction in Baton Rouge, the location of her office, was the U.S. District Court for the eastern district of Louisiana in New Orleans, presided over by Judge Wayne G. Borah. Like his famous uncle, Senator William E. Borah of Idaho, Wayne Borah was a Republican. His path to the federal bench was therefore different from that of judges normally appointed to the federal courts in a state dominated by the Democratic party, as was the entire South at the time. Without any realistic hope for elective office, those active in the Republican party in the South could look for a reward for their efforts only on those occasions when the presidency was captured by the Republicans. Republican presidents could ignore the senatorial courtesy that required Democratic presidents to appoint to federal patronage positions, including federal judgeships, only loyal Democrats supported by southern Democratic U.S. senators. Republican presidents, on the other hand, could instead fill such positions with deserving Republicans.

Wayne Borah was born in 1890 in Baldwin, Louisiana. After receiving his undergraduate education at Washington and Lee University, he obtained his law degree from Louisiana State University in 1915, when he established a law practice in New Orleans. He served in World War I as a captain of infantry, and upon his return to Louisiana he became active in Republican politics. With Republican Warren Harding in the White House, he was appointed assistant U.S. attorney for New Orleans in 1923 and two years later became the U.S. attorney. Finally, with Republican administrations continuing at the national level, Borah was appointed judge of the U.S. District Court for the eastern district of Louisiana in 1928.[38]

Wayne Borah as a district judge was well acquainted with Huey Long as a result of some encounters that had occurred between the two in the past. In the most bizarre of such encounters, Borah had issued the order requiring the Kingfish to answer charges of kidnapping in connection with the notorious Samuel Irby–James Terrell incident during Long's campaign for the U.S. Senate in 1930. Borah, however, was required to vacate the order when Irby denied being kidnapped in a radio broadcast arranged by the Kingfish and in a subsequent court hearing in the matter.[39]

If the customary practice of selecting judges to serve on a three-judge court were followed in the newspaper tax lawsuit, Judge Borah, in whose court the suit would be originally filed, would be designated to serve. The second judge on the court would be the other U.S. district judge in Louisiana, Judge Ben C. Dawkins, of the U.S. District Court for the western district of Louisiana. Ben Dawkins was born in 1881 at Ouachita City, a small community near Monroe, Louisiana. He received his undergraduate education at the Louisiana Polytechnic Institute in Ruston, where he worked as a grade school teacher, secretary, and farm hand to finance his education. In 1905, he enrolled at Tulane University Law School, and he received his law degree in 1906, when he established a practice in Monroe. Dawkins was a Democrat, and he successfully campaigned for election as judge of the Louisiana fourth judicial district court in 1912 and subsequently was elected as an associate justice of the Louisiana Supreme Court in 1918. Despite being a Democrat, Dawkins was appointed U.S. district judge by President Coolidge in 1924.[40]

Since one of the judges serving on special three-judge courts was required to be a member of the U.S. court of appeals for the circuit in which the case arose, a member of the U.S. Court of Appeals for the Fifth Circuit, headquartered in New Orleans, would be chosen. If that judge were to be a resident of Louisiana as well, as custom dictated, he would be Judge Rufus Edward Foster.

Rufus Foster had been born on his family's plantation in Mathews County, Virginia, in 1871. His father had served as a captain in the Confederate navy, but the Civil War apparently impoverished the Foster family, and at an early age Rufus was constrained to quit school to earn a living. Settling in New Orleans, he was employed in various jobs associated with the shipping industry while he attended college at night. Foster was also active in the Louisiana militia and was named the best-drilled soldier in the state, an honor that led to an invitation to participate in a national drilling competition at the World's Fair in Chicago in 1893. On the train to Chicago, Foster was accompanied by a friend who planned to attend Tulane University Law School, and he persuaded Foster to join him. At Tulane, he was a member of the university's first football team.

Foster received his law degree from Tulane in 1895 and established a law practice in New Orleans, but his professional career was interrupted by his service as a lieutenant in the Louisiana Volunteer Infantry during the Spanish-American War. Returning to New Orleans after his military service, he became active in Republican politics and his career followed a path almost identical to that of Judge Wayne Borah a generation later. Foster was appointed assistant U.S. attorney for New Orleans in 1905, and he was a member of the 1908 Republican national convention that nominated William Howard Taft for the presidency. In the same year, he was appointed U.S. attorney, and in the following year he received his appointment as a judge of the U.S. District Court for the eastern district of Louisiana. After serving sixteen years on the district bench, Foster was elevated by President Coolidge to the U.S. Court of Appeals for the Fifth Circuit in 1925.[41]

As a federal judge, Rufus Foster had clashed with Huey Long in the past. While Long was serving on the Louisiana Public Service Commission, the commission had suspended telephone rate increases imposed by the Cumberland Telephone & Telegraph Company. Still a U.S. district judge, Foster had issued a restraining order against the commission at the request of the company, but a permanent injunction against the commission could be issued only by a three-judge district court. When such a court was convened, it ruled in the commission's favor and refused to issue the injunction, but after the three-judge court disbanded, Foster reimposed his restraining order. Serving as the counsel for the Public Service Commission, Long appealed Foster's action to the U.S. Supreme Court, and in 1922 the Court ruled in favor of Long and the commission, ordering Foster's restraining order to be vacated. Remarking on Long's presentation of the Public Service Commission's case before the Supreme Court, Chief Justice William Howard Taft stated that he had rarely seen a lawyer with a greater legal mind or a better capacity to argue a legal point.[42]

After Long was elected governor of Louisiana, the state's political establishment, hoping to co-opt the fiery young governor, arranged a lavish banquet in his honor in New Orleans. At the banquet the leaders of the establishment made flattering speeches about the new governor, and Rufus Foster was among the speakers. "I have not always agreed with what this young man said or did," Foster said rather condescendingly, "and I have sometimes considered him a bad boy making faces at authority." "But," he added, "I think he has grown up." Whether Judge Foster still entertained the same opinion of the Kingfish in 1934 is unknown.[43]

With the three-judge court that would hear their case likely to be composed of Judges Rufus Foster, Wayne Borah, and Ben Dawkins, the decision to initiate the constitutional test of the newspaper tax in the federal court was made doubly attractive to the attorneys for the papers.

All three of the judges had attained their positions wholly free of any connection with or influence of the Kingfish. Indeed, two of the judges were Republicans, and Dawkins, the lone Democrat among them, had obtained appointment to the U.S. district court by operating in the state's Democratic party politics well before the rise of Huey Long. When the merits of bringing their case in the federal courts under these circumstances were weighed against initiating litigation in the Long-influenced state courts, the decision to file the suit in the federal courts could only have been a relatively easy one for newspaper counsel.

The attorneys for the newspapers were nevertheless required to show that their suit fell within the statutory jurisdiction that Congress had conferred upon the federal judiciary. On this point newspaper counsel relied on an 1875 congressional act conferring on the federal courts jurisdiction to hear any civil suit arising under the Constitution, laws, or treaties of the United States in which damages were alleged in the amount of three thousand dollars or more. In addition, they relied on an 1871 federal statute that conferred on the federal courts jurisdiction over suits for damages or injunctions in which persons were alleging that state officials had deprived them, or were about to deprive them, of their rights guaranteed by the Constitution or laws of the United States.[44]

Since their suit would be for an injunction to stop the collection of the newspaper tax on the ground that it violated the federal Constitution, newspaper counsel could contend that it was a civil suit arising under the Constitution and involving potential damages to the newspapers of an amount in excess of three thousand dollars. In addition, since they were alleging the tax violated the Equal Protection Clause of the Fourteenth Amendment and the freedom of the press, counsel could also argue that the suit involved an action to prohibit state officials from depriving the newspapers of rights secured by the Constitution and laws of the United States.

The attorneys for the press filed a complaint before Judge Wayne Borah of the U.S. District Court for the eastern district of Louisiana on September 20, 1934, seeking a restraining order prohibiting Supervisor of Public Accounts Alice Grosjean from collecting the disputed tax and requesting the convening of a three-judge court to hear arguments and consider issuing a permanent injunction against the collection of the tax. Since it was alphabetically first on the list of the publishers affected by the tax, the American Press Company, publisher of the *Lake Charles American Press*, became the lead plaintiff in the suit in the federal court—a somewhat ironic happenstance, since the *American Press* had not opposed Longism prior to 1934 and the Kingfish himself had stated that he would have exempted the Lake Charles paper from the tax if it had been possible. The case in the district court would nevertheless be styled *American Press Co.* v. *Grosjean*.[45]

In their complaint, the attorneys for the newspapers pointed out that there were approximately 163 publications selling advertising in Louisiana, with 120 of those publications being mostly rural, weekly newspapers. Yet, they pointed out, of the 163 publications in the state only the newspapers that were plaintiffs before the court had been singled out by the legislature for taxation of their gross receipts derived from the sale of advertising. The dailies affected by the tax were compelled to compete with the other publications for advertising revenues, but only the dailies were subject to the tax.[46]

Throughout the United States and in Louisiana as well, the complaint stated, there were six principal methods of advertising—advertising in newspapers, in magazines, or on radio, outdoor advertising (mostly billboards), streetcar card advertising, and motion picture advertising. With newspaper advertising nationally at $453 million a year, it was by far the most extensively used advertising medium. Newspapers, it was pointed out, derived their revenues from two principal sources, sales of papers to subscribers and advertising sales, and advertising revenues were used by the papers to subsidize sales of papers to the public because it was common for newspapers to sell their papers below cost. The rates charged by various newspapers for advertising depended upon a variety of factors, with extent of circulation being only one of them. Competitive and economic conditions in the areas served by various papers were also important considerations in the setting of advertising rates, with the result that newspapers with smaller circulations sometimes charged higher rates than papers with larger circulations. These allegations were intended to demonstrate that taxes on sales of advertising based on circulation alone, as was the Louisiana tax, would not necessarily apply to newspapers that had higher revenues from sales of advertising yet smaller circulations than papers subject to such taxes.[47]

The Louisiana newspaper advertising tax, the complaint of the newspapers continued, while purporting to be a revenue-raising measure, had not been enacted to raise revenues at all. Rather, the tax "is simply an attempted reprisal or punishment by the dominant political faction of the state—to which belong the governor, the heads of various executive departments of the state, and a majority of the members of the state legislature—against the daily press of the state for its past opposition, and a threat of further reprisals in the event of further or future opposition; all in direct violation of the freedom of the press in both federal and state constitutions." No such tax had ever before been levied in Louisiana, it was alleged, and if enforced, the present tax would raise a mere seventy-five thousand dollars in annual revenue, a relatively negligible amount when compared to the total revenues of the state.[48]

The federal courts, and indeed no court of equity having power to issue injunctions, will grant one if it can be shown that those seeking it have available an adequate legal remedy to which they can resort to solve the legal problem facing them. The newspapers in their complaint pointed out that no adequate remedy was available to them, since there was no procedure under state law by which taxes paid to the state could be recovered in a subsequent lawsuit challenging the tax. The only alternative available to the newspapers under state law was to refuse to pay the tax and then to raise their constitutional objections to the tax in prosecutions brought by the state for failure to pay the tax. This method, it was alleged, would take months if not years, while in the interim not only would the newspapers subject themselves to the risk of being penalized large amounts of money, but the agents of the papers responsible for the failure to pay the tax would also be subject to criminal prosecutions for each such failure. Injunction proceedings in the federal court, it was therefore argued, were the only viable remedy available to the newspapers subject to the tax.[49]

The Louisiana newspaper advertising tax was constitutionally invalid and should be enjoined by the federal court, the complaint concluded, because it violated article 10, section 8, of the Louisiana constitution requiring all license taxes to be imposed upon all members of businesses, professions, trades, or occupations subjected to the tax and not just on a select few. Because of its discriminatory effect, it was alleged, the tax also violated the Equal Protection Clause of the Fourteenth Amendment of the federal Constitution. Finally, the tax was alleged to be invalid because it violated both article 1, section 3, of the Louisiana constitution, which provided that "no law shall ever be passed to curtail or restrain the liberty of speech or of the press," and the Due Process Clause of the Fourteenth Amendment, which "secures against state action the freedom of the press guaranteed by the First Amendment to the Constitution of the United States."[50]

When the complaint of the newspapers was filed in the U.S. district court in New Orleans on September 20, Judge Wayne Borah ordered that the governor and attorney general be notified of the suit. At 2:30 P.M. a conference was held in Borah's chambers with a representative of the state attorney general's office and counsel for the newspapers in attendance. Following the conference, Judge Borah issued a temporary restraining order prohibiting the collection of the newspaper tax by Supervisor of Public Accounts Alice Grosjean pending a further hearing. He also certified the case as one requiring a three-judge court and scheduled the convening of that court for later in the fall. With the filing of the complaint attacking the advertising tax, counsel for the newspapers had seized the initiative, and the question now became what response the state of Louisiana would make to the newspapers' suit in the federal court.[51]

NOTES

1. T. Harry Williams, *Huey Long* (New York: Knopf, 1969), p. 722; Hodding Carter, "The Kingfish on His Way," *The New Republic* 81 (Nov. 21, 1934): 40–42.

2. *New Orleans Times-Picayune*, Aug. 19, 1934, p. 14; Hermann Deutsch, "Prelude to a Heterocrat," *The Saturday Evening Post* 208 (Sept. 7, 1935): 5–7, 84–88; William Ivy Hair, *The Kingfish and His Realm* (Baton Rouge: Louisiana State University Press, 1991), p. 301.

3. Hair, *The Kingfish*, pp. 301, 305.

4. Williams, *Long*, pp. 492–525.

5. *New Orleans Times-Picayune*, Nov. 12, 1934, p. 1.

6. Huey P. Long Scrapbooks, vol. 24, quoting the *New Orleans States*, Hill Memorial Library, Louisiana State University, Baton Rouge; Hair, *The Kingfish*, pp. 184, 292.

7. *New Orleans Times-Picayune*, Nov. 27, 1934, p. 6; Nov. 28, 1934, p. 2; Nov. 29, 1934, p. 27.

8. Ibid., Nov. 28, 1934, p. 10; *New York Times*, Nov. 18, 1934, p. 30; Nov. 27, 1934, p. 6; Nov. 28, 1934, p. 2; *The Nation* 140 (Jan. 2, 1935): 3.

9. *American Progress*, Aug. 7, 1934, p. 7.

10. Hair, *The Kingfish*, pp. 178, 207–8.

11. *American Progress*, Aug. 7, 1934, p. 7.

12. *Editor & Publisher* 69 (Feb. 15, 1936): 5.

13. *Baton Rouge Morning Advocate*, Feb. 11, 1936, pp. 1, 8; Record, *Grosjean* v. *American Press Co.*, 297 U.S. 233 (1936), pp. 1, 12 (hereafter cited as Record).

14. 1939 *Martindale-Hubbell*, Louisiana volume (New Providence, N.J.: Martindale-Hubbell); the information regarding J. J. Davidson was furnished by Ms. Gwen Horner of the law firm of Davidson, Meaux, McElligot & Swift, Lafayette, La., in a telephone interview on March 8, 1994.

15. Memorial services before the Supreme Court of Louisiana for Colonel John H. Tucker, Jr., Nov. 16, 1984, in the author's possession courtesy of T. Haller Jackson III of the firm of Tucker, Jeter, Jackson & Hickman, Shreveport, La.

16. *New Orleans Times-Picayune*, Jan. 17, 1980, sec. 1, p. 26; *Time* 27 (Feb. 24, 1936): 49–50.

17. The document "Memorandum and Discussion Relative to Validity of Act 23 of 1934 (Newspaper Advertising Tax) and Jurisdiction and Procedure to Set It Aside" is in the possession of the law firm of Davidson, Meaux, McElligot & Swift, Lafayette, La. I express my appreciation to the firm and especially Ms. Gwen Horner for making this memorandum available to me. The document will be cited as Memorandum hereafter.

18. Memorandum, pp. 4–5.

19. Ibid., pp. 5–6, 11–14.

20. Ibid., pp. 7–11.

21. Ibid., p. 11.

22. *Hammer* v. *Dagenhart*, 247 U.S. 251 (1918).

23. *Bailey* v. *Drexel Furniture Co.*, 259 U.S. 20, 37 (1922). For an excellent analysis of the litigation in the child labor cases, see Stephen B. Wood, *Constitutional Politics in the Progressive Era* (Chicago: University of Chicago Press, 1967). In sustaining the Fair Labor Standards Act of 1938, the Supreme Court reversed *Hammer* v. *Dagenhart* and upheld the validity of congressional regulation of child labor in *United States* v. *Darby*, 312 U.S. 100 (1941).
24. Memorandum, pp. 21–27.
25. Ibid., pp. 30–44.
26. Ibid., p. 46.
27. Ibid.
28. *Thompson* v. *State*, 17 Tex. 253 (1884); *Baldwin* v. *State*, 21 Tex. 591 (1886); *In re Jager*, 29 S.C. 438 (1888); *Preston* v. *Finley*, 72 F. 850 (D.C. Tex., 1896); *City of Norfolk* v. *Norfolk Landmark Publishing Co.*, 95 Va. 564 (1898).
29. *New Orleans Item-Tribune*, Feb. 12, 1936, p. 12. The quotation is probably not directly attributable to Deutsch but was likely a paraphrase of his thinking on the free-press issue.
30. *Editor & Publisher* 69 (Feb. 15, 1936): 6.
31. The results of Eberhard Deutsch's research on the free-press issue may be found in Brief of Appellee, *Grosjean* v. *American Press Co.*, 297 U.S. 233 (1936), Appendix B, pp. 48–70.
32. Memorandum, pp. 46–51.
33. Hair, *The Kingfish*, p. 316.
34. Williams, *Long*, pp. 733–36; *New Orleans Item*, Sept. 16, 1934, p. 1.
35. *Editor & Publisher* 67 (Aug. 11, 1934): 26.
36. *Ex parte Young*, 209 U.S. 123 (1908).
37. On the decision of *Ex parte Young* and the congressional response to that decision, see Richard C. Cortner, *The Iron Horse and the Constitution: The Railroads and the Transformation of the Fourteenth Amendment* (Westport, Conn.: Greenwood, 1993), pp. 125–208.
38. *New Orleans Times-Picayune*, Feb. 7, 1966, pp. 1, 3.
39. Williams, *Long*, pp. 471–77.
40. *New Orleans Times-Picayune*, May 6, 1924, p. 1; Aug. 23, 1966, p. 1.
41. Ibid., Aug. 24, 1942, p. 1.
42. *Cumberland Telephone & Telegraph Co.* v. *Louisiana Public Service Commission*, 260 U.S. 212 (1922); Williams, *Long*, pp. 105, 170–71.
43. Williams, *Long*, pp. 280–81.
44. Record, p. 10.
45. *American Press Co.* v. *Grosjean*, 10 F.Supp. 161 (D.C.E.D. La., 1935).
46. Record, pp. 3–4.
47. Ibid., pp. 4–5.
48. Ibid., pp. 5–6.
49. Ibid., p. 9.
50. Ibid., p. 6.
51. *New Orleans Times-Picayune*, Sept. 21, 1934, pp. 1, 6–7.

Chapter 6

The *Grosjean* Case before the Three-Judge Court

> The guarantees of a free press were imbedded in our constitutions, not only to prohibit censorship but specifically to prohibit any restraint of the press, especially one by taxation, such as was then prevalent in England. It was recognized then, as it must be now, that control of the press may be effected by government as well through a threat of destructive taxation, as by a licensing system or by censorship.
>
> —Newspaper counsel, November 23, 1934

> It is not essential to liberty of speech and freedom of the press, as constitutionally understood, that profit be derived from the exercise of these rights. Nor was it ever contemplated that the constitutional guarantee should extend to charging for and selling advertising.
>
> —Counsel for the state of Louisiana, November 23, 1934

♦ While the complaint attacking the advertising tax filed by the newspapers in the federal district court named Supervisor of Public Accounts Grosjean as the defendant, the responsibility for defending suits involving the state was that of the office of the Louisiana attorney general. In 1934, the occupant of that office was forty-nine-year-old Gaston Louis Porterie. Porterie was born in Mansura in Avoyelles Parish in 1885 and attended the Mansura public schools. He received a bachelor of science degree from Louisiana State University in 1904 and subsequently attended Cornell University. In 1905 he was appointed principal of Mansura high school and in 1909 became the superintendent of Avoyelles Parish schools, but he returned to Louisiana State University and earned a law degree in 1915. The following year Porterie was elected district attorney for the fourteenth judicial district, but his tenure in that position was interrupted by World War I, during which he served as a captain of the Red Cross in France.[1]

Gaston Porterie was the candidate for attorney general on the Long-selected state ticket in 1932, and he defeated the anti-Long incumbent, Percy Saint. Porterie, however, subsequently paid a heavy price for his loyalty to the Kingfish. In the elections of 1932, several amendments to the state constitution, some of which were important to the Long program, were voted on by the electorate. The Long organization therefore strongly supported the amendments, and all of them were easily approved, but the vote in their favor in New Orleans was suspiciously lopsided. Indeed, in sixteen precincts in the city, the amendments were approved by unanimous votes, and the conservative opposition to the Kingfish charged voting fraud.

The district attorney of Orleans Parish, Eugene Stanley, launched an investigation of the charges of fraud and convened a grand jury for that purpose. Stanley, who had been neutral toward the Long organization, had won office without its support and therefore owed no loyalty to it. As his investigation proceeded, Stanley was summoned to Baton Rouge by Attorney General Porterie and ordered to drop his probe of the voting fraud charges. When Stanley adamantly refused, Porterie then assumed control of the investigation himself and successfully guided the grand jury in deciding to take no effective action in the matter.[2]

Attorney General Porterie's sabotage of the voting fraud probe provoked angry protests from the anti-Long forces, and a complaint was filed with the state bar association charging the attorney general with unethical behavior in the matter. The committee on grievances of the state bar conducted an investigation and on April 24, 1933, recommended that the bar association expel Porterie from its membership. Porterie appealed the recommendation to the executive committee of the association, but in June he resigned his membership before his appeal could be acted on. The bar association, however, refused to accept his resignation, and on June 24 it formally expelled Attorney General Porterie from its ranks.[3]

Porterie's "blind obedience to the orders of his political deity, regardless of his official oath and duties," the *Times-Picayune* asserted, "led him to an awkward predicament. Therein he sat tight and dumb, patiently awaiting rescue by his overlord, Sir Crawfish." Porterie, the paper maintained, was the only attorney general in the history of the state "who ever invaded a grand jury room to block investigation of gross election frauds." He was also the only attorney general of the state to be recommended for expulsion by the state bar and the only one to "resign his bar association membership in order to avoid a hearing before his professional brethren on charges so serious as to warrant his expulsion from the bar association if substantiated."[4]

Attorney General Porterie refused to comment after his expulsion, but the Kingfish angrily denounced the bar's action, asserting that Porterie had refused to knuckle under to the corporation lawyers controlling the bar association. Porterie's expulsion, Long charged, had been engineered by "a clique of corporation lawyers whose clients have been trying to mulct the state out of several million dollars which Mr. Porterie and others keep them from getting." Other states had provided for the public election of the officers of their bar associations, he continued, and Louisiana should follow their example. "It has been an open secret for years that certain sinister corporation influences have tried to keep the attorney general's office friendly to them," the Kingfish maintained. "They will even rather let the governor's office get away from them if they can be sure of the attorney general, because it is the attorney general who must pass on the points of law and go to court to defend the state in upholding the interest of the people." Because Attorney General Porterie had performed his duties in such a manner as to save the state "many millions of dollars that some of these corporations would like to have," Long concluded, "these interests have set after him, trying to seize upon some flim flam thing to do him harm."[5]

As usual, the *Times-Picayune* observed, "the Crawfish brings his mud guns into action." His "abuse and vituperation" could not conceal the fact, however, that the state bar association had possessed the courage to condemn official obstruction of an investigation into voting fraud and "to expel from its membership the attorney general who undertook that obstructive task in the face of his oath to uphold and faithfully to execute the laws of his state." In expelling Porterie, the *Times-Picayune* declared, the bar association had performed a great service to the "high traditions of its profession" and to the cause of "fearless and impartial law enforcement" and honest elections, "whose restoration in Louisiana must be desired by every citizen who believes in decent government and democratic institutions."[6]

The *American Progress*, however, charged that a "group of corporation lawyers and lobbyists, fighting us before the legislature and before the courts and in politics, have lately prostituted the Louisiana Bar Association by slipping into the president's chair and committees lawyers and lobbyists of their interests whom we are having to tax and who are continuing to fight us in the courts and elsewhere." In an obvious reference to the disbarment of Attorney General Porterie, the *Progress* warned that the corporation lawyers had "even undertaken to browbeat and intimidate officials of the state from defending suits against their special interest clients through the corruption that they have brought about in the bar association." "In time," the *Progress* predicted, "the people can care for that condition."[7]

In fulfillment of the prediction of the *Progress*, the Kingfish restructured the state bar association in a special legislative session in November 1934. At his behest, a bill was introduced creating the Louisiana State Bar Association and requiring all practicing lawyers in the state to join. "You know," the Kingfish asserted, "this private bar association we have in Louisiana has been taken possession of by a clique of lawyers representing the corporations and special interests, and they have browbeat and intimidated young lawyers who try to bring suit against their clients." "The bar has become the vehicle of the corporate interests," he declared, "and we're going to stop it." The bill introduced in the legislature thus provided for an eight-person board of governors of the bar that would be elected by the people from each of the state's congressional districts.[8]

Explaining the bill before the house ways and means committee, Long pointed out that it provided that "any candidate for membership on the state bar governing board shall file with his qualification papers a list of the five leading corporations he has represented during the past five years, together with the amount of money paid him by these corporations." "The provision," he explained, "will give the people a chance to vote some little country lawyer as a member of the board of governors." When he concluded his remarks, Long threw back his head and erupted in gleeful laughter. The bill was enacted into law by the legislature on November 16 by large majorities in both houses, and in 1935 Attorney General Gaston Porterie was selected as the first president of the Louisiana State Bar Association.[9]

Since the complaint of the newspapers against the advertising tax was filed on September 20, Attorney General Porterie found himself the center of a major controversy when he was confronted with the suit brought by the newspapers. It would not be the attorney general, however, who would assume the principal responsibility of defending the tax in the federal courts, but rather New Orleans attorney Charles J. Rivet, serving as a special assistant attorney general in the litigation.

Rivet had befriended Huey Long when Long was preparing for the state bar exam while living a hand-to-mouth existence in a boarding house in New Orleans. Long had taken courses at Tulane University Law School, but he prepared for admission to the bar by reading law rather than graduating from law school. Rivet had graduated from the College of the Immaculate Conception (now Jesuit High School), but he did not earn a university degree. He attended Tulane University Law School for a month, but quit in disgust when a professor cited a statute as controlling authority which Rivet knew had been repealed by the legislature. Rivet pointed out the error and the professor confessed his mistake the following day, but Rivet felt that he was in law school to be educated by the faculty, not vice versa. He then read law under the supervision of a state judge instead of completing law school. Rivet was admitted to the bar in 1914 and later assisted Long in preparing for the bar exam, advising him on how best to impress the committee of examiners.[10]

Born in New Orleans in 1890, the forty-four-year-old Rivet had been visited frequently by Long after he was admitted to the bar and established a law practice in Shreveport. Apparently admiring Rivet's legal skill, Long attempted to persuade Rivet to leave New Orleans and join him in his law practice in Shreveport, guaranteeing him at least ten thousand dollars in yearly fees, at the time a handsome sum. Rivet, however, refused Long's invitation because he was a native of New Orleans and enjoyed the city where his closest friends also lived. In the mid-1920s, Long informed Rivet that he was going to run for governor and although he was not successful in his first race for that office, he did win election in 1928. After stumping the state, Long asked Rivet what he thought of his speeches, and Rivet bluntly told him that he should ask someone else to speak for him because his own speeches made him appear to be a "wild man" on the stump. After Long was elected governor, he listed Charles Rivet among those to whom he owed his success, but Rivet made no attempt to capitalize on his links to the governor after the election. Indeed, Rivet had told Long that he would not vote for him and indeed did not. "I was a conservative and Huey was not," he later explained. He could not support Long, he added, because "our views were too different."[11]

Sometime after his election as governor, the Kingfish phoned Rivet in the middle of the night and attempted to persuade him to accept appointment as counsel for the license tax collector for Orleans Parish. Rivet refused to make a decision, but he subsequently received his commission of appointment to the position. Although Rivet reluctantly accepted the appointment, he would not use his office to play favorites with the Kingfish's supporters. As a consequence he expected to be dismissed, but he apparently was never interfered with and in fact was later retained as an attorney for the secretary of state's office and the attorney general. As a special assistant attorney general, Rivet ultimately was responsible for defending the state in some four hundred corporation franchise tax cases when the corporations challenged the validity of the tax.[12]

Rivet was also called upon by the Kingfish to draft legislation, but in a meeting with Rivet and his henchmen, Long told his inner circle, "You can ask him about law but don't ask him about politics because he don't know a dang thing about politics." Long informed Rivet at one point that he considered himself to be the best lawyer in the South and probably in the country. While disagreeing with the Kingfish's exaggerated assessment of his abilities as a lawyer, Rivet thought that Long was "brilliant" though also "paranoic." He apparently never had any misgivings regarding his role as a legal technician defending the Long regime, although Rivet admitted that Long "had every characteristic of a dictator." "Of course, I like benevolent or good dictators," he added. "They simplify things."[13]

Rivet has been described as a "man with a razor-sharp mind and a somewhat sardonic manner" and one of the state's "ablest lawyers." He no doubt possessed intimate knowledge of Louisiana law, but he had only a limited acquaintance with federal constitutional law. This was not unusual for the time, since federal constitutional law affected legal questions arising in the states at relatively few points, and a lawyer could spend an entire career without encountering any important federal constitutional issue. As a result, a thorough knowledge of state law was largely all that was required for a successful legal career. Nonetheless, Rivet's lack of knowledge of federal constitutional law became obvious during his defense of the newspaper advertising tax in the federal courts.[14]

With Rivet undertaking most of the preparation, the state responded to the newspapers' complaint by filing in the federal court a motion to dismiss, strike, and an answer on September 23. Rivet's principal strategy in the motion was to attack the jurisdiction of the federal court to entertain the newspapers' case. The amount in controversy in such a case, he pointed out, had to be three thousand dollars or more, and he denied that amount was at issue for all the newspaper plaintiffs. The newspaper advertising tax was to be collected quarterly by the state, Rivet noted, and the amount due from each of the affected papers for the first quarter in which the tax was due amounted to less than three thousand dollars, with the sole exception of the *Times-Picayune*. This argument ignored, however, the other basis of jurisdiction asserted by the newspapers: the 1871 congressional statute conferring jurisdiction on the federal courts to enjoin state officers from depriving persons of their federally protected rights—a statute that did not require an allegation of a minimum amount of alleged damages.

The state's motion also denied that there was no effective and readily available remedy under state law to which the newspapers could have resorted to challenge the tax. The issue of the validity of the tax could have been contested in a single suit filed by the state to collect the tax, Rivet argued, and that suit would have been resolved finally by the Louisiana Supreme Court within a few months at most. Because an adequate remedy under state law was available to the plaintiffs, he contended, the federal court again should not assume jurisdiction or issue an injunction in the case.[15]

On the merits of the case, Rivet asserted that the statements in the newspapers' complaint alleging that the tax had been imposed as retaliation for their opposition to the Long regime, and that the Kingfish had himself characterized the tax as a "tax on lying," should all be stricken by the court. Those allegations, he said, "consist of conclusions which are impertinent, scandalous and libelous, and concern persons not connected with this suit." The newspaper tax was "a legitimate and valid exercise of the taxing power of the State of Louisiana," he argued, and the "classification adopted by its legislature is a rational one, consonant with classifications made in the newspaper and advertising business."[16]

The inclusion within the class of papers to be taxed of the newspapers with circulations of twenty thousand copies or more per week, Rivet contended, was perfectly legitimate, since those papers not included in that classification were mostly small, weekly newspapers with limited circulations. The weeklies not subject to the tax, he pointed out, were "a class of country journals, with little equipment, few employees and small assets, which use methods of operation entirely different from the metropolitan newspapers operating in the state and having a circulation of more than 20,000 copies per week." Contrary to the metropolitan dailies' assertions, he maintained, there was in fact no real competition for advertising between the dailies and the weeklies, since the "small journals are not recognized as advertising media by the large advertisers and the advertising agencies of this country."[17]

The federal court lacked jurisdiction over the newspaper tax case, Rivet reiterated, because the amount required by federal law in such cases had not been met by all of the plaintiffs and because there was an adequate remedy under state law readily available to the affected newspapers. The newspapers had also failed to raise any valid legal or constitutional basis for the invalidation of the tax, since the legislature's classification of the metropolitan dailies as the papers to be taxed was both legitimate and rational. Consequently, Rivet concluded, the state "prays that the restraining order issued herein be recalled and vacated; that the interlocutory injunction prayed for be denied, and that the plaintiffs' bill of complaint be dismissed at their cost."[18]

Notably lacking from Rivet's motion on behalf of the state was any mention of the free-press issue. This omission might have been explained by an intent on his part to minimize the importance of that issue or to imply its irrelevance to the court. But as would become apparent later, Rivet was in fact unaware that freedom of the press now applied to the states via the Fourteenth Amendment as a result of the decision in *Near* v. *Minnesota* in 1931.

As the Louisiana dailies were making preparations for initiating proceedings in the federal courts to challenge the newspaper tax, they continued to receive encouragement from the American Newspaper Publishers' Association. The group's publication, *Editor & Publisher*, predicted that the Kingfish, "like all the other vicious specimens brought to the surface by our recurring economic storms, will be hooked and on the beach long before he attains his evident ambition to rival Mussolini and Hitler." "In most praiseworthy fashion," it said, "the newspapers of Louisiana are fighting the Kingfish 2 percent advertising spite tax." When Judge Borah issued the temporary restraining order prohibiting the collection of the tax for the time being, *Editor & Publisher* also predicted that the case "ultimately will go before the U.S. Supreme Court and will be fought to a finish on the ground of constitutional press liberty." Whether this in fact would occur, however, depended on the hearing yet to come before the three-judge federal court in New Orleans.[19]

While awaiting the hearing in *American Press Co.* v. *Grosjean*, counsel for both the newspapers and the state sought to bolster their cases by supplementing the complaint and the motion to dismiss with sworn affidavits fleshing out the facts in the proceeding. In this battle of the affidavits, Charles Rivet and Attorney General Porterie attempted to strengthen the state's contention that the classification of the large metropolitan dailies in Louisiana as the papers to be taxed had been both rational and legitimate. They hoped to accomplish this by securing several affidavits from the publishers of small, weekly newspapers who indicated that the operation of their papers was almost completely different from that of the large dailies and that there was in reality no significant competition for advertising between the two kinds of papers.

These affidavits were almost identical in content, with that of Frank C. Chekal, publisher of the weekly *Caddo Citizen*, being typical. The *Caddo Citizen* was published in the town of Vivian in Caddo Parish. Checkal stated that while in the past the small weeklies did receive some advertising from national companies such as Chesterfield cigarettes and the Ford Motor Company, the revenues from those sources of advertising had largely disappeared for the weeklies. "The big daily newspapers," Chekal said, "are continually, and have been continuing, encroaching for the last few years upon the weekly paper. As a result they have practically gained all foreign [out-of-state] advertisement, due to their large circulation in the field where the country paper circulates."[20]

The large dailies, Chekal continued, delivered their papers by bus or other means throughout the state, and in their advertising they inserted the names of local businesses in the areas within the reach of their circulation. "As a result," he said, "there is less opportunity for me to get advertisement from my local merchants. The country newspapers, if they depended upon foreign and local advertising could not exist. The majority must do, in addition to publishing a paper, a certain amount of job printing. This is our salvation and the only way that we can eke a livelihood." His investment in the *Caddo Citizen*, including a town lot, newspaper building, and printing equipment, was $6,500, Chekal pointed out. His annual income was only $4,500, which left little profit and a very small allowance for salaries. "To operate my business," he said, "I do all the work I can myself. My wife does part of the writing, proof-reading, and attends to some collections. The only force in addition to my wife and myself which I employ consists of one apprentice."[21]

Through affidavits such as Chekal's, counsel for the state hoped to demonstrate to the federal court that the small weeklies not only did not compete with the dailies for advertising but were very different in the size and scope of their operations. The contention of the dailies that the tax was discriminatory because it singled them out for differential treatment from the weeklies, the state could argue, was wholly without merit, since differential treatment of the dailies was fully justified by the marked differences between them and the weeklies.

In addition to bolstering their argument that the classification adopted by the legislature was a reasonable one, Rivet and Porterie also sought to strengthen the contention that the federal court should not hear the case because an adequate and readily available remedy could be obtained by the newspapers under state law. This was done by Charles Rivet swearing to an affidavit himself, pointing out his extensive experience as a special assistant attorney general representing the state in tax litigation in the state courts. His experience had demonstrated, Rivet stated, that the time span from the filing of a tax case in a trial court to the final disposition of appeals in the case by the Louisiana Supreme Court was at most only a few months. Rather than facing a delay of perhaps years before their objections to the advertising tax could have been resolved in the state courts, the plaintiff newspapers could find in those courts a speedy and effective remedy. Counsel for the state argued that the federal court should consequently not exercise jurisdiction in the case.[22]

Counsel for the newspapers countered with affidavits of their own. In their affidavits, newspaper counsel attempted to demonstrate that the daily papers in fact did face competition for advertising from the weeklies and other dailies in the state not subject to the tax; that the advertising tax was intended by the Long regime as a retaliation against and punishment of the affected papers for their opposition; and that the effect of the tax would be to reduce significantly the ability of the affected dailies to disseminate information and news to the public and thus would violate the freedom of the press.

Affidavits were filed from many of the publishers of the dailies subject to the advertising tax, with the affidavit of Frank Smith, publisher of the *Lake Charles American Press*, being typical. Smith stated that the American Press Company, as the publisher of the Lake Charles paper, had a circulation of over twenty thousand copies per week and that the revenues of the paper consisted almost entirely of money paid by subscribers and advertisers. The *Lake Charles American Press*, he continued, competed for advertising revenues with the *Crowley Signal*, a daily paper published in Crowley in Acadia Parish, and with weekly papers in Allen, Beauregard, Vermillion, Vernon, Jefferson Davis, and Acadia parishes. All of these competitors had circulations of less than twenty thousand copies weekly and were therefore exempt from the advertising tax. The *Lake Charles American Press*, Smith pointed out, had received $82,613.26 in gross receipts from advertising sales during the period from October 1, 1933, to September 30, 1934.[23]

The editor in chief of the *New Orleans Item* and *Tribune*, Marshall Ballard, and J. Walker Ross, the editor in chief of the *New Orleans States*, stated in their affidavit that they had been close observers of the contemporary political and economic scene in Louisiana. They confirmed that all of the newspapers affected by the newspaper advertising tax had opposed the Long regime and its policies, with the exception of the *Lake Charles American Press*, which had joined the other papers in opposition after the tax had been adopted by the 1934 legislature. The dominant political faction in the state, Ballard and Ross pointed out, had for many years been led by "Huey P. Long, ex-governor of the state and present United States Senator from the state; that all of the executive departments of the state have been since the year 1930, and are at present, controlled by said faction; that the present governor of the state, Oscar K. Allen, is a member, and one of the leaders of said faction; that a majority of the members of the legislature of 1934 were members of said faction."[24]

During the 1934 legislative session that enacted the newspaper tax, Ballard and Ross continued, the leaders and various members of the Long faction "openly and vehemently denounced . . . [the opposition] newspapers in political addresses, in speeches on the floor of the legislature, and in circulars widely distributed through the employees of various state departments under their control." While the legislature was considering the newspaper advertising tax, Long and Allen had distributed a circular denouncing the "lying newspapers," Ballard and Ross pointed out, and defended the newspaper tax as a "tax on lying, at 2 cents per lie." They then quoted excerpts from the "lying newspapers" circular and asserted that a copy of the circular was placed on the desk of every member of the legislature while the advertising tax was being considered. In September 1934, after the tax had been adopted by the legislature, Ballard and Ross concluded, Long delivered a public address in Calcasieu Parish in which he admitted that he would have preferred to exempt the Lake Charles paper from the tax and stated that "we would have done it if we could." Counsel for the newspapers hoped that through the facts alleged by Ballard and Ross they could convince the federal court that the newspaper tax was not a genuine revenue measure at all but was rather a direct punishment of the opposition press that violated freedom of the press.[25]

An additional affidavit of the business managers of the Item Company and the Times-Picayune Publishing Company, Arthur G. Newmyer and John F. Tims, was filed by newspaper counsel. Newmyer and Tims attested to the fact that the only newspapers in Louisiana having circulations of more than twenty thousand copies per week were those affected by the advertising tax, while there were four dailies in the state having slightly smaller circulations, in addition to the 120 weeklies. All of these papers, they claimed, competed for advertising among themselves, but advertising rates and revenues were not exclusively dependent on circulation. It was frequently the case, Newmyer and Tims noted, that a "daily newspaper with a much smaller volume of circulation than another has advertising rates as high as, and in some instances, considerably higher than, those of the other newspapers having greater circulation, and accordingly obtains an annual income from advertising published in its columns larger than that obtained by the other newspaper of a greater circulation." The purpose of the Newmyer-Tims affidavit was obviously to strengthen the argument that the use of circulation alone as a basis for classifying newspapers for the purpose of taxing advertising gross receipts was irrational and unrelated to the realities of the newspaper business. A tax based on a circulation classification alone would therefore result in discrimination against those papers affected by the tax.[26]

The final affidavits filed in the federal court by the attorneys for the newspapers reflected their ability to obtain the assistance of the American Newspaper Publishers' Association (ANPA) in securing the testimony of leaders in national press circles. The affidavits of Howard Davis, the business manager of the *New York Herald Tribune* and president of the ANPA, and Carl W. Ackerman, the dean of the faculty of journalism at Columbia University, reinforced the contention that Louisiana's advertising tax directly inhibited the ability of the affected newspapers to disseminate news to the public and thus infringed on freedom of the press. Both Davis and Ackerman maintained that revenues from the sale of advertising by newspapers subsidized the sales of newspapers to the public, since the price of newspapers to the public was customarily less than the cost of production. In order for newspapers to provide the widest dissemination of news to the public, both said, advertising revenues must supply the major costs of production. Any factor that adversely affected advertising revenues of newspapers, they therefore argued, directly diminished their ability to furnish news to the broadest possible segment of the public.[27]

As the battle of the affidavits ended, the attorneys for the newspapers, Charles Rivet, and Attorney General Porterie stipulated that they would not present any live witness testimony at the hearing before the three-judge court. They agreed that they would allow the court to decide the *Grosjean* case on the basis of the plaintiffs' complaint, the state's motion to dismiss and answer, and the supplementing affidavits that they had submitted to the court. Judge Borah had initially scheduled the hearing before the three-judge court for September 29, but the hearing was delayed as some difficulties were encountered in arranging for all three of the judges to be present for the hearing. Finally, however, Judge Rufus Foster of the U.S. court of appeals and Judges Wayne Borah and Ben Dawkins of the district courts convened in New Orleans to hear the case on November 23.[28]

The importance of the *Grosjean* case to national press interests was emphasized when on the eve of the hearing before the three-judge court, the American Newspaper Publishers' Association dispatched its general counsel, Elisha Hanson, to New Orleans to observe the proceedings. Hanson was joined by Bennett Clark, a U.S. senator from Missouri, who had a personal interest in the proceedings. Clark's sister, Genevieve, was the wife of James Thomson, publisher of the *New Orleans Item* and *Tribune*.[29]

Elisha Hanson's newspaper career began when he became a reporter for the *Peoria (Ill.) Journal* in 1907. He subsequently served as the Washington correspondent for the *Chicago Tribune* from 1915 to 1917. Hanson then became the secretary to Illinois senator Medill McCormick and also secured a legal education. Admitted to the bar in Washington in 1924, he became the general counsel of the ANPA.[30]

The ANPA had been largely oblivious to free-press issues prior to the 1920s and had concentrated its energies instead on the economic problems facing newspapers across the country. Almost single-handedly, Colonel Robert McCormick of the *Chicago Tribune* had aroused the association to an awareness of the importance to its interests of defending freedom of the press and had persuaded the association to establish a committee on freedom of the press in 1928. The subsequent litigation in *Near* v. *Minnesota,* which McCormick and the *Chicago Tribune* had largely financed, also substantially contributed to raising the ANPA's consciousness of the importance of freedom of the press as a constitutional issue.

With the election of Franklin D. Roosevelt as president in 1932 and his initiation of New Deal programs to combat the Depression and fundamentally reform American life, the ANPA also perceived new threats to the principle of freedom of the press. This was especially so when the Roosevelt-sponsored National Industrial Recovery Act (NIRA) of 1933 was applied to newspaper publishers. Intended to bring about the recovery of the industrial and commercial sector of the economy, the NIRA required that "codes of fair competition" be formulated to cover business enterprises. The NIRA codes were to establish among other things minimum-wage and maximum-hour standards, the regulation of child labor, a guarantee of the right of workers to organize into unions free of employer interference, production controls where appropriate, and provisions outlawing unfair practices of competition.

The ANPA recommended to its membership in July 1933 that they should refrain from "subscribing to a code under the recovery act at the present time," because the NIRA was perceived by the association as threatening the national licensing of the press. Pressure to join the recovery effort under the NIRA nevertheless led the ANPA to submit a draft NIRA code covering the newspaper industry in August, but the draft reflected publishers' fears that participation in the recovery effort might pose dangers to freedom of the press. The ANPA draft code thus provided that "because of the limitations of the First Amendment to the Constitution of the United States nothing in this code shall be construed as authorizing the licensing of publishers and/or newspapers or as permitting injunction proceedings which would restrain the publication of newspapers." The ANPA also resisted the provision of the NIRA guaranteeing the right of employees to organize unions free of employer interference. Its draft code also provided that press employees could not be required to join any organization as a condition of employment, and it retained the right of publishers and press employees to bargain individually concerning terms and conditions of employment.[31]

The National Recovery Administration (NRA), the agency required to enforce the NIRA, resisted the ANPA's attempts to qualify its participation in the recovery effort by including the free-press guarantee in the newspaper code and limiting the right of its workers to organize into unions. Colonel Robert McCormick of the ANPA free-press committee was the author of the free-press provision, which General Hugh Johnson, the administrator of the NRA, characterized as a "synthetic dead cat." The ANPA, however, remained adamant about including both the free-press guarantee and the labor qualifications in the newspaper code. The ANPA general counsel, Elisha Hanson, especially insisted that the qualification regarding the right of press employees to organize was "vital if this code is to be signed by the publishers of daily newspapers," but in the end it was eliminated. The publishers were successful, however, in retaining the freedom of the press provision in the final newspaper code.[32]

Encouraged by the NIRA, editorial employees of newspapers around the country began to organize into unions, a movement that led to the founding of the American Newspaper Guild in 1933. Initially, *Editor & Publisher*, as the voice of the ANPA, welcomed this development and acknowledged that real abuses existed in the industry with regard to editorial employees. As the American Newspaper Guild attempted to bargain collectively with various publishers, however, it found itself almost uniformly resisted and by 1934 *Editor & Publisher* was denouncing the guild as a "radical trades union." Press organizations, and ultimately the ANPA itself, soon began to link the unionization of newspaper editorial employees with freedom of the press, contending that the two were incompatible. This linkage became a central tenet of the ANPA's opposition to the unionization of editorial employees during the 1930s, and the association's increased focus on free-press issues was undoubtedly a factor in the dispatch of its general counsel, Elisha Hanson, to New Orleans to observe the proceedings in the *Grosjean* case. A victory for the press in the *Grosjean* case was apparently perceived as important to strengthening the hand of publishers in resisting the unionization of editorial employees.[33]

Although all seven of the attorneys employed by the newspapers were present when Judges Foster, Borah, and Dawkins convened the three-judge federal court on November 23, the presentation of the newspapers' case against the validity of the tax was made by Esmond Phelps and Eberhard Deutsch. The state of Louisiana and Supervisor of Public Accounts Alice Grosjean were represented by Charles Rivet and Attorney General Gaston Porterie. Tragedy marred the occasion, however, as Attorney General Porterie had to leave the courtroom abruptly soon after proceedings had begun when he was informed that his fourteen-year-old son had met with a fatal accident. The burden of defending the state's interest in the proceedings thus fell solely on Charles Rivet.[34]

Arguing on behalf of the state, Rivet again contended that the three-judge court lacked jurisdiction to hear the *Grosjean* case because the three-thousand-dollar minimum in alleged damages had not been shown by each of the plaintiff newspapers and because Louisiana law afforded them a speedy and effective remedy in the state courts. At the time the newspapers filed their complaint in the federal court on September 20, Rivet pointed out, none of them in fact owed any tax to the state, since their first payment would not have been due until October 1. When the suit was filed, he thus argued, the three-thousand-dollar jurisdictional amount required for the federal court did not exist for any of the newspapers. Even if the amount of tax each newspaper would have owed on October 1 were accepted as the amount each would have suffered in damages without federal judicial relief, he also noted, only the amount owed by the *Times-Picayune* would have been three thousand dollars or more.[35]

Counsel for the newspapers responded that the amount of damages the newspapers would suffer during the first year of the tax would have amounted to more than the jurisdictional amount for six out of the nine publishers affected by the tax. The remaining three publishers would have incurred more than three thousand dollars in damages during the same period if the attorneys' fees and penalties they would have owed for failure to pay the tax were added to the taxes themselves. But even if counsel for the state were correct in asserting that the jurisdictional amount simply had not been met by the plaintiffs, counsel for the newspapers pointed out that their complaint had also been based on the congressional act conferring jurisdiction on the federal courts to hear suits for injunctions to prevent state officials from depriving persons of their federally protected rights. Because this statute did not require any jurisdictional amount, newspaper counsel argued, the federal court still had jurisdiction in the case.[36]

The state's response to this latter point revealed a fundamental misunderstanding of the federal rights that the newspapers were asserting against the advertising tax. Counsel for the state argued that the newspapers were claiming that their rights under the Privileges and Immunities Clause of the Fourteenth Amendment were violated by the advertising tax. The Privileges and Immunities Clause prohibits the states from denying the privileges and immunities of U.S. citizenship, but this clause had been rendered essentially a dead letter by the Supreme Court's decision in the *Slaughter House Cases* in 1873. Since that decision the Court had consistently refused to interpret the Privileges and Immunities Clause as embracing any significant rights as limitations on the states.[37]

The state nevertheless insisted that the rights the newspapers were asserting against the advertising tax and asking the federal court to enjoin Louisiana officials from violating were rights derived from the Privileges and Immunities Clause. As counsel for the state correctly pointed out, the Court had long since held that corporations were not considered U.S. citizens within the meaning of the Privileges and Immunities Clause. Since the newspaper publishing companies in the *Grosjean* case were corporations, the state therefore argued that they could not validly assert rights under the clause. The congressional statute giving federal courts jurisdiction to enjoin state officers from violating federally protected rights, state counsel concluded, was inapplicable in the *Grosjean* case, since the newspaper publishing companies, as corporations, had no federally protected rights. The federal court consequently had no jurisdiction.[38]

Counsel for the newspapers answered the state's contentions by arguing that counsel for the state had entirely misunderstood the rights the newspapers were asserting against the advertising tax. The newspapers, they pointed out, were not asserting any rights under the Privileges and Immunities Clause, but were rather asserting that the tax denied them both the equal protection of the laws, in violation of the Equal Protection Clause, and freedom of the press, which was protected from invasion by the states under the Due Process Clause of the Fourteenth Amendment. Both the Equal Protection and Due Process Clauses, newspaper counsel noted, protected "persons" from the denial by the states of the equal protection of the laws or of "liberty" without due process of law. The Supreme Court as early as 1886 had held that corporations were "persons" within the meaning of those two clauses of the Fourteenth Amendment. While corporations could not validly invoke the rights of U.S. "citizens" that were protected by the Privileges and Immunities Clause, they could validly invoke both the Equal Protection Clause and the Due Process Clause against state action because they were "persons" within the meaning of those clauses. Newspaper counsel concluded that both clauses covered federally guaranteed rights that Congress had authorized the federal courts to protect by the issuance of injunctions against state officers who were threatening to deprive "persons," including corporations, of those rights.[39]

To the state's contention that an adequate remedy was available to the newspapers under the law of Louisiana in the state courts, Esmond Phelps responded: "We're confronted with all kinds of harassment. Each publisher if he refuses [to comply with the statute], is subject to a six months' prison sentence for each violation, six months for failure to report to the supervisor of public accounts [gross receipts from sales of advertising], and an additional six months for failure to pay the tax." "On this basis," Phelps maintained, "the plaintiffs might be sent to prison for five years." Unless the federal court acted, the newspapers would face harassment by the state through a multiplicity of suits both civil and criminal in the state courts. To prevent irreparable harm to the newspapers and their officers and agents, an injunction should therefore be issued. "If the suit is dismissed," newspaper counsel asserted, "nine civil suits could be brought each three months and during each such period eighteen criminal proceedings could be brought against the plaintiffs, and a like number against their principal officers. The entire controversy can and should be settled in this one suit."[40]

Answering the newspapers' assertion that the advertising tax denied them the equal protection of the laws, the state maintained that the Equal Protection Clause only required the state to demonstrate that its classification of subjects to be taxed was a rational one and that the burden was on those challenging the classification to prove that it was completely arbitrary and irrational. "There is no innovation in the classification adopted by the legislature of Louisiana" in the advertising tax, counsel for the state argued. "It was long theretofore an established and recognized fact that the small country journal, with a circulation of less than 20,000, could not be compared, hence is not in the same class, as the city newspaper with its large circulation and more extensive field of operation." The affidavits of the publishers of small weekly papers filed by the state with the court, it was pointed out, clearly demonstrated "the sharp distinction that exists between the business of the newspapers which fall within the statute and those which are without. The character of the business, the source of revenue, the field of operation are entirely different." By distinguishing between large urban dailies with circulations of twenty thousand copies per week and newspapers of smaller circulations, the state maintained, the classification adopted by the legislature in the advertising tax was clearly a rational one and thus did not deny the equal protection of the laws. The advertising tax, Charles Rivet told the federal court, did not apply to the "little two bit country newspapers. Surely you cannot compare these small papers with the large metropolitan newspapers."[41]

Counsel for the state also disputed the newspapers' contention that the advertising tax was violative of article 10, section 8, of the Louisiana constitution. Article 10, section 8, the state asserted, did not prohibit the legislature from classifying trades, professions, vocations, and so on for purposes of taxation, and that was all the legislature had done in the advertising tax. Counsel for the newspapers, however, responded that the Louisiana Supreme Court had uniformly held under article 10, section 8, that license taxes must be applied to all members of a trade, vocation, profession, and so on, that was the object of taxation. By applying the advertising tax to only 13 of 163 newspapers publishing advertising in Louisiana, they contended, the legislature had plainly violated the Louisiana constitution. Citing decisions of the U.S. Supreme Court interpreting the Equal Protection Clause, counsel for the newspapers additionally argued that the Court had invalidated as denying the equal protection of the laws state taxes that applied to some of those engaged in certain trades while exempting others engaged in the same trade. The Court had held, they maintained, that it condemned taxes that were "a positive and direct discrimination between persons engaged in the same class of business which each may do." Newspaper counsel added, "We join with the Supreme Court of the United States in saying that 'if such legislation does not deny the equal protection of the laws, we are unable to see what legislation would.' "[42]

During the hearing before the three-judge court, Esmond Phelps raised the freedom of the press issue by asserting that out of "163 newspapers published in Louisiana, there are thirteen with circulations of more than 20,000 copies per week. This statute is deliberately aimed at punishing these thirteen papers for their political stands." Freedom of the press, he continued, was protected by both article 1, section 3, of the Louisiana constitution and the Due Process Clause of the Fourteenth Amendment of the federal Constitution, which "secures against state action that freedom of the press guaranteed by the First Amendment of the Constitution of the United States." This point had been established by the Supreme Court's decision in *Near* v. *Minnesota* in 1931, Phelps pointed out, and he quoted the holding of Chief Justice Hughes in the *Near* case that it "is no longer open to doubt that the liberty of press and speech is within the liberty safeguarded by the due process clause of the Fourteenth Amendment from invasion by State action. It was found impossible to conclude that this essential personal liberty of the citizen was left unprotected by the general guaranty of fundamental rights of person and property."[43]

In response to Phelps, Charles Rivet asserted that the newspapers were arguing that the court had jurisdiction on the ground that "this is a federal question because the federal Constitution guarantees the freedom of the press." "There is no guarantee under the federal Constitution of freedom of the press insofar as the states are concerned," Rivet asserted. "That is only a prohibition insofar as the federal government is concerned. There is nothing in the Constitution of the United States that prohibits the states themselves from absolutely destroying the press. That prohibition is only found in the state constitution so far as the states are concerned and therefore it is strictly a question to be decided by the state courts." Seizing upon Rivet's apparent ignorance of the Supreme Court's decision in *Near* v. *Minnesota*, Esmond Phelps replied that if "Mr. Rivet had read the case of *Near* versus *Minnesota* he could never have argued against the freedom of the press. The Supreme Court in that case clearly decided that the federal Constitution guaranteed that freedom [against impairment by the states]."[44]

Apparently stung by Phelps's comments, Rivet subsequently quoted the First Amendment and maintained that "we are at a loss to understand how anyone can challenge our assertion that this prohibition is directed only against Congress and in no wise affects the states. If this amendment were the sole prohibition the state could abridge the freedom of speech and suppress all publications." The newspapers had nonetheless claimed a right of freedom of the press against state action under the Fourteenth Amendment, Rivet conceded. But he again misstated the source of the rights claimed by the press and misinterpreted the Supreme Court's *Near* decision when he maintained that the freedom of the press the papers were asserting derived from the Privileges and Immunities Clause of the Fourteenth Amendment. As he had argued on the jurisdictional issue, he pointed out that corporations could not validly assert the Privileges and Immunities Clause against state actions because they were not "citizens" within the meaning of the clause. "Hence," Rivet said, "the Fourteenth Amendment secures to the plaintiffs here no privileges, immunities or liberty which the state is prohibited from affecting."[45]

"If the plaintiffs, instead of charging us . . . with not having read *Near* v. *Minnesota*," Rivet continued, "had themselves given closer attention to that case, they would have discovered that the statute of Minnesota was directed against natural persons," who, unlike the corporations involved in the *Grosjean* case, possessed privileges and immunities as citizens of the United States "which the law of a state could not abridge, impair or destroy." "Furthermore," he added, "as pointed out in *Near* v. *Minnesota*, the chief purpose of the constitutional protection of liberty of the press is to prevent previous restraints upon publications, and nowhere has it ever been held that a person or corporation engaged in the publishing business is exempt from taxation. The authorities are to the contrary."[46]

Despite Rivet's contention that the newspapers in the *Grosjean* case could not properly invoke the freedom of the press against the advertising tax, Esmond Phelps continued to attack the tax on that ground. "Freedom of the press is guaranteed against state impairment by the constitutions of both Louisiana and the United States," he maintained. "These constitutional guarantees prohibit licensing of the press, or regulation thereof through the subterfuge of taxation. Historically interpreted, the constitutional guarantees of a free press preclude subjection of the press to any form of taxation not levied against all members of a general class. Given the power to tax the press, the legislature would have the power to destroy the press. [The advertising tax] . . . is accordingly unconstitutional in that it abridges the freedom of the press."[47]

All of the newspapers affected by the advertising tax, with the exception of the *Lake Charles American Press*, had opposed the Long regime, Phelps continued, and Senator Long himself had admitted that he would have preferred to exempt the Lake Charles newspaper from the tax for that reason. Long and Governor Allen had also published a circular describing the advertising tax as a tax on lying, at two cents a lie, he added, and that circular had been on the desks of the Louisiana legislators when the tax was being considered. Eberhard Deutsch also read the Long–Allen circular to the three-judge court and contended that the contemporary "political history of Louisiana indicates that the statute is a reprisal [against the press] by the dominant political faction of the state for its past opposition, and a threat of further reprisals through the exercise of the power of destruction by taxation in the event of continued opposition." The contents of the Long–Allen circular he had read to the court, Deutsch continued, "indicate the real underlying purpose of the legislation in question, as distinguished from its declared purpose of raising revenue." "In a long line of decisions," he continued, "the Supreme Court of the United States has held that it will determine the validity of legislation by its real and underlying purpose, rather than by its superficial or declared purpose, and that prohibited power of regulation may not be exercised through the subterfuge of taxation."[48]

"A dominant political faction announces to the press that its policies have been offensive to it and that it will mete out punishment through tax legislation," newspaper counsel said in describing the situation to the court. "The tax legislation is adopted by the faction-controlled legislature in the full knowledge that its purpose is one of reprisal for the past, and warning for the future. It is simply a statement of the legislature to the press: 'Because you have sought to impede our political path, we hereby punish you with a tax on your advertising. If you do not discontinue your opposition and support our policies, whatever they may be, we shall burden you with further and additional taxes of this nature.' "[49]

"The applicability to the freedom of the press, of the doctrine that the power to tax is the power to destroy, is emphasized by the constitutional history of the freedom of the press," newspaper counsel told the court. "The guarantees of a free press were imbedded in our constitutions, not only to prohibit censorship but specifically to prohibit any restraint of the press, especially one by taxation, such as was then prevalent in England. It was recognized then, as it must be now, that control of the press may be effected by government as well through a threat of destructive taxation, as by a licensing system or by censorship."[50]

Counsel for the state, however, argued that the motives of the Louisiana legislature in passing the advertising tax could not properly be considered by the federal court. The allegations by the newspapers that the state government and legislature were dominated by the Long regime and that the advertising tax was a reprisal for the opposition of the press to that regime, state's counsel maintained, consist "entirely of a libel against the majority of the members of the legislature of Louisiana, who are not parties to these proceedings, by ascribing to them improper and illegal motives in the enactment of the statute under consideration." Even if the motives ascribed to the legislature by the newspapers were true, it was argued, the court could not pass upon such allegations. "Assuming that the dominant political party in Louisiana, through the distribution of patronage, or the withholding thereof, or by other means, induced the majority of the members of the legislature to enact the statute under consideration, such practice is not peculiar to state politics," counsel for the state pointed out. "Whether the federal Congress or a state legislature has responded to pressure from a dominant political party in the enactment of laws, presents no matter open to judicial inquiry."[51]

Eberhard Deutsch shouldered most of the burden of presenting the freedom of the press issue to the three-judge court. He began by reciting the history of the struggle of the press in England to escape from suppression first by licensing and then by taxation. The newspapers conceded that freedom of the press did not exempt the press from taxes that were applicable to business generally, and they admitted that income taxes, property taxes, or franchise taxes that were applicable to all businesses were not invalid when applied to the press. The power to single out the press for special taxation, however, Deutsch warned, was the power to destroy the press. "What, then, is freedom of the press and what constitutes abridgment thereof?" he asked. "Freedom of the press is the right of the people to have a press free from governmental restraint, or threat of such restraint, affecting the performance of its function in gathering and disseminating information. A statute which imposes, or tends to impose, any restraint on the performance of that function abridges the freedom of the press. The function of the press is to gather and disseminate information in the form of news, comment and advertising. The press has but two sources of revenue from this function, advertising and circulation. The revenue from advertising must, therefore, carry the substantial burden of the newspaper function."[52]

Citing the affidavits of the president of the American Newspaper Publishers' Association and the dean of the Columbia University faculty of journalism, Deutsch maintained that the "press must be viewed as an entity. A tax on newspaper advertising is just as invalid as a tax on circulation," since the cost of newspapers to the public was subsidized by the revenues from the sale of advertising. "The power to tax is the power to destroy," he continued. "Once that power is invoked against any newspaper, any part of a newspaper, any part of a newspaper's function, or against that newspaper's subsistence, the service of that newspaper is impaired. To accomplish its destruction, it is only necessary to increase the degree or extent of impairment." "A tax on advertising published in the press is just as invalid as a tax on circulation, a tax on news columns, a tax on the expression of opinion, or a tax on newspaper publishers as a whole," Deutsch argued. "A tax on the entity, or any of its component functions, is illegal and must be so held. A power over a man's purse is a power over his will."[53]

In England, Deutsch pointed out, the press had historically been restrained by three methods, licensing, censorship, and taxation, "and of these the most efficient weapon of attack and control was taxation," while the most effective control of the press "was a tax on advertising." The Louisiana advertising tax was intended to suppress the state's newspapers that had opposed the Long regime, Deutsch argued, just as surely as the licensing system and taxes on newspapers and advertising in England had had political censorship as their purpose. Licensing of the press had been abandoned in England in 1694, he pointed out, and the newspaper taxes, the taxes on knowledge, had also been subsequently abandoned. The Louisiana advertising tax nevertheless "purports to levy a license tax on advertising—the lifeblood of a newspaper—for the privilege of engaging in business in the state." The advertising tax, he asserted, "goes even further than to threaten the ultimate exercise of the power to destroy the press through taxation. It provides a direct means to that end through the infliction of sentences and fines or imprisonment on the publisher, his managing agents and officers for failure to pay this 'license tax for the privilege of doing business.' " Again alluding to the history of freedom of the press, Deutsch declared that there "can be no better illustration of the applicability to the freedom of the press, of the doctrine that the power to tax is the power to destroy, than the history of these constitutional guarantees." "The brief of plaintiffs contains quotations from the speeches and writings of those founders of our government who were successful in making the promise of a bill of rights a condition of ratification [of the Constitution]," he told the court. "These amply evidence their demand for a liberty-of-the-press provision on the ground that the absence of such a provision would leave the press open to restraint through taxation, then so effectively used for that purpose in England."[54]

"In 1925, in *Gitlow* v. *New York,* and in a number of subsequent opinions culminating in the leading decision of *Near* v. *Minnesota* in 1931," Deutsch continued, "the Supreme Court of the United States held that liberty of the press was a . . . [right] safeguarded by the Fourteenth Amendment from invasion by the states." The Louisiana advertising tax, he noted, "is no novel attempt at restraint of freedom of the press. This form of restraint was originally conceived as a political measure in 1712 in England, existed for an historical moment in Massachusetts, was swept out of being in England only after a century and a half of struggle for liberty of thought and expression with the repeal of this 'tax on knowledge' in 1853, and was barred in the United States through constitutional provisions adopted before the end of the eighteenth century." The Louisiana advertising tax, he concluded, "is nothing more nor less than a restraint on the business of publishing newspapers in Louisiana, and must, accordingly, be declared invalid."[55]

Answering the free-press arguments of the newspaper counsel, counsel for the state pointed out that freedom of the press obviously did not mean freedom of the press to escape paying its fair share of taxes. If freedom of the press meant freedom from taxation, "the income tax law of the United States, which takes a part of every penny collected as income from the business of publishing a newspaper, would be clearly unconstitutional as Congress, by the First Amendment to the Constitution, is distinctly forbidden to make a law abridging freedom of the press." The newspapers admitted that they were legitimately subject to income taxes, property taxes, and franchise taxes, it was noted, yet they claimed the Louisiana advertising tax was somehow different and consequently unconstitutional. "It is not essential to liberty of speech and freedom of the press, as constitutionally understood," counsel for the state argued, "that profit be derived from the exercise of these rights. Nor was it ever contemplated that the constitutional guarantee should extend to charging for and selling advertising."[56]

Freedom of the press, the state contended, was limited to the "right of the citizen to speak and publish his views, subject to punishment for the abuse of that privilege. Liberty of speech and of the press is not an absolute right." Even if the plaintiff newspaper corporations were considered citizens "entitled to protection under the Fourteenth Amendment," counsel for the state concluded, "extended argument would seem to be unnecessary to demonstrate that there is no substance to the complaint that the statute under consideration infringes upon the freedom of the press."[57]

At the close of the hearing on November 23, the three-judge federal court took the *Grosjean* case under advisement, but it did not issue its decision for almost four months. Finally, on March 22, 1935, the decision of the court was announced in an opinion by Judge Wayne Borah—a decision that represented a defeat for the state, but only a partial victory for the daily newspapers. Although attorneys for the state and for the newspapers had hotly contested the issue of whether or not the federal court had jurisdiction in the case, the court in its opinion gave that issue short shrift. The court limited its discussion to the single comment that it was "of the opinion that defendant's plea to the jurisdiction should be dismissed."[58]

The court noted that there were 163 publications in Louisiana selling advertising and that the advertising tax applied to only 13 of them, the ones published by the nine companies that were plaintiffs in the case. It also pointed out that the plaintiff newspapers derived virtually all of their incomes from subscriptions and sales of advertising. While the advertising tax had been denounced both in Louisiana and in the national press as a blatant violation of freedom of the press, and while the free-press issue had been vigorously contested by the counsel for the state and the newspapers, the court chose to ignore the issue in its opinion, noting only that the tax had been assailed on that ground by the newspapers.[59]

The court instead limited its opinion to addressing the discrimination issue raised by the newspapers. "We think . . . [the advertising tax] not only violates the Constitution of this state," the court said, "but that it is also violative of the Fourteenth Amendment of the Constitution of the United States in that it does not represent a legitimate exertion of the power of classification, is purely arbitrary, and denies the equal protection of the laws to those against whom it discriminates." The court rejected the contention of the state that the differences between the rural weekly press and the urban dailies justified the classification adopted by the legislature in the advertising tax. "If the state, upon the same classification which it is seeking to uphold," the court said, "had reversed the process and taxed the country journals and exempted the metropolitan newspapers, the inequality probably would be readily conceded, but the constitutional infirmity, though more strikingly apparent, would have been the same."[60]

While it recognized that the states had the power to adopt a broad range of classifications for purposes of taxation, the court continued, "it must be remembered that the equal protection of the laws is guaranteed, and that such equal protection is denied where as here the act makes positive and direct discrimination between persons engaged in the same class of business." "No one will presume to say," it concluded, "that a newspaper whose circulation is 20,000 copies per week is not doing precisely the same business as one whose circulation is slightly below that figure."[61]

In holding that the advertising tax was violative of the Equal Protection Clause, the court cited only two decisions of the Supreme Court. In the first, the Court, over the dissents of Justices Holmes, Brandeis, Stone, and Sanford, held invalid under the Equal Protection Clause a Kentucky tax that was levied on mortgages that matured after five years, while exempting from taxation mortgages maturing within five years. In the second decision, the Supreme Court, over the dissents of Justices Cardozo, Stone, and Brandeis, invalidated under the Equal Protection Clause another Kentucky tax on gross sales of businesses graduated by volume of sales. The Court held that gross sales did not necessarily reflect the profitability of a business, with the result that under the Kentucky tax, a business with a greater volume of gross sales but which was losing money would be taxed at a greater rate than a business with a smaller volume of gross sales but which was making a profit. The three-judge court's citation of the latter case seemed to indicate that a contention of the counsel for the newspapers, that volume of circulation as a basis of taxation did not necessarily reflect the profitability of a newspaper, had had an impact on the thinking of the court.[62]

On April 4, the temporary restraining order issued by Judge Borah against the advertising tax was supplanted by an order of the three-judge court issuing a temporary injunction against Supervisor of Public Accounts Alice Grosjean prohibiting the collection of the tax. Counsel for the state and the newspapers then stipulated that the court could decide whether to make the injunction permanent on the basis of the record already before the court. On April 8 the court accordingly issued a permanent injunction prohibiting Supervisor of Public Accounts Grosjean from collecting the tax.[63]

While the newspapers affected by the advertising tax had won the case and were now no longer under any obligation to pay the tax, their victory nevertheless was not wholly satisfactory. The court had invalidated the advertising tax both under the Louisiana constitution and under the Equal Protection Clause of the Fourteenth Amendment, but it was possible that the discriminatory feature of the tax could be remedied by the passage of legislation simply applying the tax to all publications in Louisiana. As a result the dailies would find themselves in the same situation they had been in at the outset of the litigation.

The fact that the advertising tax might be revived by legislative action was troubling to the newspapers, but also disappointing was the avoidance of the freedom of the press issue by the federal court. That aspect of the decision was especially disappointing to Eberhard Deutsch, who initially had been alone among the newspaper attorneys in contending that the advertising tax was invalid on free-press grounds. Commenting on the decision of the three-judge court, Deutsch pointed out that a "ruling on the press freedom issue would have ended the newspaper tax forever in Louisiana. Under the decision, however, the state can amend the statute to remove the discriminatory feature." If the legislature in fact passed such an amendment, he continued, the new statute "could be attacked by the publishers, too, because the court left undecided the free press issue. On the other hand, the state can appeal the entire decision to the Supreme Court and all issues can be reopened."[64]

The court had resolved the jurisdictional issue in the *Grosjean* case in favor of the newspapers, Deutsch also pointed out. He suggested that the court might have rested its jurisdictional decision on the congressional statute giving the court the power to protect federal rights by injunction regardless of the amount of damages. If this were so, he suggested, it "is possible that the jurisdictional holding involves an affirmative decision that the tax impairs the freedom of the press guaranteed by the Fourteenth Amendment of the Constitution." Deutsch, however, was whistling in the dark on this point, since it was highly unlikely that the three-judge court would have resolved the important free-press issue in the *Grosjean* case by indirection in a jurisdictional ruling.[65]

Although it ignored the litigation in the *Grosjean* case, the *American Progress* did continue its ridicule of the leading personalities associated with the state's daily press while the case was pending decision in the federal court. A *Progress* cartoon portrayed these individuals as performers in a circus, among whom were "Leonard the Liverwurst," "Sir Esmond the whiner," "John the Squirt," and "Hilda, the antique queen, the Picayune damsel," who was a "cross between a lemon and a fog horn." The Long paper also published a mock analysis by "Professor Marmaduke Dingbat" of the handwriting of individuals associated with the dailies. The handwriting of "Pinky Jim Thomson" was pronounced to be that of a person with a "bad memory" who was engaged in the "rag business," while the handwriting of "Liverwurst Nicholson" was said to reveal a person "who is led around by the hand." "Gutfoot Ballard," the *Progress* analyst said, "writes in a dream and the unintelligible jargon is as meaningless as are his editorials." "Shinola Phelps" in his handwriting "crowded his words into one corner to save paper," and "he does not dot the i's or cross the t's in order to save paper. Obviously this is the handwriting of a very stingy man." Hilda Phelps Hammond was reported to write with "a fanatical hieroglyphic of an outraged woman driven into a frenzy," using a "stick dipped in mud. Two things must have caused her present condition, maybe she lost two jobs."[66]

The decision of the three-judge court in the *Grosjean* case was noted by *The Nation* magazine, which observed that much "has been heard of late from publishers about freedom of the press, which the public has been told depends on the right to fire reporters and engage children to peddle newspapers." "The Louisiana decision is a victory for a free press in realms of reality," it continued, "and is of historic importance. The right to tax the press is the right to destroy it, and as such it has not been exercised in Anglo-Saxon countries since the middle of the last century in England. Then the tax on newspapers was conspicuously applied to keep journalism from criticizing the government." "Huey Long revived the practice because he was defied by the press in his last campaign," *The Nation* added. "It was his practical application of fascism, and it should be noted by those who believe that Huey is a democrat merely because he says so."[67]

Editor & Publisher applauded the decision of the federal court in the case, while also expressing disappointment that the court had avoided the free-press issue. The advertising tax had been a punitive measure directed at "newspapers that had committed lese majesty against the self-anointed King," it said. "Just what action the State of Louisiana will now take is in doubt. It may pass a statute at a special session to cure the discriminatory features of the law which is now declared unconstitutional." If that occurred, *Editor & Publisher* continued, "publishers must push the free press case to a finish. This infamous principle must not catch root in this country." As both Eberhard Deutsch and *Editor & Publisher* had acknowledged, the initiative in the *Grosjean* case had now passed to the counsel for the state of Louisiana, and the important question that remained was whether they would appeal the court's decision. If they did, newspaper counsel would have an opportunity to argue the freedom of the press issue before the Supreme Court itself.[68]

NOTES

1. *New Orleans Times-Picayune*, March 25, 1953, pp. 1, 3.
2. T. Harry Williams, *Huey Long* (New York: Knopf, 1969), pp. 654–59.
3. *New Orleans Times-Picayune*, June 21, 1933, p. 1; June 25, 1933, p. 1.
4. Ibid., June 21, 1933, p. 8.
5. Ibid., June 26, 1933, pp. 1, 2.
6. Ibid., June 27, 1933, p. 6.
7. *American Progress*, Aug. 24, 1933, p. 4.
8. Huey P. Long Scrapbooks, vol. 23, Hill Memorial Library, Louisiana State University, Baton Rouge.
9. *New Orleans Times-Picayune*, Nov. 13, 1934, p. 6; Nov. 14, 1934, p. 12; Nov. 15, 1934, pp. 1, 8; Nov. 17, 1934, pp. 1, 4; March 25, 1953, p. 3.
10. Williams, *Long*, p. 78.
11. T. Harry Williams interview with Charles J. Rivet, June 27, 1959, in New Orleans, in the Hill Memorial Library, Louisiana State University, Baton Rouge.
12. Ibid.
13. Ibid.
14. Williams, *Long*, p. 78.
15. Record, *Grosjean* v. *American Press Co.*, 297 U.S. 233 (1936), pp. 60–61 (hereafter cited as Record).

16. Ibid., pp. 58-60.
17. Ibid., p. 60.
18. Ibid., p. 61.
19. *Editor & Publisher* 67 (Aug. 15, 1934): 30; 67 (Oct. 6, 1934): 24.
20. Record, pp. 69–70.
21. Ibid., p. 70.
22. Ibid., pp. 67–68.
23. Ibid., pp. 17–19.
24. Ibid., pp. 41–42.
25. Ibid., pp. 42–43.
26. Ibid., pp. 48–52.
27. Ibid., pp. 53–55.
28. Ibid., p. 99; *New Orleans Times-Picayune*, Nov. 24, 1934, p. 1.
29. John Wilds, *Afternoon Story: A Century of the New Orleans States-Item* (Baton Rouge: Louisiana State University Press, 1976), p. 211.
30. *New York Times*, Aug. 12, 1962, p. 81.
31. *Editor & Publisher* 66 (July 22, 1933): 5; 66 (Aug. 12, 1933): 5.
32. Ibid., 66 (Feb. 24, 1934): 36; Richard C. Cortner, *The Wagner Act Cases* (Knoxville: University of Tennessee Press, 1964), pp. 53–56.
33. *Editor & Publisher* 66 (Sept. 23, 1933): 24; 67 (Sept. 13, 1934): 24; National Labor Relations Board, Division of Economic Research, *Collective Bargaining in the Newspaper Industry*, Bulletin No. 3 (Washington, D.C.: Government Printing Office, Oct. 1936), pp. 68, 143; Cortner, *The Wagner Act Cases*, pp. 53–56.
34. *New Orleans Times-Picayune*, Nov. 24, 1934, pp. 1, 3; *New Orleans Item*, Nov. 23, 1934, pp. 1, 8. In discussing the arguments of counsel in the *Grosjean* case, I have combined the coverage of those arguments in the *Times-Picayune* and the *Item* with the arguments found in the briefs filed with the court by counsel on both sides.
35. Brief of the State, pp. 1–5. The record of the materials presented by the parties in the *Grosjean* case before the three-judge court are located in the National Archives Southwest Regional Records Center, Ft. Worth, Texas, and are filed under *American Publishing Co.* v. *Grosjean*, No. 315 in Equity. Included in these materials are the Brief of the State, Original Brief of the Plaintiffs, Reply Brief of the Plaintiffs, and the Notice of Appeal. The citation of these materials will hereafter be designated with the letters NA.
36. NA, Original Brief of the Plaintiffs, pp. 16–17, 21–26.
37. *Slaughter House Cases*, 16 Wall. 36 (1873).
38. *Orient Insurance Co.* v. *Daggs*, 172 U.S. 557, 561 (1899); *Berea College* v. *Kentucky*, 211 U.S. 45 (1908); *Liberty Warehouse Co.* v. *Burley Tobacco Marketing Association*, 276 U.S. 71, 89 (1928); NA, Brief of the State, pp. 3–6; *New Orleans Times-Picayune*, Nov. 24, 1934, pp. 1, 4.
39. *Santa Clara County* v. *Southern Pacific Railroad Co.*, 118 U.S. 394 (1886); Original Brief of Plaintiffs, pp. 21–26; NA, Reply Brief of Plaintiffs, pp. 9–12.
40. *New Orleans Item*, Nov. 23, 1934, pp. 1, 8; NA, Brief of the State, pp. 9–12; NA, Original Brief of the Plaintiffs, pp. 26–27; NA, Reply Brief of the Plaintiffs, pp. 5–7.
41. NA, Brief of the State, pp. 19, 22; *New Orleans Times-Picayune*, Nov. 24, 1934, pp. 1, 4.
42. NA, Brief of the State, pp. 23–24; NA, Original Brief of the Plaintiffs, pp. 27–33, 34–40.
43. *New Orleans Times-Picayune*, Nov. 24, 1934, pp. 1, 4; *Near* v. *Minnesota*, 283 U.S. 697 (1931).

44. *New Orleans Times-Picayune*, Nov. 24, 1934, pp. 1, 4; *New Orleans Item*, Nov. 23, 1934, pp. 1, 8; *Editor & Publisher* 67 (Dec. 1, 1934): 9, 38.

45. NA, Brief of the State, pp. 16–18.

46. Ibid., p. 17.

47. *New Orleans Times-Picayune*, Nov. 24, 1934, pp. 1, 4.

48. Ibid.

49. NA, Original Brief of the Plaintiffs, p. 54.

50. Ibid., p. 69.

51. NA, Brief of the State, pp. 13–15.

52. *New Orleans Times-Picayune*, Nov. 24, 1934, pp. 1, 4.

53. Ibid.; *New Orleans Item*, Nov. 23, 1934, pp. 1, 8.

54. *New Orleans Times-Picayune*, Nov. 24, 1934, pp. 1, 4; *New Orleans Item*, Nov. 23, 1934, pp. 1, 8.

55. *New Orleans Times-Picayune*, Nov. 24, 1934, pp. 1, 4; *New Orleans Item*, Nov. 23, 1934, pp. 1, 8; NA, Original Brief of the Plaintiffs, p. 90.

56. NA, Brief of the State, p. 18.

57. Ibid.

58. *American Press Co.* v. *Grosjean*, 10 F.Supp. 161 (D.C., E.D. La., March 22, 1935); *New Orleans Times-Picayune*, March 23, 1935, p. 2.

59. 10 F.Supp. 161, 163.

60. 10 F.Supp. 161, 163–64.

61. 10 F.Supp. 161, 164.

62. *Louisville Gas & Electric Co.* v. *Coleman*, 277 U.S. 32 (1928); *Stewart Dry Goods Co.* v. *Lewis*, 294 U.S. 550 (1935).

63. NA, Order for Temporary Injunction, April 4, 1935; NA, Order Issuing Permanent Injunction, April 8, 1935.

64. *Editor & Publisher* 67 (March 30, 1935): 9.

65. Ibid.

66. *American Progress*, Jan. 4, 1935, p. 8; Feb. 1, 1935, p. 3.

67. *The Nation* 140 (April 3, 1935): 373–74.

68. *Editor & Publisher* 67 (March 30, 1935): 24.

Chapter 7

The Appeal to the Supreme Court

> Of all the forces that conspired, incited and urged the removal of Huey P. Long from politics in Louisiana there is none whose hands are so stained with his blood as the daily newspapers of Louisiana. The people know only too well now, and it will never be forgotten as long as decent people dwell in Louisiana, that these very newspapers exposed Huey Long to the death he experienced.
>
> —*American Progress,* October 24, 1935

> Huey Long was a Hitler in every sense but one. Hitler controls the press of Germany. Huey Long did not control the press of Louisiana, and, in particular, he did not control the more influential papers. He knew, and so did every intelligent citizen of Louisiana, that in that fact, and in that fact alone, lay the possibility of his overthrow.
>
> —*Chicago Tribune,* February 12, 1936

♦ Between the Civil War and the 1920s, the United States Supreme Court periodically faced burdensome caseloads that threatened to impede the performance of its function within the governmental system. When Melville W. Fuller became chief justice in 1888, for example, the Court had a three-year backlog of cases pending on its docket because litigants were appealing more cases to the Court than it could possibly decide during each term. Congress finally responded to the Court's plight by passing the U.S. courts of appeals act in 1891, creating intermediate courts of appeals to hear appeals of cases from the lower federal courts before they reached the Supreme Court. If litigants had one appellate review of lower federal court decisions at a level below the

Supreme Court, it was believed, fewer litigants would seek review of their cases in the Supreme Court. This proved to be the case, and within a short time after the passage of the courts of appeals act, the Supreme Court was abreast of its docket.[1]

The act of 1891, however, proved to be only a temporary remedy to the overcrowding of the Supreme Court's docket, and by the 1920s the proliferation of federal litigation again resulted in the Court being unable to keep up with its caseload. When William Howard Taft became chief justice in 1921, the Court was lagging two years behind its docket. Chief Justice Taft responded by appointing a committee of the justices to draft legislation to alleviate the problem, and the result was the "Judges' bill," which was passed by Congress as the Judiciary Act of 1925. The act provided that most cases appealable to the Supreme Court would reach the Court via petitions for writs of certiorari. Since the Court had the option of issuing a writ of certiorari or of not doing so, the effect of the Judiciary Act of 1925 was to give the Court discretionary control over most of its docket by deciding whether writs of certiorari should be issued in cases appealed to it. A denial of certiorari by the Court simply meant that it would not hear the case, and in only those cases the Court considered of sufficient public importance was certiorari granted.[2]

Although most cases were appealed to the Court by petitions for writs of certiorari after 1925, there remained some cases that were brought to the Court by "appeal," and technically the Court was required to hear them. Among the appeal cases were ones brought to the Court directly from the special three-judge district courts that had been mandated by Congress in 1910. Following the decision of the three-judge court in the *Grosjean* case, Attorney General Gaston Porterie and Charles Rivet therefore had to decide whether the state should appeal the case to the Supreme Court by filing an "appeal" rather than a petition for a writ of certiorari.

The permanent injunction against the Louisiana advertising tax had been issued by the three-judge court on April 8, 1935, and Attorney General Porterie and Charles Rivet had ninety days from that date during which to consider whether to appeal the decision. Consequently, there ensued over two months of uncertainty for counsel for the newspapers as they waited to learn if they would be afforded the opportunity of renewing their free-press challenge of the advertising tax before the high court. Finally, however, on June 20, Porterie and Rivet filed with the district court a notice of appeal of *Grosjean* v. *American Press Co.*, as the case would now be styled, insuring that the battle over the constitutionality of the advertising tax would continue before the Supreme Court in Washington.[3]

During the months that the *Grosjean* case was being litigated, Huey Long appeared to be determined to fully live up to the label that most

Louisiana newspapers had long since conferred upon him—that of dictator. During a breathtaking series of sessions of the legislature in 1934–35, he won approval of measure after measure centralizing control of almost all governmental power in the hands of the state—that is, himself. Local self-government and any centers of political power other than his own were effectively destroyed in Louisiana.

In addition to the measures designed to control the dissemination of information by newspapers and movies, the Kingfish centralized under state control the police forces of the state. New Orleans was stripped of the control of its police force and firemen in 1934 when the legislature approved a measure placing those forces in the hands of a state board of police commissioners, and the state civil service commission was given the power to hire and fire police and firemen outside New Orleans. The Bureau of Criminal Identification (BCI), a special branch of the state police, was expanded and its power strengthened, with members of the BCI remaining anonymous to the public and known only by a few members of the Long organization. Also in 1934, the appointment of all parish deputy sheriffs was required to be approved by the BCI, and in 1935 the hiring and firing of all parish and municipal employees were placed in the hands of the state civil service commission. The Louisiana attorney general was authorized to supersede local district attorneys at any time on behalf of the state. Finally, after the governor was granted power to call out the National Guard for any reason and to grant reprieves from any court orders, the Guard could be used for any purpose free of judicial limitation.[4]

Local power from independent sources of revenue was undermined by legislation depriving local units of government of the power to issue liquor licenses and centralizing that function in the hands of the supervisor of public accounts. A state tax commission was also created with the power to change any local tax assessments. A state bond and tax board was granted power to approve any loan, grant, or bond issue proposed by parish and municipal governments, which thus effectively placed federal aid to local units of government in the hands of the state. Smashing one of the few pockets of resistance to his supreme rule, Long secured legislation prohibiting New Orleans from collecting real estate, license, or other taxes. Deprived of any source of revenue, the New Orleans city government was consequently forced to surrender on any terms the Kingfish dictated.[5]

Striking at local control of the public schools, the Kingfish secured legislative approval of a state budget committee with the power to hire, fire, and set the salaries of all public school teachers, with the resultant destruction of the most significant powers of local school boards. Since Baton Rouge was another pocket of resistance, Long also obtained passage of legislation specifing that one-half of the members of the East Baton Rouge Parish government were to be appointed by the governor. In Alexandria, where Long had been greeted with rotten eggs in the fall of 1933, the mayor's office was declared vacant by additional legislation. In Shreveport, also a center of opposition to the Kingfish, leaders complained that the city was receiving little benefit from the road construction program. "What we ought to do," Long arrogantly replied, "is send a crew of men out with dynamite and pickaxes to tear up the roads you have."[6]

Although his attempt to tax oil refined in the state had triggered the legislative revolt that had led to his impeachment in 1929, in December 1934 Long nevertheless struck at his old enemy Standard Oil by securing legislative approval of a five-cents-per-barrel tax on the refining of oil. Standard Oil subsequently surrendered to the senator, and the Kingfish approved a compromise under which the company would receive a rebate of 80 percent of the oil tax in return for its agreement to use Louisiana oil in 80 percent of its refining operations in the state. On another front, Long contacted mobster Frank Costello and struck a deal by which Costello would control gambling in New Orleans in return for a kickback from the proceeds to the Long organization.[7]

As this accumulation of power in the hands of one man occurred in a manner unprecedented in the history of the Republic, the stunned enemies of the Kingfish could only observe from the political sidelines. His domination of the legislature was absolute, and as the *New York Times* reported, watching "Long and his legislature at work is like stepping through the looking glass with Alice." "The dictator's vagaries, abuses and tyrannous excesses have been carried to such extremes that no aggression of his causes surprises nowadays," the *Times-Picayune* complained during this period. "But all decent Americans here in Louisiana and throughout the United States stand amazed at the abject servility and obedience to the royal whims, rendered by majorities in both houses." Representative Rupert Payton of Caddo Parish conceded in frustration that since "we are plainly headed for Hitlerism in Louisiana, we might as well give the agents of Senator Long the right to shoot down people." Beginning with the summer of 1934, the thoroughly routed anti-Long forces in Louisiana increasingly turned from hopeful talk of defeating Long electorally to rather open discussion of his assassination and the use of force to reclaim the governmental process in the state. There came to be, as one anti-Longite said, a certain "wildness in the air."[8]

During 1934–35, the anti-Long opposition organized a paramilitary organization, the Square Deal Association, which debated using violence and assassination to recapture the state government from the Long forces. The largest concentration of Square Dealers was in East Baton Rouge Parish, and when the state ordered the firing of all parish employees there in January 1935, heavily armed Square Dealers seized and occupied the parish courthouse. Governor O. K. Allen, acting on the Kingfish's orders, called out the National Guard to occupy Baton Rouge, which was placed under martial law until the following July. Under martial law decrees, two or more persons were forbidden to gather in public places and the Manship papers were prohibited from publishing anything critical of the state government. On January 26, the Square Dealers and the National Guard clashed briefly at the Baton Rouge airport, but the Square Dealers were quickly routed with tear gas and most surrendered, while one was shot and wounded.[9]

A formal hearing to investigate the Square Dealers was convened by Attorney General Gaston Porterie, and with the Kingfish himself conducting the questioning of witnesses, informers who had infiltrated the Square Deal Association claimed that its members had plotted to assassinate Long. One witness said he had been offered ten thousand dollars to carry out the assassination. Reporting on the investigation of the alleged plot, the *American Progress* asserted that the Square Deal Association had been involved in "one of the most sensational conspiracies in the annals of American politics." Standard Oil and the state's newspapers were responsible for inciting violence against Long, the *Progress* added. "The lying newspapers of Louisiana stand today with blood dripping from their presses." Not only had the press been inciting the use of violence against the Kingfish, but it had remained silent and failed to condemn the Square Deal assassination plot. "The newspapers have convinced even the most charitable minded citizens," the *Progress* charged, "that there is nothing they would rather do than print their sheets with blood instead of printer's ink."[10]

If his enemies had come to despair of ever defeating Huey Long electorally, he himself had come to mistrust elections and to doubt the permanence of his hold on the voters of Louisiana. Ordering the legislature summoned to another special session in April 1935, he moved to block any possibility that he could be ousted by the voters in any forthcoming election. Since the only real selection of political leaders in the state occurred in the Democratic primary elections, the Kingfish obtained passage of legislation centralizing the counting of primary election ballots in the hands of the state. Supervisors of elections were created in each parish, two out of three of whom were to be appointed by the governor, and they were empowered to select the election commissioners and poll watchers in each parish. The counting of votes would henceforth be in the grasp of the Long organization.[11]

As the Kingfish's election measures were being passed by the legislature, Representative Mason Spencer of Madison Parish spoke in opposition to them in what he admitted was a futile effort. He was "not simple enough to believe that what I am about to say will change a single vote in the house," Spencer said. "However, I desire to sound a warning and go on record before the people of this state and particularly the people of my parish." Looking directly at Long, who was on the house floor as usual, Spencer warned that when "this ugly bill is boiled down in its own juice it disfranchises white people of Louisiana. I am no prophet, but I know that any attempt of this legislature to disfranchise the white voter of Louisiana will 'ride through the state on the pale horse of Death.' "[12]

"I maintain that the right to vote means the right to count the vote," Spencer continued. "To deprive the people of this right is putting too much power in the hands of one man who is mortal." Alluding to recent events in the state, he charged that the people of Baton Rouge and Alexandria had been deprived of their rights and that there had been "murmurs and plots—these are the privileges of slaves." "We have soldiers here with guns and we have armed men in this capitol," he concluded. "The great leader walks among us and there are shouts of 'Hail Caesar.' I am not one who shouts 'Hail Caesar' because I have read history and know what happened to Caesar."[13]

The Kingfish attended the 1935 session of Congress, which lasted from January to August, and during the session he opposed most of Roosevelt's second New Deal program, frequently by filibustering in the Senate. On the last day of the session on August 26, Long filibustered the appropriations needed by the administration to launch the Social Security program that he had opposed, forcing the administration to divert funds from other programs for that purpose. When Congress adjourned, Long traveled by train to New York, then to Pennsylvania, and on to Missouri and Oklahoma, where he addressed a Labor Day crowd in Oklahoma City. He then entrained for Dallas, drove by car to Shreveport, and arrived in Baton Rouge on September 3, when he promptly ordered Governor Allen to summon yet another special session of the legislature.[14]

Among the measures the Kingfish intended to have enacted during the special session were ones requiring the registration of sawed-off shotguns, rifles, and gas grenades with the Bureau of Criminal Identification and prohibiting any federal official or employee from spending federal funds in the state if in the opinion of state officials the expenditures would violate states' rights under the Tenth Amendment of the Constitution. An additional measure was designed to gerrymander the judicial district of Judge B. Henry Pavy, one of the few state district judges who remained an open opponent of Longism. Pavy's reelection was to be prevented by combining the judge's home parish of St. Landry with three pro-Long parishes to form a new judicial district. Although the evidence is conflicting, it was possible that Long also intended to attack Pavy personally by claiming that the Pavy family was tainted with black ancestry, a tactic he frequently used against his enemies.[15]

On the evening of September 8, the Kingfish was on the floor of the house as was his custom during legislative sessions, and as he was leaving, he spotted Representative Mason Spencer, who had warned him of the deadly danger the election control legislation would create. Joking with Spencer, Long told the legislator, "You remind me of [an] old nigger woman." Long then proceeded out of the house chamber to the governor's office, only to reappear moments later. He reentered the corridor outside the governor's office, where he was shot by Dr. Carl Austin Weiss, a Baton Rouge ear, nose, and throat surgeon. The Kingfish's bodyguards immediately pumped a fusillade of shots into Weiss, continuing to fire into his body as it lay lifeless on the floor of the corridor.[16]

Long was rushed to Our Lady of the Lake Hospital, where he underwent surgery, but his internal hemorrhaging continued and doctors considered the senator too weak for additional surgery. Early in the morning of September 10, Huey Long died after having survived the shooting for thirty hours. An estimated 175,000 people attended his funeral on September 12, as he was buried in a sunken garden near the high-rise capitol building he had built. He was forty-two years old.[17]

Why Carl Austin Weiss assassinated Huey Long, or even if he did, remains a puzzle to the present time. Essentially apolitical, Dr. Weiss was highly successful in his profession, and he appeared to be living a happy and contented life in Baton Rouge with his wife and recently born son. Yvonne Weiss was the daughter of Judge Henry Pavy, whose reelection was to be prevented by the gerrymander Long sponsored, and it has been speculated that Weiss acted out of resentment of the Kingfish's treatment of his father-in-law. Another explanation for Weiss's behavior, and probably a more likely one, was that he had learned of Long's plan to charge the Pavy family with black ancestry and had attacked the senator to protect his family from what he considered disgrace. Others have speculated that Weiss did not shoot Huey Long at all and that the Kingfish was killed instead by a bullet fired by his bodyguards after Weiss accosted the senator in the capitol. Still others have suggested that Long was shot by both Weiss and one of his bodyguards. The possibility of finding out the motive for the Kingfish's assassination ended in the fusillade of bullets that killed Weiss on September 8. He was buried the day following his death, and as James

Clarke, the leading expert on American assassins, has said, his funeral was "the largest of any assassin in American history."[18]

Huey Long, the *American Progress* proclaimed, was the "president who was assassinated before he was elected," and his assassin had been "incited by a steady campaign of slander and lies." Comparing the Long and Lincoln assassinations, the *Progress* maintained that the assassins of both had been inspired by contemporary newspapers that had falsely accused both of being tyrants. In an editorial titled "They Print Their Newspapers with Blood!" the *Progress* charged that during the "past five years the newspapers of Louisiana, that is, the big daily papers, not the honest country weeklies, have been printing articles defaming the late Senator Huey P. Long. While he was alive every day you could read in their lying sheets stories about the 'dictator,' the 'tyrant,' the 'czar,' the 'kaiser of Louisiana' and all their other terms of abuse."[19]

Contrary to the distortions that had appeared in the press, the *Progress* argued, the people had overwhelmingly approved everything Huey Long had done on their behalf. "[W]e say today, October 24, 1935, in this newspaper on this page that when the lying daily newspapers of Louisiana unqualifiedly, systematically and persistently declared Huey Long to be a liberty-destroyer, a dictator and a tyrant, we say that they were lying when they said it, we say that they knew in their black hearts they were lying, and furthermore—Of all the forces that conspired, incited and urged the removal of Huey P. Long from politics in Louisiana there is none whose hands are so stained with his blood as the daily newspapers of Louisiana." "The people know only too well now," the *Progress* declared, "and it will never be forgotten as long as decent people dwell in Louisiana, that these very newspapers exposed Huey Long to the death he experienced."[20]

Huey Long thus did not live to learn the fate of his attempt to censor the Louisiana dailies, but his death did not affect the decision of Attorney General Porterie to appeal the *Grosjean* case to the Supreme Court. Counsel for the state and the newspapers were notified that oral arguments in the case would be heard by the Court on January 14, 1936. Charles Rivet, still acting as a special assistant attorney general, was designated by Attorney General Porterie to make the oral argument on behalf of the state of Louisiana.

For the newspapers challenging the advertising tax, the choice of which counsel should present the oral argument was a more difficult one. Eberhard Deutsch had not only mapped out the strategy that had guided counsel for the newspapers thus far, but it was also his research on the history of freedom of the press that had guided the free-press arguments against the tax. The Louisiana publishers, however, wished to impress upon the Supreme Court that the issues raised by the advertising tax were not merely of local but of national importance. It was decided that this could best be accomplished if the oral argument was made in part by Elisha Hanson, the general counsel of the American Newspaper Publishers' Association. Esmond Phelps was also designated to make the oral argument on behalf of the Louisiana newspapers. Eberhard Deutsch, therefore, did not participate in the argument, since the rules of the Court allowed no more than two attorneys to be heard on each side of a case. Deutsch did have the satisfaction, however, of having the fruits of his research on the history of freedom of the press included in an appendix to the brief filed by newspaper counsel in the *Grosjean* case.[21]

When Charles Rivet, Esmond Phelps, and Elisha Hanson arrived in Washington to argue the *Grosjean* case in January 1936, for the first time since the Civil War era the Supreme Court was meeting in new quarters. From the Civil War era to 1935, the Court heard arguments in the old senate chamber in the basement of the Capitol. The old senate chamber provided a small albeit decorous courtroom, but the accommodations for the Court in the Capitol did not afford sufficient working space for the nine justices. Consequently, until the 1930s, the justices customarily maintained their own offices and libraries in their homes, where most of the work of the Court was done.

Chief Justice William Howard Taft, however, possessed strong convictions regarding the important role the federal judiciary performed in the governmental system, and he concluded that the dignity and independence of the Supreme Court as the third branch of the national government required that the Court should have its own building. Taft therefore undertook an intensive lobbying campaign to convince Congress to appropriate money for one, and his lobbying proved successful when Congress appropriated money in 1929 to acquire a site just east of the Capitol for a building for the Court. Taft was also successful in winning congressional approval of construction funds for the new building, which was finally completed in 1935. Beginning with the fall term that year, the Supreme Court for the first time in its history had its own building providing not only a courtroom where the Court heard oral arguments but also adequate office space for all of the justices and their clerks and staff.[22]

The Court before which Rivet, Phelps, and Hanson would argue on January 14 was deeply divided along ideological lines and was increasingly becoming the focal point of a national debate regarding the proper role it should play in the governmental system. There were four ardently conservative justices—George Sutherland, James McReynolds, Willis Van Devanter, and Pierce Butler—who were ideologically opposed to governmental regulation of economic affairs and consequently were generally hostile to much of the New Deal program sponsored by President Franklin Roosevelt. Three members of the Court—Louis Brandeis, Benjamin N. Cardozo, and Harlan Fiske Stone—were usually identified as constituting the liberal bloc on the Court, and as the 1930s progressed these justices were frequently aligned in favor of upholding the constitutional validity of New Deal measures. Chief Justice Charles Evans Hughes and Justice Owen J. Roberts tended to occupy a more centrist position, and the vote of at least one of them was crucial in determining the outcome in closely divided cases. As New Deal programs began to be challenged before the Court during 1935–36, either Hughes or Roberts, or both of them, frequently sided with the Court's conservatives, with the result that key New Deal measures were declared unconstitutional.[23]

In 1935, however, the Court was unanimous in declaring unconstitutional the centerpiece of the New Deal's economic recovery program, the National Industrial Recovery Act (NIRA) of 1933. Adopting what President Roosevelt denounced as a "horse and buggy definition of interstate commerce," the Court held that the NIRA exceeded the power of Congress to regulate interstate commerce and involved an unconstitutional delegation of legislative power to the executive branch.[24] When the *Grosjean* case was pending, the Court was also confronted with several other key cases raising the question of the proper scope of governmental power to regulate the economy. Two laws were being challenged before the Court: the New Deal's recovery program for agriculture, the Agricultural Adjustment Act of 1933, and the Bituminous Coal Conservation Act, which was intended to stabilize prices and labor relations in the coal industry. Also pending before the Court was a case challenging the validity of the Tennessee Valley Authority, a government-controlled program designed to provide inexpensive electrical power for the southeastern region of the country. Touching a sensitive issue of economic regulation was an additional challenge to New York's legislation setting minimum wages for women workers. Finally, in the field of civil liberties, the Court would face not only the free-press issues raised by the *Grosjean* case but also the constitutional validity of the use of coerced confessions in a state capital case from Mississippi.

Opening the argument on behalf of the state of Louisiana in the *Grosjean* case on January 14, Charles Rivet attacked the decision of the three-judge court and again asserted that the lower court had been without any legitimate jurisdiction in the case. The three-judge court in its decision, he argued, "made no reference whatsoever to the pleadings and the affidavits filed on behalf of . . . [Supervisor of Public Accounts Grosjean], but proceeded with its findings of fact and conclusions of law practically as though no defenses or proof whatsoever had been urged or presented by her." The lower court had ignored the affidavits filed by the state, he pointed out, which indicated that there were significant differences between the small, weekly newspapers that were exempt from the advertising tax and the large metropolitan dailies that were subject to it. Those differences, Rivet argued, fully justified the legislature's classification applying the tax to newspapers which sold twenty thousand copies or more per week while exempting those papers whose circulations were more limited.[25]

As he had in the lower court, Rivet again contended that the *Grosjean* case did not meet the requirements of federal jurisdiction because each of the newspapers affected by the advertising tax had not shown that it would suffer at least the three thousand dollars in damages that were required. "Though this serious question of jurisdiction was called squarely to the attention of the statutory [three-judge] court," he charged, "it gave no consideration to it in its written reasons other than to say: 'The court is of the opinion that defendant's plea to the jurisdiction should be dismissed.' " Notwithstanding the clear lack of jurisdiction, he continued, "the three judges enjoined defendant from attempting to collect the tax even by suit, instead of dismissing the bill [of complaint] for want of jurisdiction."[26]

Even if valid jurisdiction had existed in the case, Rivet also again asserted, the lower court should not have exercised its power to enjoin the collection of the advertising tax because the affected newspapers had an adequate remedy in the state courts. In proceedings to enforce the tax in the state courts, "all available defenses could be presented and all federal questions disposed of in due course of law. The pretense that equitable relief is necessary in order to avoid a multiplicity of suits, finds no support in fact or under settled jurisprudence," Rivet argued. If the tax had not been enjoined by the lower court, "the issue herein would have been settled by one suit in a court of competent jurisdiction in the state, which suit would have long since been settled by final judgment of the Supreme Court of Louisiana."[27]

Before the Court, Esmond Phelps presented the arguments regarding jurisdiction and equal protection, while Elisha Hanson argued the free-press objections to the advertising tax. Answering Rivet's jurisdictional contentions, Phelps pointed out that the three-thousand-dollar amount had been met by most of the newspapers. Even if none had met it, however, the congressional statute would apply that conferred upon the federal courts jurisdiction to hear suits for injunctions against state officials who had violated, or were threatening to violate, federally protected rights regardless of the amount alleged in damages. Challenging the advertising tax in the state courts, Phelps again pointed out, would have exposed the newspapers and their agents to multiple civil and criminal suits by the state. At no time while the *Grosjean* case was pending in the lower court had the state sought permission from the federal court to bring an enforcement suit with an offer to stay further proceedings against the newspapers and their agents. Consequently, he maintained, the three-judge court had properly exercised jurisdiction in the case and enjoined the collection of the tax by Supervisor of Public Accounts Grosjean.[28]

On the issue of equal protection, Charles Rivet argued that the affidavits from the publishers of weekly newspapers submitted by the state in the lower court clearly demonstrated not only that the weeklies were distinct in both the size and mode of their operations but also that there existed no significant competition for advertising between the metropolitan dailies and the state's weeklies. The three-judge court had ignored this evidence, he pointed out, and because "the state in taxing metropolitan newspapers did not include the small country journals, and notwithstanding the differences disclosed by the record between the two businesses, the lower court held that if one newspaper was taxed for the privilege of selling advertising, all newspapers must be so taxed."[29]

"Long ago this Court announced the principle, from which it has never departed, that the restriction which requires that the essential power of taxation in the states shall not be so exercised as to deny the equal protection of the laws does not compel the adoption of an iron rule of equal taxation, nor prevent variety or differences in taxation, or discretion in the selection of subjects, or of the classification for taxation of properties, businesses, trades, callings or occupations," Rivet pointed out. "That a discrimination in favor of a certain class does not make a statute arbitrary if the discrimination is founded upon a reasonable distinction, or if any state of facts reasonably can be conceived to sustain it, and that such differences need not be great . . . [are] made abundantly clear by the past decisions of this Court."[30]

"We respectfully submit that the state legislature reasonably might have determined that there was fair ground for distinction between newspapers having a circulation of more than 20,000 copies per week, and those falling below that number," Rivet told the Court. On the record presented in the lower court, "there is no basis for holding that . . . [the legislature's] action was arbitrary, capricious, or wholly unreasonable." Furthermore, he contended, "the plaintiffs have utterly failed to show just ground in support of their complaint that the statute here involved deprives them of the equal protection of the laws."[31]

Disputing Rivet's equal-protection contentions, Esmond Phelps asserted that the Louisiana advertising tax "is clearly in conflict with the settled jurisprudence of this Court that a classification must be reasonable, not arbitrary, and must rest upon some ground of difference having a fair and substantial relation to the object of the legislation, so that all persons similarly circumstanced shall be treated alike." The advertising tax did not meet these standards, Phelps maintained, because it applied only to the sale of advertising by the thirteen metropolitan dailies out of 163 publications in the state, while ignoring other forms of advertising such as radio, streetcar, and billboard ads, and that published by the state's weeklies.[32]

Rivet's contention that the differences between the weeklies and the dailies justified the taxing of the latter but not the former, Phelps argued, was without merit and was unsupported by the record in the case. "On the contrary," he said, "the affidavits filed by the . . . [state] fail to show that there is any substantial difference between . . . [the weeklies and the dailies] except as to the size of business and as to the volume of national advertising appearing therein. There is not even a suggestion that the country newspapers do not still continue to carry a substantial volume of local advertising." Raising the possibility that the application of the tax to the dailies but not the weeklies might serve a legitimate state policy, Justice Brandeis suggested during oral argument that the state might be seeking to foster a diverse rural press. "That would be a dangerous doctrine," Phelps responded. "This Court has never held that mere size is a ground for discrimination."[33]

On the freedom of the press issue, Charles Rivet continued his rather puzzling strategy of denying that the federal Constitution guaranteed freedom of the press against impairment by the states. "The First Amendment to the federal Constitution imposes no restriction upon the states with reference to abridging the freedom of the press. The prohibition is directed only against Congress," he told the Court. "Complainants contend that by effect of the Fourteenth Amendment, legislatures of the states are prohibited from passing laws infringing the freedom of the press. This theory finds no support in the jurisprudence of this Court." Again Rivet asserted that the newspapers were claiming a right of freedom of the press as a privilege and immunity of national citizenship. The newspapers affected by the advertising tax were corporations, and corporations were not "citizens" whose privileges and immunities were protected by the Privileges and Immunities Clause of the Fourteenth Amendment from impairment by the states, he argued. There was nothing to the contrary in *Gitlow* v. *New York* and *Near* v. *Minnesota* "upon which . . . [the newspapers] relied below as in each of these cases the complainant was a citizen of the United States and not an artificial person." "Suppose Congress passed a law prohibiting publication of a newspaper in the City of Washington by a corporation, would that violate freedom of the press?" Justice Sutherland asked. Rivet conceded that it would, but pointed out that the Louisiana statute did not prohibit publication and only taxed the sale of advertising by newspapers.[34]

Moving to more solid ground, Rivet argued that "as pointed out in *Near* v. *Minnesota*, the chief purpose of the constitutional protection of liberty of the press is to prevent previous restraints upon publication." The advertising tax clearly did not impose a requirement of governmental approval or censorship of material prior to its publication, he pointed out, but merely taxed the gross receipts of newspapers from the sale of advertising. "Nowhere has it ever been held that a person or corporation engaged in the publishing business is exempt from taxation." Indeed, in order to "avoid insurmountable objections," he maintained, the newspapers conceded the validity of property, franchise, and income taxes as applied to the press, but unaccountably contended that a tax on advertising was somehow unconstitutional.[35]

"If there is any burden upon liberty of speech and freedom of the press, it is imposed by the . . . [newspaper] corporations who are profiting by engaging in the business of selling or charging for the use of their columns for expression of views or the presentation of the merit of commercial products," Rivet told the Court. "The state statute does not censure or restrict free expression of opinions. It merely requires of those who engage in the profitable business of making others pay for the expression of their views, or for advertising their business, a small contribution for the support of government," he concluded. "There is neither substance, nor a federal question, in the complaint that the statute under consideration abridges liberty of speech or the freedom of the press."[36]

To demonstrate to the Court that the advertising tax was in fact intended as a restraint on the expression of political opinions in the Louisiana press, Esmond Phelps read the "lying newspapers" circular which had been distributed by the Long forces during the 1934 legislative session. The passage from it in which Senator Long and Governor Allen had characterized the advertising tax as a "tax on lying, two cents per lie" aroused considerable amusement among the justices. Phelps also quoted Long's subsequent speech in which he admitted that the Lake Charles newspaper had not opposed him and that he would have preferred exempting the paper from the tax for that reason. Phelps used the quotes from Long to indicate that the tax had been intended to punish the affected newspapers for the opinions they had published.[37]

Picking up on the point Phelps had made, Elisha Hanson argued that there could be no other conclusion from the record in the *Grosjean* case than that the advertising tax was intended to punish the newspapers that had opposed the Long regime. The tax "is limited in its applicability to but thirteen newspapers out of a total of 163 in the State of Louisiana, . . . of which thirteen newspapers twelve were active in their opposition to the dominant political group in the state, which group controlled the legislature and at whose dictates the legislature passed the law," Hanson pointed out. Justice Butler interrupted to ask if the advertising tax would be valid if it applied to all of the newspapers in the state, and Hanson replied, "No, sir. I don't believe such a tax is within the Constitution." The advertising tax "would tend to curtail circulation, would it not?" Justice Sutherland asked. "Yes," Hanson responded. "It would also turn the business of one newspaper group over to another."[38]

In *Near* v. *Minnesota*, the Court had squarely held that the freedom of the press was protected from abridgment by the states by the Due Process Clause and not the Privileges and Immunities Clause, Hanson pointed out. The state was attempting "to distinguish between persons and corporations in the application of the Fourteenth Amendment to the sacred fundamental rights guaranteed under the Bill of Rights," he argued. "This Court, many years ago, held that corporations are persons within the meaning" of the Fourteenth Amendment. "Newspaper publishers, whether natural or artificial persons, were not given this great right as a matter of personal right to the exclusion of others," he told the Court. "Rather, they occupy the position of trustees of a right granted to all of the people. By reason of their peculiar position, it is their solemn duty to protect the press against hostile action. They and only they can do so."[39]

The record in the *Grosjean* case amply demonstrated that newspapers were dependent for their economic survival upon two sources of revenue, that from subscribers and that from advertisers, Hanson pointed out. Both sources of revenue "constitute the lifeblood of a newspaper and anything which depletes the revenues of a newspaper from either source, impairs the ability of that paper to serve its function," he continued. "The principle that the power to tax is the power to destroy has been imbedded in our jurisprudence since the decision of this Court in *McCulloch* v. *Maryland*. . . . When the power to tax exists, there is no limit on the legislature's discretion as to the amount of the tax. If it has the right to tax at all, it has the right, if it so desires, to tax the particular business right out of existence," he argued. "If the legislature can tax advertising, when published in a newspaper, it can tax news, or it can tax comment as and when they are published. If the legislature can tax advertising receipts two percent, as it did in this case, it can tax advertising right out of existence." "But . . . [the advertising tax] has not been raised," Justice Stone interjected. "Because it has been enjoined," Hanson replied. "We were told if it did not shut us up it would be raised."[40]

The history of freedom of the press consisted in large part of the struggle of the press in England to free itself from political restraints, including licensing, censorship, seditious libel, and taxation, Hanson pointed out. "The historical background of the First Amendment was fully discussed by the Court in its decision in *Near* v. *Minnesota*," he continued. "The real issue there, as here, was over the attempt by the legislature to exercise a power prohibited by the Constitution." The generation that established the Constitution was well aware that a principal method of political control of the press in England was through taxation. The demand for a bill of rights in the Constitution was in part motivated by a fear that unless press freedom were protected, the press might be subjected to similar taxation in this country, Hanson argued.[41]

"Therefore, it must be concluded, that the framers of the Bill of Rights had no mental reservations when they drafted the First Amendment," Hanson said in conclusion. "That amendment was written to protect the people in their right to have a press free from restraint from whatsoever hostile source the threat of restraint might spring, and from any method sought to be applied—whether that method be censorship, licensing, taxation, seditious libel, injunction, writ of attachment or anything else."[42]

With the conclusion of the arguments in the *Grosjean* case, the fate of the Louisiana advertising tax was in the hands of the Court. Assuming the objections to the jurisdiction of the lower court were rejected, the Court could, as the three-judge court had done, choose to decide the case on the equal-protection issue alone. If this were the course chosen by the Court, the *Grosjean* case would have little lasting significance, but would merely join a host of other cases in which state taxes were held to run afoul of the Equal Protection Clause of the Fourteenth Amendment. Only if the Court chose to reach the freedom of the press issue in the case, therefore, would the *Grosjean* case assume the status of a landmark in the jurisprudence of the Court.

The probability of a divided Court in the *Grosjean* case, and most likely a closely divided Court, seemed unavoidable regardless of whether the case were decided on free-press or equal-protection grounds. The Court in *Near* v. *Minnesota* had divided five to four on the question of the constitutionality of the Minnesota gag law, and with the exception of Benjamin N. Cardozo, who had replaced Oliver Wendell Holmes in 1932, the membership of the Court remained the same as when the *Near* case was decided.

On the other hand, the Court had also been increasingly divided over the application of the Equal Protection Clause to the constitutional validity of state taxing policies. The Court's conservatives—Sutherland,

Van Devanter, Butler, and McReynolds—favored subjecting state tax classifications to substantially more stringent standards under the Equal Protection Clause than did the Court's liberals—Brandeis, Stone, and Cardozo. The Court consequently had a tendency to divide ideologically when deciding the validity of state taxing policies on equal-protection grounds just as it did when confronted with other issues involving governmental regulation of economic affairs. While the Court's conservatives had generally prevailed in cases involving challenges to state taxes on equal-protection grounds during the 1920s, the liberals, joined by Chief Justice Hughes and Justice Roberts, began to score some victories in these cases during the 1930s. In any event, if the justices reached the equal-protection issue in the *Grosjean* case, there was the likelihood of a badly divided Court.[43]

In the conference of the Court following the oral arguments in the *Grosjean* case, the justices apparently voted to invalidate the Louisiana advertising tax on equal-protection grounds and the majority opinion was assigned to Justice Sutherland. Justice Cardozo disagreed with equal protection as the basis for invalidating the tax, but rather argued in a concurring opinion that the tax should be invalidated as a violation of freedom of the press. Cardozo's concurring opinion was apparently so persuasive that Sutherland redrafted his opinion to incorporate most of Cardozo's language holding the advertising tax invalid on free-press grounds, and this redrafted opinion ultimately won the unanimous support of the justices. Announced on February 10, the redrafted opinion of Justice Sutherland for the Court was substantially a replica of the free-press arguments that Eberhard Deutsch had mustered in his memorandum outlining the strategy newspaper counsel should follow in attacking the advertising tax.[44]

Sutherland rejected Charles Rivet's objections to the jurisdiction of the federal courts to hear the case as well as his contention that there was an adequate remedy available to the newspapers under state law. Proceeding to a consideration of the free-press issue, Sutherland said that it "presents a question of the utmost gravity and importance; for, if well made, it goes to the heart of the natural right of the members of an organized society, united for their common good, to impart and acquire information about their common interests." The First Amendment's guarantee of freedom of the press, he acknowledged, had originally applied as a restriction on the powers of the national government alone, but the Court had concluded "that certain fundamental rights, safeguarded by the first eight amendments against federal action, were also safeguarded against state action by the due process of law clause of the Fourteenth Amendment." "That freedom of speech and of the press are rights of the same fundamental character, safeguarded by the due process of law clause of the Fourteenth Amendment against abridgment by state legislation," Sutherland continued, "has . . . been settled by a series of decisions of this court, beginning with Gitlow v. New York . . . , and ending with Near v. Minnesota."[45]

Sutherland conceded that as corporations, the publishers of the Louisiana dailies could not invoke the Privileges and Immunities Clause of the Fourteenth Amendment, as Charles Rivet had argued, but he pointed out that the freedom of the press claimed by the publishers was protected by the Due Process Clause and that corporations were among the "persons" protected by that clause. He then turned to a brief outline of the history of freedom of the press, an outline that closely tracked the research of Eberhard Deutsch which had been submitted to the Court as an appendix to the brief of newspaper counsel. He noted that after the abandonment of the licensing of the press in England, the Parliament had resorted to taxation as a method of controlling the press for political purposes, a method that had also been briefly copied in Massachusetts in the 1780s when stamp taxes on newspapers as well as taxes on newspaper advertising were levied. There was no question, he said, that the purpose of the English taxes on newspapers and advertising "was to prevent, or curtail the opportunity for, the acquisition of knowledge by the people in respect of their governmental affairs. It is idle to suppose that so many of the best men of England would for a century of time have waged, as they did, stubborn and often precarious warfare against these taxes if a mere matter of taxation had been involved. The aim of the struggle was not to relieve taxpayers from a burden, but to establish and preserve the right of the English people to full information in respect of the doings or misdoings of their government. Upon the correctness of this conclusion the very characterization of the exactions as 'taxes on knowledge' sheds a flood of corroborative light."[46]

"The framers of the First Amendment were familiar with the English struggle, which then had continued for nearly eighty years and was destined to go on for another sixty-five years, at the end of which time it culminated in a lasting abandonment of the obnoxious taxes," Sutherland pointed out. "The framers were likewise familiar with the then recent Massachusetts episode; and while that occurrence did much to bring about the adoption of the amendment . . . the predominant influence must have come from the English experience."[47]

At this point, Sutherland also rejected Charles Rivet's contention that the constitutional guarantee of freedom of the press was limited to prohibiting only prior restraints. In doing so, Sutherland and the Court broadened the protection of freedom of the press beyond any previous interpretation that the guarantee had been given in decisions of the Court. "It is impossible to concede that by the words 'freedom of the press' the framers of the amendment intended to adopt merely the narrow view then reflected by the law of England that such freedom consisted only in immunity from previous censorship; for this abuse had then permanently disappeared from English practice," Sutherland said. "It is equally impossible to believe that it was not intended to bring within the reach of these words such modes of restraint as were embodied in the two forms of taxation already described. Such belief must be rejected in the face of the then well known purpose of the exactions and the general adverse sentiment of the colonies in respect to them." Constitutional guarantees, he continued, may at times be construed in light of their definition under the common law that existed at the time of their adoption, but such a construction must be "one not rejected by our ancestors as unsuited to their civil and political conditions." The Court had relied on freedom of the press as a prohibition of prior restraints in *Near* v. *Minnesota*, Sutherland conceded, but it had been careful in that case "not to limit the protection of the right to any particular way of abridging it." "In the light of all that has now been said," he continued, "it is evident that the restricted rules of the English law in respect of the freedom of the press in force when the Constitution was adopted were never accepted by the American colonists."[48]

Nothing in the holding of the Court, Sutherland noted, should be construed to suggest that newspaper publishers were "immune from any of the ordinary forms of taxation for support of the government. But this is not an ordinary form of tax, but one single in kind, with a long history of hostile misuse against the freedom of the press." "The predominant purpose of the grant of immunity here invoked was to preserve an untrammeled press as a vital source of public information," he continued. "The newspapers, magazines and other journals of the country, it is safe to say, have shed and continue to shed, more light on the public and business affairs of the nation than any other instrumentality of publicity; and since informed public opinion is the most potent of all restraints upon misgovernment, the suppression or abridgment of the publicity afforded by a free press cannot be regarded otherwise than with grave concern."[49]

"The tax here involved is bad not because it takes money from the pockets of the appellees," Sutherland maintained. "If that were all, a wholly different question would be presented. It is bad because, in the light of history and of its present setting, it is seen to be a deliberate and calculated device in the guise of a tax to limit the circulation of information to which the public is entitled in virtue of the constitutional guarantee." "A free press stands as one of the great interpreters between the government and the people," he declared. "To allow it to be fettered is to fetter ourselves."[50]

"In view of the persistent search for new subjects of taxation, it is not without significance that, with the single exception of the Louisiana statute, so far as we can discover, no state during the one hundred fifty years of our national existence has undertaken to impose a tax like that now in question," Sutherland continued. "The form in which the tax is imposed is itself suspicious. It is not measured or limited by the volume of advertisements. It is measured alone by the extent of circulation of the publication in which the advertisements are carried, with the plain purpose of penalizing the publishers and curtailing the circulation of a selected group of newspapers." Having reached the conclusion that the Louisiana advertising tax was unconstitutional because "it abridges the freedom of the press," Sutherland concluded, "we deem it unnecessary to consider the further ground assigned that it also constitutes a denial of the equal protection of the laws." The decree of the lower court enjoining the collection of the advertising tax, he said, was "affirmed."[51]

The Louisiana advertising tax, which Huey Long had boasted was "my own stuff" when it was introduced during the 1934 session of the legislature, had thus been repudiated by a unanimous Court as an unconstitutional abridgment of freedom of the press. Ironically, when the Court's decision was announced on February 10, Rose McConnell Long appeared in the U.S. Senate to be sworn in to serve out the term of her late husband, as her sons Russell and Palmer and daughter Rose looked on from the Senate gallery. Indicating the bitterness that still lingered in Louisiana as part of the legacy of Huey Long, however, Hilda Phelps Hammond, in commenting on Mrs. Long's appointment, maintained that it "no longer is an honor to go to the United States Senate. . . . It is composed of an aggregation of the cheapest politicians who have neither courage nor honesty."[52]

The Louisiana dailies, as well as the national press, greeted the Supreme Court's decision with jubilation, and the *New Orleans Item* declared the decision to be "a great victory of the American press" over "terrorism." The *Grosjean* decision, it said, was "the most sweeping and ungrudging judicial recognition that we can recall to the value of the press as a prime instrument of human liberty, and its consequent right to protection from any and every form of oppression and intimidation." The victory in the case, the *Item* properly observed, was due in large part to the "learning and industry of Eberhard Deutsch, our own counsel." While the attorneys for the Louisiana dailies had felt that the advertising tax violated the freedom of the press, "only Mr. Deutsch was hopeful of getting the courts to agree that it did," the *Item* pointed out. "Most of the consultants attached only minor import to his contention, as a long shot." After exhaustive research, Deutsch had "brought in a brief embracing an astonishing chain of historical data and legal precedent in

England and the American colonies; all supporting his point, and covering Louisiana's gag-tax like a glove," the *Item* continued. With the Supreme Court's unanimous decision, it said, a "young lawyer's faith in the logic of American and English history and precedent had moved a mountain."[53]

Commenting on the *Item*'s praise of Eberhard Deutsch, *Time* pointed out that seldom "is a newspaper's lawyer a hero in the editorial rooms. Even more seldom does a local barrister achieve note among the platoon of silk-hatted, wing-collared, stripe-trousered counsel which is attracted to an important constitutional case." Justice Sutherland's opinion in the *Grosjean* case, *Time* continued, closely followed Deutsch's original free-press arguments and had resulted in a "decision which surpassed even the Minnesota Gag Law case for liberality" and established a "resounding precedent for freedom of the press in the U.S."[54]

The publishers of the Louisiana dailies that had been targets of the advertising tax also issued statements uniformly praising the decision of the high court. Frank Smith, the publisher of the *Lake Charles American Press*, which had been the lead plaintiff against the tax, said, "Thank God again for the Supreme Court. . . . Messrs. Phelps, Deutsch and Hanson deserve the highest praise for their brilliant preparation and presentation of the rights of 120 million people when these rights were challenged." Leonard Nicholson, president of the *Times-Picayune*, observed that with the *Grosjean* decision every "editor can now feel free to inform his readers of the actions of political officers, both national and state, without having the threat or fear of being taxed out of business." The Louisiana press, he said, "is proud and glad to have been the instrument of service to our brother publishers."[55]

In Baton Rouge, Charles Manship and his *Morning Advocate* and *State-Times* maintained that as long as the advertising tax had been the law no newspaper in the country could feel free, but with the Court's decision, the "newspapers of America now know they are free." "The decisión was not given to the papers that they might escape the punitive measure for themselves," the Manship papers said, "but given because the long history of the English people, dating back through the English Kings and the early history of the American colonies, shows that a free press is essential to the liberties of the people." John Ewing of the *Shreveport Times* declared that the *Grosjean* case would be "a perpetual bar to political interference with the free press of this country through taxation." "I am sorry the first case of this kind in the history of this country had to arise in Louisiana," Ewing added. "But I am proud of the Supreme Court's stirring defense of a free and untrammeled press."[56]

The Ewing papers in Monroe, the *News-Star* and *Morning World*, echoed John Ewing's sentiments, while denouncing the advertising tax as a measure adopted for "the express purpose of punishing newspapers that had dared to oppose a dictatorial administration." "The Louisiana law was one of the elements of ruthlessness invoked to insure the process of shackling the people to the chariot of a dictatorship," the Monroe papers maintained. The Court's invalidation of the law had set Louisiana "free from a menace that would in its very essence [have] led to destruction of the state as one of the commonwealths in a Union founded on liberty, justice and equality."[57]

Adding to the praise heaped on the *Grosjean* decision by the Louisiana dailies, R. C. Jarreau, publisher of the *Alexandria Daily Town Talk*, predicted that the decision would be "received with unusual favor by the people, not only in Louisiana, but in the other states of the Union, who believe in the freedom of the press." The publisher of the *Lafayette Advertiser*, Thomas Callahan, acknowledged that the Supreme Court's decision would "give reason to those who have been seeking to hamper . . . freedom [of the press] to think seriously," but he warned that the decision also imposed on the "newspaper publishers of the nation a greater responsibility." "They must ever keep in mind," Callahan said, "that theirs is a sacred trust."[58]

Among the members of the national press praising the *Grosjean* decision, Colonel Robert McCormick's *Chicago Tribune*, which had spearheaded the fight against the Minnesota gag law in *Near* v. *Minnesota*, harshly attacked not only the Louisiana advertising tax but also the late Kingfish. "Huey Long was a Hitler in every sense but one. Hitler controls the press of Germany. Huey Long did not control the press of Louisiana, and, in particular, he did not control the more influential papers," the *Tribune* said. "He knew, and so did every intelligent citizen of Louisiana, that in that fact, and in that fact alone, lay the possibility of his overthrow." With the *Grosjean* decision joining the decision of the Court in the *Near* case, the courts had "gone as far as they can go to protect the citizens of the United States against fascism and any other form of tyranny," the *Tribune* declared. "Neither the federal government nor any state government can directly or through subterfuge abridge the liberty of the press. If we develop Hitlers and Mussolinis in this country it will be despite the Constitution and despite the courts."[59]

Elisha Hanson, the general counsel for the American Newspaper Publishers' Association (ANPA), expressed his gratitude to the Louisiana publishers who had allowed him to argue the *Grosjean* case before the Supreme Court. The Louisiana publishers, he said, had been "true to their trust when the right of their subscribers to have a free press was challenged. The privilege of arguing the freedom of the press phase of the case before the Supreme Court of the United States which was granted to me by the Louisiana publishers and their counsel will always stand out as the high point of my professional career." "I am deeply gratified," Hanson added, "for such an opportunity to be of service to the people and the press of this country."[60]

The ANPA's *Editor & Publisher* had consistently encouraged the Louisiana dailies in their attack on the advertising tax, and it was predictably effusive in its praise of the *Grosjean* decision. In its opinion in the case, it said, the Court had "dipped deeply into the pages of history, and wrote into the law of the land what is probably the most comprehensive outline of what is embraced in the press freedom clause of the Constitution that has been judicially pronounced in the history of the United States." J. D. Barnum, publisher of the *Syracuse Post-Standard* and ANPA president, fully concurred in *Editor & Publisher*'s assessment of the importance of the *Grosjean* case. "The Supreme Court," he said, "has lighted a torch for the oppressed peoples of the world and rekindled the fires of liberty in the United States." The ANPA itself also subsequently adopted a resolution commending the Louisiana dailies "for their courageous and successful resistance to the attempt of a corrupt government to suppress that dissemination of information on public questions which is the first duty of a free press; and . . . for obtaining the statement of the highest court of the land of the principle that the freedom of the press includes freedom from unjust and discriminatory taxation by which hostile political factions may seek to stifle criticism through attempting the economic destruction of their critics."[61]

Ruminating subsequently on the events that had led to the *Grosjean* case, *Editor & Publisher* observed that the Supreme Court's "brilliantly incandescent" opinion in the case had repudiated a measure deliberately designed by a leader "mad with power" to destroy newspapers that opposed a "brazen dictatorship." But the victory of the press left in its wake disturbing questions regarding the American political system. Huey Long was "dead, his un-American machine well-nigh broken," *Editor & Publisher* observed, but how "citizens of Louisiana could have supinely permitted the upstart arriviste, whose conduct revolted the sensibilities of normal free people, to disgrace them and their commonwealth by vandal assaults upon the pillars of American life, is a question left unanswered. How can patriotism run so thin, intelligence run so small?" Today, as in 1936, the career of Huey Long still raises the same troubling questions. Perhaps, however, Cassius was correct: "The fault, dear Brutus, is not in our stars, but in ourselves."[62]

NOTES

1. Felix Frankfurter and James M. Landis, *The Business of the Supreme Court* (New York: Macmillan, 1928), pp. 56–102.

2. Ibid., pp. 255–94; Alpheus T. Mason, *William Howard Taft: Chief Justice* (New York: Simon and Schuster, 1964), pp. 88–120.

3. Notice of Appeal, June 20, 1935. The record of the materials presented by the parties in the *Grosjean* case before the three-judge court are located in the National Archives Southwest Regional Records Center, Ft. Worth, Texas, and are filed under *American Publishing Co.* v. *Grosjean*, No. 315 in Equity. Included in these materials are the Brief of the State, Original Brief of the Plaintiffs, Reply Brief of the Plaintiffs, and the Notice of Appeal. The citation of these materials will hereafter be designated with the letters NA.

4. William Ivy Hair, *The Kingfish and His Realm* (Baton Rouge: Louisiana State University Press, 1991), pp. 279–81, 289, 292, 305.

5. Ibid., pp. 279, 289–90, 301, 305.

6. Ibid., p. 292; *New York Times*, Sept. 2, 1934, sec. 6, pp. 3, 10.

7. Hair, *The Kingfish*, pp. 292–95.

8. Ibid., p. 279; *New York Times*, Sept. 2, 1934, sec. 6, pp. 3, 10; *New Orleans Times-Picayune*, Aug. 16, 1934, p. 1.

9. Hair, *The Kingfish*, pp. 296–98; *New Orleans Times-Picayune*, Jan. 26, 1935, pp. 1, 2; Jan. 27, 1935, pp. 1, 9.

10. *American Progress*, Feb. 1, 1935, pp. 11–12; Hair, *The Kingfish*, pp. 299–300.

11. *New Orleans Times-Picayune*, April 18, 1935, p. 1; Hair, *The Kingfish*, pp. 301–2.

12. *New Orleans Times-Picayune*, April 18, 1935, p. 1.

13. Ibid.

14. Hair, *The Kingfish*, pp. 310–16.

15. Ibid., pp. 316–22.

16. Ibid., pp. 324–25.

17. Ibid.

18. James W. Clarke, *American Assassins: The Darker Side of Politics* (Princeton, N.J.: Princeton University Press, 1982), p. 238; Hair, *The Kingfish*, 322–26; T. Harry Williams, *Huey Long* (New York: Knopf, 1969), pp. 867–88.

19. *American Progress*, October, 24, 1935, p. 3.

20. Ibid.

21. *New Orleans Item*, Feb. 12, 1936, p. 12; Brief of Appellees, *Grosjean* v. *American Press Co.*, 297 U.S. 233 (1936), pp. 47–68 (hereafter cited as Brief of Appellees).

22. Mason, *Taft*, pp. 133–37; Merlo Pusey, *Charles Evans Hughes* (New York: Macmillan, 1952), 2:288–90.

23. Richard C. Cortner, *The Wagner Act Cases* (Knoxville: University of Tennessee Press, 1964), pp. 141–49.

24. *Schechter Poultry Corp.* v. *U.S.*, 295 U.S. 495 (1935).

25. Brief of Appellant, *Grosjean* v. *American Press Co.*, 297 U.S. 233 (1936), pp. 6–7 (hereafter cited as Brief of Appellant).

26. Ibid., pp. 14–22.

27. Ibid., pp. 26–32.

28. Brief of Appellees, pp. 10–19.

29. Brief of Appellant, p. 47.

30. Ibid., p. 50.

31. Ibid., p. 56.

32. Brief of Appellees, p. 24.

33. Ibid., pp. 24–25; *New Orleans Times-Picayune*, Jan. 14, 1936, p. 28.

34. Brief of Appellant, pp. 41–42; *New Orleans Times-Picayune*, Jan. 14, 1936, p. 28.

35. Brief of Appellant, pp. 43–45.

36. Ibid., p. 46.

37. *New Orleans Times-Picayune*, Jan. 14, 1936, p. 28; Brief of Appellees, pp. 26–27.

38. Brief of Appellees, p. 26; *New Orleans Times-Picayune*, Jan. 14, 1936, p. 28; *Chicago Tribune*, Jan. 15, 1936, p. 4.

39. Brief of Appellees, pp. 29, 35–36.

40. Brief of Appellees, pp. 29–30; *New Orleans Times-Picayune*, Jan. 14, 1936, p. 28.

41. Brief of Appellees, p. 27.

42. Ibid., p. 29.

43. Compare *Louisville Gas & Electric Co.* v. *Coleman*, 277 U.S. 32 (1928), and *Stewart Dry Goods Co.* v. *Lewis*, 297 U.S. 550 (1935), with *State Board of Tax Commissioners* v. *Jackson*, 283 U.S. 527 (1931), *Liggett* v. *Lee*, 288 U.S. 517 (1933), *Concordia Fire Insurance Co.* v. *Illinois*, 292 U.S. 575 (1934), and *Fox* v. *Standard Oil Co.*, 294 U.S. 87 (1935).

44. See Leon Friedman and Fred L. Israel (ed.), *The Justices of the United States Supreme Court 1789–1969: Their Lives and Major Opinions*, 3: 2287–2317 (New York: Chelsea House, 1969); *Grosjean* v. *American Press Co.*, 297 U.S. 233 (1936).

45. 297 U.S. 233, 240–44.

46. 297 U.S. 233, 244–48.

47. 297 U.S. 233, 248.

48. 297 U.S. 233, 248–49.

49. 297 U.S. 233, 250.

50. 297 U.S. 233, 250.

51. 297 U.S. 233, 250–51.

52. *New Orleans Item*, Feb. 10, 1936, p. 1; *Time* 27 (Feb. 10, 1936): 12.

53. *New Orleans Item*, Feb. 13, 1936, p. 12.

54. *Time* 27 (Feb. 24, 1936): 49–50.

55. *Editor & Publisher* 69 (Feb. 15, 1936): 6.

56. Ibid.

57. Ibid.

58. Ibid.

59. *Chicago Tribune*, Feb. 12, 1936, p. 14.

60. *Editor & Publisher* 69 (Feb. 15, 1936): 41.

61. Ibid., pp. 5, 41; *New Orleans Times-Picayune*, Jan. 25, 1937, p. 6.

62. *Editor & Publisher* 69 (Feb. 15, 1936): 26; William Shakespeare, *Julius Caesar*, act 1, scene 2, lines 141–42.

Chapter 8

Epilogue

> [T]he constitutional guarantees of free speech and free press do not permit a State to forbid or proscribe advocacy of the use of force or of law violation except where such advocacy is directed to inciting or producing imminent lawless action and is likely to incite or produce such action.
>
> —U.S. Supreme Court, *Brandenburg* v. *Ohio*, June 9, 1969

> [There is] a profound national commitment to the principle that debate on public issues should be uninhibited, robust, and wide-open, and that it may well include vehement, caustic, and sometimes unpleasantly sharp attacks on government and public officials.
>
> —Justice William Brennan, *New York Times* v. *Sullivan*, March 9, 1964

♦ During its 1935–36 term, the Supreme Court offered a stirring defense of freedom of the press in the *Grosjean* case, and in another important advance for civil liberties, it unanimously reversed the murder convictions of three Mississippi black tenant farmers whose confessions had been beaten from them. The focus of national attention, however, was on the decisions of the Court involving challenges to New Deal programs and other measures involving governmental regulation of economic affairs. In this regard, the term was a disaster for the New Deal and the government's power to regulate the economy. The Court invalidated the New Deal's Agricultural Adjustment Act in January and the Bituminous Coal Conservation Act in May. In doing so, the Court narrowly construed the power of the national government to tax and spend and to regulate commerce, thereby excluding control of production activities from the scope of legitimate congressional power. While the validity of the Tennessee Valley Authority was upheld on technical grounds, on June 1 the Court also invalidated New York's minimum-wage law for women by a five to four vote. The Court's liberals protested what they considered to be the majority's distorted interpretations of the Constitution, but to no avail. "We finished the term of the Court yesterday," Justice Harlan Fiske Stone wrote privately. "I think in many ways one of the most disastrous in its history. At any rate it seems to me that the Court has been needlessly narrow and obscurantic in its outlook." The Court, he added, has "tied Uncle Sam up in a hard knot." "We did indeed have a hard year in the court," Justice Benjamin Cardozo agreed with his colleague. "Next year may be bad, but certainly can't be worse."[1]

Despite what appeared to be impenetrable constitutional barriers erected by the Court to the implementation of his New Deal program, Franklin Roosevelt was overwhelmingly reelected in the fall of 1936. With two measures crucial to the New Deal, the National Labor Relations Act (NLRA) and the Social Security Act, well on their way to being challenged before the Supreme Court, Roosevelt took a new approach. On February 5, 1937, he suddenly proposed legislation that if adopted by Congress would increase the number of justices on the Court from nine to fifteen, thus giving the president six additional appointments to the bench. This so-called "court-packing" plan was of course designed to allow Roosevelt to obtain a pro–New Deal majority on the Court. During the spring and summer of 1937, an intense national debate erupted over the merits of the court-packing measure and the proper role of the Supreme Court in the governmental system.[2]

The Court itself, however, effectively undermined support for Roosevelt's plan during the spring of 1937 when in an about-face it began to uphold the constitutionality of the New Deal and other measures it had been against only a year previously. On March 29, the Court upheld the validity of Oregon's minimum-wage law for women, even though it had invalidated New York's minimum-wage law the previous term. But the crucial turning point in the Court's confrontation with Roosevelt and the New Deal occurred on April 12, when in five cases it upheld the constitutionality of the National Labor Relations Act of 1935.[3]

The NLRA guaranteed the right of workers to organize unions and to bargain collectively free of employer interference, and it created the National Labor Relations Board (NLRB) to enforce its provisions. The act had encountered the bitter opposition of employer groups when under consideration by Congress, and the National Association of Manufacturers, the Automobile Manufacturers' Association, and the Iron and Steel Institute, among others, denounced the act as patently unconstitutional. The American Newspaper Publishers' Association

(ANPA), which had been resisting the unionization of newspaper editorial employees since the days of the National Industrial Recovery Act, joined in the condemnation of the NLRA as "unfair and one-sided legislation, which amounts, in practical application, to a labor dictatorship." The act was amended at the insistence of publishers to include a provision that nothing in its contents "would abridge freedom of speech or the press as guaranteed by the First Amendment," but under pressure from the American Newspaper Guild, that amendment was dropped from the bill before its final passage.[4]

Although *The Nation* magazine had pronounced the Supreme Court's decision in the *Grosjean* case as "excellent," it had also pointed out the opposition to the NLRA by the newspaper publishers' association and its general counsel, Elisha Hanson. "The freedom involved [in the *Grosjean* case] is indicated by the fact that Elisha Hanson was its advocate," *The Nation* warned. "His presence foreshadows the uses to which the decision may be put." When the NLRB began to apply the NLRA to newspaper employees during the fall of 1936, as *The Nation* had predicted, Elisha Hanson issued a legal brief advising publishers on free-press grounds to "flatly refuse to have anything to do with the National Labor Relations Board, other than to notify it it is without power under the Constitution to interfere with their business." "There is in so far as the business of the press is affected by . . . [the NLRA's] terms," Hanson advised publishers, "the question as to whether Congress has the power to vest an agency of the government with authority to dictate to publishers whom they shall or shall not employ. If the law is valid, that authority has been conferred on a Board, and without limitation. Such a power is now being exercised by the Hitler government in Germany." The ANPA's standing committee on labor also assured publishers that the NLRA was unconstitutional and advised them to "tell any National Labor Relations Board representative coming into contact with them that the Board is without jurisdiction and to refuse to deal with such representative." Publishers were especially urged not to sign closed-shop contracts with their employees, contracts that would mean the "regimentation of . . . news or editorial employees in favor of any political party or other pressure group."[5]

Among the five cases brought before the Supreme Court by the NLRB to test the constitutionality of the NLRA, one involved the Associated Press (AP), which was charged with violating the act by dismissing AP reporter Morris Watson because of his activities in the American Newspaper Guild. When the *Associated Press* case was argued before the Court, counsel for the AP, John W. Davis, assailed the application of the NLRA to publishers as a violation of freedom of the press, citing the *Near* and *Grosjean* cases. "Can freedom and independence of the press be maintained," Davis asked the Court, "if a federal bureau may dictate to the American newspapers the persons they employ to prepare their news reports?" Newspapers were the interpreters between the government and the people, he said, and the power to name who should write the news "is no different either in principle or in result from naming what shall be written or published. Here the author and the product are one and inseparable. If one is to be free, so must the other."[6]

In an amicus curiae brief filed in the *Associated Press* case, Elisha Hanson also relied on the *Near* and *Grosjean* cases in arguing on behalf of the ANPA that membership in labor unions on the part of reporters was incompatible with the objectivity of reporting and thus threatened freedom of the press. The affiliation of "newspaper reporters or editorial writers with an organization which can demand or command adherence to and support of any particular program affecting broad public interest or assistance to one party or another in a controversy cannot be countenanced by a publisher who desires to preserve the integrity of his news columns," Hanson told the Court. If a publisher believed that an employee had become unsuited for employment because of such affiliations, he added, "no agency of government either has the power or can be endowed with the power by Congress to interfere with the exercise of that judgment, whatever the nature of the employee's affiliations or activities may be."[7]

On April 12, 1937, the Supreme Court by a five to four vote upheld the constitutionality of the NLRA in all five of the cases appealed to it to test the act's validity, including the *Associated Press* case. The lead case was *NLRB* v. *Jones & Laughlin Steel Corp.*, in which the Court held that the act was a valid exercise of the power of Congress to regulate interstate commerce and that it did not deny employers due process of law. Writing for the Court in the *Associated Press* case, Justice Owen Roberts held that the NLRA prohibited employers from dismissing employees for union membership or activities, as the record clearly indicated the Associated Press had done. The Associated Press or any publisher, he said, could freely dismiss an employee for bias or lack of objectivity in reporting the news, but those grounds could not be used to mask a publisher's dismissal of an employee for union activities or affiliation. Stating the rule that the Court has since consistently followed in free-press cases, Roberts held that the "business of the Associated Press is not immune from regulation because it is an agency of the press. The publisher of a newspaper has no special immunity from the application of general laws. He has no special privilege to invade the rights and liberties of others."[8]

Joined by Justices Butler, McReynolds, and Van Devanter, Justice Sutherland, the author of the opinion of the Court in the *Grosjean* case, filed an eloquent dissent in the *Associated Press* case contending that freedom of the press had been abridged by the application of the NLRA to publishers. "Do the people of this land—in the providence of God, favored, as they sometimes boast, above all others in the plenitude of their liberties—desire to preserve those so carefully protected by the First Amendment: liberty of religious worship, freedom of speech and of the press, and the right of freemen peacefully to assemble and petition the government for a redress of grievances?" Sutherland asked. "If so, let them withstand all *beginnings* of encroachment. For the saddest epitaph which can be carved in memory of a vanished liberty is that it was lost because its possessors failed to stretch forth a saving hand while yet there was time." Despite Sutherland's eloquence, however, the attempt of Elisha Hanson and the ANPA to use the *Grosjean* case as a constitutional barrier to the unionization of press employees ended in failure in the *Associated Press* case.[9]

With decisions upholding the NLRA in April and sustaining the validity of the Social Security Act in May, the Supreme Court had effectively undermined much of the rationale for Roosevelt's court-packing plan. The announcement of the retirement of Justice Van Devanter at the end of the term, giving the president his first appointment to the Court, also slowed the momentum for Roosevelt's plan. The court-packing plan was finally defeated in the Senate during the summer, and the constitutional crisis of 1937 passed. But in 1937 and in the years that followed, the Court repudiated the constitutional barriers that it had erected against governmental power to direct and regulate the nation's economic affairs.[10]

The expansion of the constitutional protection of civil liberties, of which the *Grosjean* case had been an important benchmark, was not abandoned by the Court after 1937, however, but was instead accelerated. In free-press cases the Court adhered to the rule enunciated by Justice Roberts in the *Associated Press* case, and it rejected arguments that would have exempted publishers from the antitrust laws and the Fair Labor Standards Act. In doing so the Court again emphasized that freedom of the press did not confer upon the press special exemptions from laws applicable to business generally. More recent decisions of the Court have applied the same rule to reporters who may be required to testify before grand juries and to searches of newspaper offices under validly issued search warrants, procedures that are equally applicable to all persons. Also rejected were contentions that freedom of the press allowed greater access by the press to governmental facilities, such as jails and prisons, than was allowed to the public generally.[11]

Laws that single out the press for special treatment, however, as in the *Grosjean* case, must be shown to be necessary to fulfill a compelling governmental purpose, as illustrated by a Minnesota tax challenged before the Court in 1983 by the *Minneapolis Star-Tribune*. The Minnesota legislature exempted newspapers from the application of the state's sales tax, but imposed a use tax on ink and paper consumed by publishers, exempting those who used less than one hundred thousand dollars worth of paper and ink per year. The result was that only eleven to fourteen newspapers out of over three hundred in Minnesota incurred any tax liability under the act. Unlike the *Grosjean* case, there was no indication that the legislature was seeking to punish newspapers or suppress the dissemination of information by the press. Speaking for a majority of seven members of the Court, Justice Sandra O'Connor nonetheless wrote an opinion invalidating the tax as an abridgment of freedom of the press.[12]

Although the Court reiterated its rule that freedom of the press did not exempt the press from laws generally applicable to businesses, it held that a taxing scheme which singled out the press for differential treatment must be justified by an overriding governmental interest that cannot be achieved without such differential treatment. The Minnesota ink and paper tax was invalid, the Court held, because such taxes are not subject to the usual political restraints on taxes of general applicability. "Further," it said, "differential treatment suggests that the goal of the regulation is not unrelated to suppression of expression, and such a goal is presumptively unconstitutional."[13]

"Differential taxation of the press, then, places such a burden on the interests protected by the First Amendment that we cannot countenance such treatment unless the state asserts a counterbalancing interest of compelling importance that it cannot achieve without differential taxation," the Court continued. As the publishers had argued in the *Grosjean* case, it also pointed out that freedom of the press was threatened not only by differential treatment but also by the possibility, if the differential treatment were upheld, of more burdensome treatment in the future. The Minnesota tax was also invalid, the Court further held, because it applied not to all of the press but only to a relatively small number of newspapers. "Whatever the motive of the legislature in this case," it concluded, "we think that recognizing a power in the state not only to single out the press but also to tailor the tax so that it singles out a few members of the press presents such a potential for abuse that no interest suggested by Minnesota can justify the scheme." The special legal treatment of the press thus continues to receive strict scrutiny by the Court, as it had for the first time in the *Grosjean* case.[14]

Although the *Grosjean* case involved a tax on gross receipts derived by newspapers from the sale of advertising, the tax was invalidated because it was perceived as an attempt to curtail the dissemination of information by the press. At the time, however, advertising itself, or commercial expression, had not been recognized by the Court as being constitutionally protected under the First Amendment. Indeed, in 1942 the Court held that advertising was not entitled to First Amendment protection at all. Beginning in 1975, however, the Court reversed course and began to hold that advertising involved commercial expression of information important to consumers in a free-market system and was thus entitled to First Amendment protection. The Court has since recognized on the other hand that commercial expression does not enjoy the broad scope of protection under the First Amendment that extends to political, religious, and other forms of traditional expression. In order to receive First Amendment protection, advertising and commercial expression must be for a lawful purpose and not be false or misleading, the Court has held. If these criteria are met, governmental regulation of commercial expression must further substantial governmental interests and be narrowly tailored for that purpose.[15]

The status of freedom of the press as a right guaranteed by the Fourteenth Amendment against abridgment by the states, which had remained rather tenuous after the Court's decision in *Near* v. *Minnesota* in 1931, was assured of permanence with the decision in the *Grosjean* case in 1936. The most significant advance in the field of freedom of the press and expression that the *Grosjean* case contributed, however, was the freeing of the First Amendment from the restricted interpretation that limited its protection to primarily prohibiting prior restraints.[16] Justice Sutherland's forthright rejection of that narrow interpretation of the First Amendment in his opinion in the *Grosjean* case in effect was an acknowledgment that the views of the Jeffersonians, who had argued that the Sedition Act of 1798 was unconstitutional, had at last prevailed in First Amendment jurisprudence. With the *Grosjean* decision, freedom of the press and freedom of expression finally became what James Madison had argued they should be at the time of the Sedition Act—the "right of freely examining public characters and measures, and of free communication among the people thereon, which has ever been justly deemed the only effectual guardian of every other right." In a very real sense, the *Grosjean* case marked the beginning of the modern scope of protection afforded freedom of expression in U.S. constitutional law.

Freed of the previous restrictive interpretation of the First Amendment, the Court in recent years has scrutinized the most common forms of subsequent punishment that are imposed in the field of free expression—punishments for advocacy of unlawful action, publication of obscenity, and libel. Regarding punishments imposed for the advocacy of unlawful action, the Court in *Brandenburg* v. *Ohio* in 1969 adopted an interpretation of freedom of expression that essentially tracked the one supported by Justices Holmes and Brandeis in their pioneering dissents many years previously. The advocacy of unlawful action itself, the Court held, was protected by the First Amendment. The "constitutional guarantees of free speech and free press do not permit a State to forbid or proscribe advocacy of the use of force or of law violation," it held, "except where such advocacy is directed to inciting or producing imminent lawless action and is likely to incite or produce such action."[17]

In the field of obscenity, the Court's efforts have produced more muddled results. It has agreed that obscenity is not afforded protection under the First Amendment because it does not involve the communication of ideas of redeeming social value, but the difficulty has come in the Court's attempts to define obscenity with sufficient specificity to afford protection for freedom of expression. The Court's current definition—that a work is obscene if, taken as a whole, to the average person applying contemporary, local community standards, the work is patently offensive, appeals predominantly to the prurient interest in sex, and lacks serious literary, artistic, political, or scientific value—is to say the least far from satisfactory. There is considerable force to Justice William Brennan's criticism that the definition fails to inform individuals with sufficient specificity of what the law forbids and does not forbid to permit it to meet standards of due process and the First Amendment.[18]

The Court's reconciliation of the law of libel with the protection of the First Amendment, on the other hand, produced a landmark victory for free expression in 1964 in *New York Times* v. *Sullivan*. In the opinion for the majority, Justice Brennan again rejected the narrow concept of free expression that had been reflected in the Sedition Act of 1798 and acknowledged that the Jeffersonian "attack upon its validity has carried the day in the court of history." Modern views of the scope of freedom of expression, he said, "reflect a broad consensus that the Act, because of the restraint it imposed upon criticism of government and public officials, was inconsistent with the First Amendment." There was now, he continued, "a profound national commitment to the principle that debate on public issues should be uninhibited, robust, and wide-open, and that it may well include vehement, caustic, and sometimes unpleasantly sharp attacks on government and public officials."[19]

The expression or publication of unintentional falsehoods during debates over public affairs or about public officials, Brennan held, must be constitutionally protected under the First Amendment, or otherwise the fear of large damage awards for libel would lead to self-censorship by the participants to the detriment of the "robust debate" protected by the First Amendment. "The constitutional guarantees require, we think," he continued, "a federal rule that prohibits a public official from recovering damages for defamatory falsehood relating to his official conduct unless he proves that the statement was made with 'actual malice'—that is, with knowledge that it was false or with reckless disregard of whether it was false or not."[20]

The public official is therefore required to prove in a libel suit not only that statements about him are false but also that the publisher of the falsehoods knew they were false or evidenced reckless disregard of their truth or falsity. This "*New York Times* rule" was subsequently extended by the Court to libel suits by public figures as well as public officials. In a 1988 decision that would have been warmly applauded by the *Louisiana Progress* and the *American Progress*, the Court also applied the *New York Times* rule to parodies of public officials and figures that were alleged to intentionally inflict emotional distress. "Were we to hold otherwise," Chief Justice Rehnquist said for a unanimous Court, "there can be little doubt that political cartoonists and satirists would be subjected to damages awards without any showing that their work falsely defamed its subject. . . . The appeal of the political cartoon or caricature is often based on exploitation of unfortunate physical traits or politically embarrassing events—an exploitation often calculated to injure the feelings of the subject of the portrayal. The art of the cartoonist is often not reasoned or evenhanded, but slashing and one-sided." Given the history of the use of parody and satire of public officials and figures as part of the national dialogue protected by the First Amendment, the Court held, the *New York Times* rule should be extended to that legitimate form of expression.[21]

By forthrightly rejecting the restricted interpretation of freedom of the press that had been inherited by the United States from English law, the Supreme Court's decision in the *Grosjean* case thus constituted the beginning of what has been a general expansion and liberalization of the modern law of the First Amendment. Those who had participated in the litigation of the *Grosjean* case had consequently been involved in an event of historic importance in U.S. constitutional law that was at least one positive result of the legacy of Huey Long.

Although they had steadfastly defended the Louisiana advertising tax, Attorney General Gaston Porterie and Charles Rivet had met defeat at the hands of the Supreme Court. Gaston Porterie nonetheless was reelected as Louisiana attorney general in 1936, and he also continued to serve as a member at large of the Democratic state central committee in Louisiana until 1940. He was elected president of the National Association of Attorneys General in 1936, serving in that position until 1939, and he was vice president of the Interstate Commission on Crime during 1938–39. President Franklin Roosevelt appointed Porterie as U.S. district judge in Louisiana in 1939, and he served on the federal bench until 1953.

Gaston Louis Porterie died at the age of sixty-eight at his home in Alexandria on March 24, 1953.[22]

Charles Rivet, who had argued the *Grosjean* case in the Supreme Court on behalf of the state of Louisiana, continued to practice law in New Orleans after 1936 and to serve as an assistant to the Louisiana attorney general until 1940. He was active in establishing civil service systems in New Orleans and at the state level, serving twelve years on the state civil service commission. He had begun teaching courses at Loyola University Law School in 1919 and continued to do so until 1959, having been awarded an honorary doctor of laws degree from Loyola in 1953. Charles Rivet practiced law until only two weeks prior to his death at the age of ninety on September 3, 1981.[23]

Esmond Phelps, who had been one of the lead attorneys on behalf of the Louisiana dailies in the *Grosjean* case, continued his practice of law in New Orleans following the victory of the press in that case in 1936. He also remained president of the board of administrators of the Tulane University Educational Fund as well as a member of the board of directors of the *Times-Picayune*. Esmond Phelps died in his law offices in New Orleans at the age of sixty-two on October 18, 1950. Classes at Tulane University were suspended the following day in honor of his long service to the university.[24]

Elisha Hanson, who had also argued the *Grosjean* case in the Supreme Court, continued to serve as general counsel of the American Newspaper Publishers' Association until his retirement from that position on April 26, 1962. He was succeeded as general counsel by his son, Arthur Briggs Hanson. Elisha Hanson died at the Georgetown University Hospital in Washington on August 11, 1962, at the age of seventy-eight.[25]

Eberhard P. Deutsch was without question largely responsible for the victory of the press in the *Grosjean* case, since he mapped out the free-press strategy for a successful attack on the advertising tax. Indeed, the free-press arguments he developed were essentially duplicated by Justice Sutherland's opinion for the Court in the case. Deutsch continued to practice law in New Orleans after 1936, but his practice was interrupted by his service in World War II. He had served in the First Illinois Cavalry in World War I and had risen to the rank of lieutenant. With the outbreak of World War II, he again enlisted in the army with the rank of major and was a participant in twelve major battles during the war, including the invasion of Sicily. He was also among the American airborne troops who parachuted into Normandy behind German lines on D-Day.[26]

By the end of the war, Deutsch had risen to the rank of colonel. He subsequently became a colonel of military intelligence, receiving sixteen American and foreign service medals. During the postwar period, he was the principal legal adviser to General Mark Clark, who commanded the military administration of Austria. Returning to civilian life, Deutsch served as a special assistant to the U.S. attorney general, defending damage claims against the government arising from a disastrous explosion of fertilizer with an ammonium nitrate base at Texas City, Texas, on April 16 and 17, 1947—at the time the largest civil litigation in the world. He was subsequently given the highest civilian award the secretary of the army could bestow, the Distinguished Civilian Service Award, which commended his "superior initiative, outstanding leadership, and many accomplishments which reflect great credit to him and the military services." Deutsch was also active in the American Bar Association, serving on its standing committee on admiralty and maritime law and as chair of the American Bar Association's standing committee on peace and law through the United Nations. Eberhard Paul Deutsch died at the age of eighty-two in New Orleans on January 16, 1980. In addition to his outstanding service to his country during World War II, he also left a lasting legacy as the architect of a landmark advance in American civil liberties in *Grosjean* v. *American Press Co.*[27]

NOTES

1. *Brown* v. *Mississippi*, 297 U.S. 278 (1936); see also Richard C. Cortner, *A "Scottsboro" Case in Mississippi: The Supreme Court and Brown v. Mississippi* (Jackson: University Press of Mississippi, 1986); *U.S.* v. *Butler*, 297 U.S. 1 (1936); *Carter* v. *Carter Coal Co.*, 298 U.S. 238 (1936); *Ashwander* v. *TVA*, 297 U.S. 288 (1936); *Morehead* v. *New York*, 298 U.S. 587 (1936); Alpheus T. Mason, *Harlan Fiske Stone* (New York: Viking, 1956), pp. 425–26; George S. Hellman, *Benjamin N. Cardozo: American Judge* (New York: McGraw-Hill, 1940), p. 231.

2. Joseph Alsop and Turner Catledge, *The 168 Days* (Garden City, N.J.: Doubleday, 1938); Leonard Baker, *Back to Back: The Duel between FDR and the Supreme Court* (New York: Macmillan, 1967).

3. *West Coast Hotel Co.* v. *Parrish*, 300 U.S. 379 (1937).

4. Richard C. Cortner, *The Wagner Act Cases* (Knoxville: University of Tennessee Press, 1964), pp. 78, 84.

5. *Editor & Publisher* 69 (Oct. 10, 1936): 7, 49; 69 (Oct. 17, 1936): 9; 69 (Dec. 12, 1936): 13; Cortner, *The Wagner Act Cases*, p. 97.

6. Brief for the Associated Press, *Associated Press* v. *NLRB*, 301 U.S. 103 (1937), pp. 99–102; Cortner, *The Wagner Act Cases*, p. 160.

7. Brief for the American Newspaper Publishers' Association as *Amicus Curiae*, *Associated Press* v. *NLRB*, 301 U.S. 103 (1937), pp. 8–9, 12; Cortner, *The Wagner Act Cases*, p. 160.

8. *NLRB* v. *Jones & Laughlin Steel Corp.*, 301 U.S. 1 (1937); *Associated Press* v. *NLRB*, 301 U.S. 103, 132–33 (1937). The remaining cases in which the NLRA was upheld by the Court were *NLRB* v. *Fruehauf Trailer Co.*, 301 U.S. 49 (1937); *NLRB* v. *Friedman-Harry Marks Clothing Co.*, 301 U.S. 58 (1937); and *Washington, Virginia and Maryland Coach Co.* v. *NLRB*, 301 U.S. 142 (1937).

9. 301 U.S. 103, 141.

10. The cases upholding the Social Security Act were *Steward Machine Co.* v. *Davis*, 301 U.S. 548 (1937), and *Helvering* v. *Davis*, 301 U.S. 619 (1937); Cortner, *The Wagner Act Cases*, pp. 176–78.

11. *Associated Press* v. *U.S.*, 326 U.S. 1 (1945); *Citizen Publishing Co.* v. *U.S.*, 327 U.S. 186 (1969); *Oklahoma Press Publishing Co.* v. *Walling*, 327 U.S. 186 (1946); *Branzburg* v. *Hayes*, 408 U.S. 665 (1972); *Zurcher* v. *Stanford Daily*, 436 U.S. 547 (1978); *Houchins* v. *KQED*, 438 U.S. 1 (1978).

12. *Minneapolis Star and Tribune Co.* v. *Commissioner of Revenue*, 460 U.S. 575 (1983).

13. 460 U.S. 575, 585.

14. 460 U.S. 575, 591–92.

15. *Valentine* v. *Chrestensen*, 316 U.S. 52 (1942); *Bigelow* v. *Virginia*, 421 U.S. 809 (1975); *Virginia Pharmacy Board* v. *Virginia Citizens Consumer Council*, 425 U.S. 748 (1976); *Bates* v. *State Bar of Arizona*, 433 U.S. 350 (1977); *Central Hudson Gas & Electric Corp.* v. *Public Service Commission*, 447 U.S. 557 (1980); *Board of Trustees* v. *Fox*, 492 U.S. 469 (1989).

16. Prior restraints of course remain presumptively unconstitutional as applied to freedom of expression. See *New York Times* v. *U.S.*, 403 U.S. 713 (1971), in which the Court held unconstitutional the attempt of the Nixon administration to enjoin the publication of the Pentagon Papers detailing the decision-making process involved in the Vietnam War.

17. *Brandenburg* v. *Ohio*, 395 U.S. 444 (1969); see also *Texas* v. *Johnson*, 491 U.S. 397 (1989), and *U.S.* v. *Eichman*, 496 U.S. 310 (1990).

18. *Miller* v. *California*, 413 U.S. 15 (1973); see Justice Brennan's dissenting opinion in *Paris Adult Theater* v. *Slaton*, 413 U.S. 49, 74 (1973).

19. *New York Times* v. *Sullivan*, 376 U.S. 254, 270, 276 (1964); see also Anthony Lewis, *Make No Law* (New York: Random House, 1991), an excellent case study of the litigation in *New York Times* v. *Sullivan*.

20. 376 U.S. 254, 279–81.

21. *Hustler Magazine* v. *Falwell*, 485 U.S. 46 (1988); see also Rodney A. Smolla, *Jerry Falwell v. Larry Flynt* (Chicago and Urbana: University of Illinois Press, 1988).

22. *New Orleans Times-Picayune*, March 25, 1953, pp. 1, 3.

23. Ibid., Sept. 5, 1981, sec. 1, p. 23.

24. *New Orleans Times-Picayune*, Oct. 19, 1950, p. 1.

25. *New York Times*, Aug. 12, 1962, p. 81.

26. *New Orleans Times-Picayune*, Jan. 17, 1980, sec. 1, p. 26.

27. Ibid. The litigation arising from the Texas City disaster was decided favorably to the government by the Supreme Court in *Dalehite* v. *United States*, 346 U.S. 15 (1953).

Bibliographical Essay

♦ Although there are numerous accounts of the career of Huey P. Long and his domination of the political life of Louisiana during the 1920s and 1930s of varying quality and assistance to one who undertakes to write on an aspect of Long's career, I have relied primarily on three biographies of Huey Long that have been published in more recent years. The first of these is T. Harry Williams, *Huey Long* (New York: Knopf, 1969), a biography that won a Pulitzer Prize. Despite the acclaim with which it was received, I found Williams's biography to be unduly complimentary of Long's career and deeds, offering apologias for most of the Kingfish's actions regardless of how seriously they may have breached fundamental American democratic and constitutional values. An example, highly relevant to the subject matter analyzed in my work, is the fact that Williams mentions the adoption of the newspaper advertising tax in 1934 at Long's behest in only a few sentences and disposes of the decision of the U.S. Supreme Court in the *Grosjean* case in a footnote, ignoring the fact that the tax was one of the most serious assaults upon freedom of the press in this century (pp. 716, 721, note 3).

Several years ago, William Ivy Hair published his biography of Long, *The Kingfish and His Realm* (Baton Rouge: Louisiana State University Press, 1991), a biography that I found to be a more balanced treatment of Long's life and career and more critical of the Kingfish's excesses than the previous Williams biography. More recently, Glen Jeansonne's *Messiah of the Masses: Huey P. Long and the Great Depression* (New York: Harper

Collins, 1993) has also been published. Although it is a briefer treatment of Long than those of Hair and Williams, concentrating as it does on Huey Long's career during the Depression, I also found the Jeansonne work to offer a more balanced treatment of Long's career than the Williams biography. A much briefer, but nonetheless insightful, treatment of Huey Long may also be found in Arthur M. Schlesinger, Jr., *The Age of Roosevelt: The Politics of Upheaval* (New York: Houghton Mifflin, 1960), chapter 4, "The Messiah of the Rednecks."

Since this work is focused on the relationship between Huey Long and the daily press of Louisiana, two works proved especially useful in providing information and insights in the evolution of particular New Orleans papers as well as the personalities associated with them. These works are John Wilds, *Afternoon Story: A Century of the New Orleans States-Item* (Baton Rouge: Louisiana State University Press, 1976), which provides good sketches of Colonel Robert Ewing and James Thomson of the *New Orleans States* and *Item*, and Thomas Ewing Dabney, *One Hundred Great Years: The Story of the Times-Picayune from Its Founding to 1940* (Baton Rouge: Louisiana State University Press, 1944), which provides useful information on one of Huey Long's greatest newspaper antagonists, the *New Orleans Times-Picayune*.

In order to present a thorough analysis of the reactions of the urban daily press of Louisiana to the events covered in this work, I relied primarily on the portrayal of those events in the New Orleans and Baton Rouge newspapers—the *New Orleans Times-Picayune*, *States*, *Item*, and *Tribune* and the *Baton Rouge Morning Advocate* and *State-Times*. I supplemented the coverage of events by the New Orleans and Baton Rouge papers with the coverage contained in the *Shreveport Times* and *Journal*, *Monroe News-Star* and *Morning World*, *Alexandria Daily Town Talk*, *Lake Charles American Press*, and the *Lafayette Daily Advertiser*. For the attitude toward the press of the Long camp and of Huey Long himself, Long's personal newspaper, the *Louisiana Progress* (after 1933, the *American Progress*) proved indispensable, and I read every issue of the *Progress* from its beginning in 1930 until it ceased publication.

I supplemented the coverage of events by the Louisiana press with the coverage by the national press as well, including the *New York Times*, the *Chicago Tribune*, and others. I also relied on material culled from the Huey P. Long Scrapbooks, which consist of newspaper and magazine clippings related to almost every aspect of Huey Long's career. These scrapbooks unfortunately at times contain undated articles and some articles which contain no identification of their sources, but when dates and sources were available I have cited those in my notes. The Long Scrapbooks are available in the Hill Memorial Library, Louisiana State University at Baton Rouge, which also has a complete microfilm record of all issues of the *Louisiana Progress* and *American Progress.* The Hill Library also has transcripts of the more than two hundred interviews conducted by T. Harry Williams with individuals having knowledge of Huey Long's career, and I consulted several of these interview transcripts in my research as well. In addition, I have relied extensively on the coverage of Long's attack on the press in *Editor & Publisher,* the official voice of the American Newspaper Publishers' Association (now the American Newspaper Association).

While articles in the periodical literature on Huey Long and Louisiana politics are voluminous, most do not deal with Long's clash with the Louisiana press or the litigation in the *Grosjean* case and are therefore not very useful for the events covered in this work. I did, however, find certain articles that contained useful insights or information regarding the subject matter covered herein: Walter Davenport, "Catching up with Huey," *Collier's* 92 (July 1, 1933): 12, 45–46; Hodding Carter, "Kingfish to Crawfish," *The New Republic* 77 (Jan. 24, 1934): 302–5; Hodding Carter, "The Kingfish on His Way," *The New Republic* 81 (Nov. 21, 1934): 40–42; Hermann Deutsch, "Prelude to a Heterocrat," *The Saturday Evening Post* 208 (Sept. 7, 1935): 5–7, 84–88; and commentary in *The Nation* 140 (April 3, 1934): 373–74, and *Time* 27 (Feb. 24, 1936): 49–50.

Since the U.S. Supreme Court's decision in *Near* v. *Minnesota,* 283 U.S. 697 (1931), was crucial to the result of *Grosjean* v. *American Press Co.,* I have relied on my own research on the *Near* case, which was published in my *The Supreme Court and the Second Bill of Rights* (Madison: University of Wisconsin Press, 1981), as well as Fred Friendly's *Minnesota Rag* (New York: Random House, 1981). I have supplemented the information from these sources on the *Near* case with correspondence between J. M. Near and the American Civil Liberties Union, which is contained in the ACLU Archives in the Seeley Mudd Library at Princeton University.

On the development of the constitutional protection of freedom of the press in the United States generally, I have relied on Leonard Levy, *Emergence of a Free Press* (New York: Oxford University Press, 1985). James Morton Smith, *Freedom's Fetters* (Ithaca, N.Y.: Cornell University Press, 1956) and Stanley Elkins and Eric McKitrick, *The Age of Federalism* (New York: Oxford University Press, 1993), describe the effect of the Sedition Act of 1798 on freedom of the press. On the effects of the World War I "Red scare" on civil liberties including freedom of the press, I consulted Julian F. Jaffe, *Crusade against Radicalism* (Port Washington, N.Y.: Kennikat Press, 1972) and Paul L. Murphy, *The Meaning of Freedom of Speech* (Westport, Conn.: Greenwood Press, 1972). The contribution of Justice Oliver Wendell Holmes to the modern constitutional protection of freedom of expression is well documented in Richard Polenberg, *Fighting Faiths: The Abrams Case, the Supreme Court, and Free Speech* (New

York: Viking, 1987). Also valuable in understanding the modern meaning of freedom of the press is Anthony Lewis's excellent analysis of *New York Times* v. *Sullivan*, 376 U.S. 254 (1964), in his *Make No Law* (New York: Random House, 1991).

For my analysis of the litigation in *Grosjean* v. *American Press Co.*, 297 U.S. 233 (1936), I found that the litigation strategy of counsel for the Louisiana dailies, and especially Eberhard Deutsch's position on the free-press issue in the *Grosjean* case, are well documented in his "Memorandum and Discussion Relative to Validity of Act 23 of 1934 (Newspaper Advertising Tax) and Jurisdiction and Procedure to Set It Aside." This document is in the possession of the law firm of Davidson, Meaux, McElligot & Swift in Lafayette, Louisiana. The record of the *Grosjean* case before the three-judge federal court and the briefs of counsel on both sides filed in that court are preserved in the National Archives Southwest Regional Records Center, Ft. Worth, Texas, and I have heavily relied on these materials in analyzing the proceedings before the three-judge court. For the briefs and record in the *Grosjean* case filed in the U.S. Supreme Court, I have relied on the microcard edition of briefs and records in Supreme Court cases available from Information Handling Services, Englewood, Colorado.

The Supreme Court of the 1930s that decided the *Grosjean* case is perhaps best approached through biographies of the justices who served on that Court. Justice George Sutherland has been the subject of a biography by Joel Francis Pascal, *Mr. Justice Sutherland: A Man against the State* (Princeton, N.J.: Princeton University Press, 1951). The standard biography of Chief Justice Charles Evans Hughes is Merlo Pusey, *Charles Evans Hughes* (New York: Macmillan, 1952). Justices Owen J. Roberts and Louis D. Brandeis are also the subjects of biographical treatment in Charles A. Leonard, *A Search for a Judicial Philosophy: Mr. Justice Roberts and the Constitutional Revolution of 1937* (Port Washington, N.Y.: Kennikat Press, 1971) and Alpheus T. Mason, *Brandeis: A Free Man's Life* (New York: Viking Press, 1946). Justice Benjamin N. Cardozo's life is covered in George S. Hellman, *Benjamin N. Cardozo: American Judge* (New York: McGraw-Hill, 1940). The judicial biography which supplies the greatest insights into the Supreme Court of the 1930s, however, is Alpheus T. Mason, *Harlan Fiske Stone* (New York: Viking, 1956). A good description of the confrontation between President Franklin D. Roosevelt and the Supreme Court in 1937 is Leonard Barker, *Back to Back: The Duel between FDR and the Supreme Court* (New York: Macmillan, 1967). The crucial litigation that marked the turning point in the constitutional crisis of the New Deal era is covered in my own *The Wagner Act Cases* (Knoxville: University of Tennessee Press, 1964).

Index

ABOUT THE AUTHOR

RICHARD C. CORTNER is Professor of Political Science at the University of Arizona in Tucson. He is the author of eleven books, including most recently, *The Iron Horse and the Constitution: The Railroads and the Transformation of the Fourteenth Amendment* (Greenwood, 1993).

ISBN 0-313-29842-4

90000>

EAN

9 780313 298424

HARDCOVER BAR CODE